# THE SECRETS OF JUDAS

# THE SECRETS OF JUDAS

*The Story of the Misunderstood Disciple and His Lost Gospel*

JAMES M. ROBINSON

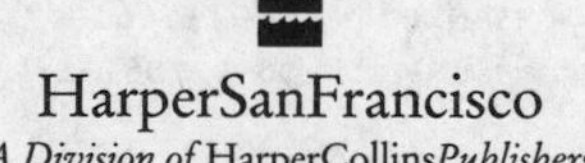

HarperSanFrancisco
*A Division of* HarperCollins*Publishers*

Bible quotations, unless the author's own or otherwise noted, are from the New Revised Standard Version of the Bible, copyright © 1989 by the Division of Christian Education of the National Council of Churches of Christ in the U.S.A.



HarperCollins books may be purchased for educational, business, or sales promotional use. For information please write: Special Markets Department, HarperCollins Publishers, 10 East 53rd Street, New York, NY 10022.

HarperCollins Web site: http://www.harpercollins.com
HarperCollins®, ®, and HarperSanFrancisco™
are trademarks of HarperCollins Publishers.

FIRST EDITION
*Designed by Joseph Rutt*

Library of Congress Cataloging-in-Publication Data is available.

ISBN: 978-0-06-117064-5
ISBN-10: 0-06-117064-X

07 08 09 10 11 RRD(H) 10 9 8 7 6 5 4 3

# Contents

*The Gospel of Judas*

# Preface

The *Gospel of Judas,* a long-lost second-century fictional account that elevated Judas to almost hero status in the story, has been rediscovered! But it was kept under wraps until Easter 2006 to maximize the financial gain for its Swiss owners and American agents. The grand exposé was performed by the National Geographic Society, timed for the greatest public impact, at Easter. Until then, those on the inside were sworn to silence on a stack of Bibles—or on a stack of papyrus leaves.

But it is amazing how much could be known about it by those of us on the outside looking in. This little book that you have in your hands has been written by an outsider who was not privy to the details about how the *Gospel of Judas* was being published. Many of you will read my book because you have read or heard about or seen on television what the National Geographic Society was doing; indeed, you may well have read its two books marketed with all the hoopla.

But I have a distinct advantage over those of you who have only read the "official" story, which is why, after all, you must read this book if you want to know what is really going on with the *Gospel of Judas.* My narration is not expurgated, sanitized, or cleaned up to make it an appetizing story. What has transpired in this money-making venture is not a pleasant story—it is about how all this has been sprung upon us, the reading and viewing public—and you have a right to know what has been going on.

I write as a scholar and, as you will see as you read my narration, I have been involved to a considerable extent over the past generation in this adventure. Yet you will also see me, in my capacity as scholar, expressing dismay, even disgust, over much of what has gone on. I lay it all out, with as much documentation as I can muster, for you to see for yourself.

I cannot promise you happy reading, but I am sure it will be exciting reading!

For the second, paperback edition, we planned to include a fresh translation of the *Gospel of Judas,* now that the Coptic transcription has become accessible to the scholarly community at large online at the National Geographic Society's Web site. The distinguished dean of Yale Divinity School, Harold W. Attridge, himself a leading authority on Gnosticism and involved in the odyssey of the *Gospel of Judas* from very early on, was enlisted to make such a fresh translation. His is a considerable improvement over the translation published by the National Geographic Society at Easter 2006. But then the copyright to the online Coptic transcription, held by the Maecenas Foundation for Ancient Art, blocked this translation of the *Gospel of Judas* from being published. To quote the language of the lawyers of the National Geographic Society:

> This transcription is not simply a transcription of the legible Coptic words on the papyrus, but the result of restoration and interpretation based on the scholarly work and expertise of Professors Kasser, Wurst and others....
>
> It is a copyright-protected work that is the product of original scholarship by Professors Rodolphe Kasser, Gregor Wurst and others, commissioned by the Maecenas Foundation of Ancient Art....
>
> It would be a violation of that copyright for a person or publisher to publish a translation of the transcription.

But the situation is quite different in Europe and South America, where new translations are being published on all sides. To list but a few: Uwe-Karsten Plisch, *Was nicht in der Bibel steht: Apokryphe Schriften des frühen Christentums* (Brennpunkt Bibel 3; Stuttgart: Deutsche Bibelsgesellschaft, 2006), presents a new German translation, 168–77, which is being reprinted in *Zeitschrift für antikes Christentum*. Peter Nagel is publishing an annotated German translation in *Zeitschrift für die neutestamentliche Wissenschaft* 98 (2007), fascicle 2. A Dutch translation that sold out in a month and is being reprinted was published by Johannes van Oort, *Het Evangelie van Judas: Inleiding, Vertaling, Toelichting* (Kampen: Uitgeverij Ten Have, 2006), with translation and commentary, 85–185. Three Spanish translations have been published, the most distinguished being that of José Montserrat Torrents, *Evangelio da Judas: Versión directa del copto, estudio y comentario* (Madrid, Buenos Aires, San Juan, Santiago: EDAF Arca de Sabiduría, 2006), with his translation, 63–82. Van Oort told me on October 29, 2006, that he assumed that the lawyers of the National Geographic Society were merely bluffing.

At a colloquium on "The Gospel of Judas: The Historical and Literary Context of a New Apocryphon," held at the Sorbonne in Paris on October 27–28, 2006, the insider Gregor Wurst announced that anyone is free to publish their own translation, and that Mario Roberty, head of the Maecenas Foundation for Ancient Art that owns the Codex Tchacos, had reassured him of this fact. At the meeting Wurst distributed to the participants the final transcription and English translation of the critical edition of all four tractates of the Codex Tchacos that he had just submitted to the National Geographic Society for publication, along with the facsimiles, in 2007. (It is a considerable improvement over what the National Geographic published at Easter 2006.)

I have updated somewhat the text of the first edition, which had been written before the *Gospel of Judas* was made public by the National Geographic Society with such fanfare at Easter 2006. Of course I have wanted to take any new information into account. But there were really no surprises. What I expressed in the future tense and stated only as "probable" can now be put in the past tense as fact. New is an introduction reporting on "The Extravaganza of Easter 2006." The sequence of the chapters is then revised, to report first on what led up to the extravaganza: "The *Gospel of Judas* Surfaces in Geneva," "The Peddling of the *Gospel of Judas,"* and "The Publication and Significance of the *Gospel of Judas*." Only then do I turn to the more academic topics: "The Judas of the New Testament," "The Historical Judas," and "The Gnostic Judas." The new final chapter, "The *Gospel of Judas,"* does put the newly published text into its second-century context in a way that of course could not be done until the new text became available.

Integrated into the jacket design of this book and provided as a sort of frontispiece to this Preface is an image of the last page of the *Gospel of Judas.* The lines on the last page, below the part that is too fragmentary to reconstruct in a meaningful way, are the heart of Judas's story and read as follows:

And their high priests murmured because [. . .] had gone into the guest room for his prayer. But some of the scribes were there watching carefully in order to arrest him during the prayer. For they were afraid of the people, since he was regarded by all as a prophet. And they approached Judas and said to him, "What are you doing here? You are Jesus' disciple." He answered them as they wished. And Judas received money and handed him over to them. >>>>>>>>>>>>>>>>>>>

>>>>>>>>>>>>>>>>>>>>>>>>>>>>>>>>>>>>>>>>>>>>>>>>

You can decipher the title at the bottom just by using the photograph that faces the first page of the Preface, if you can remember the shape of the Greek letters found on the fraternity and sorority houses of college campuses. This is because the Copts used the Greek letters in writing Coptic, and indeed often used Greek loanwords when they didn't have appropriate Coptic synonyms. The most obvious thing in the picture is a hole in the papyrus about the size of a penny. Just to the left of the hole, you can read, if you try hard, the Greek letters *PEUA*. So, you are ready to transcribe and translate. Ignore the P, since that is just the Coptic definite article *The.* But what follows, *EUA,* is the beginning of the Greek word for *Gospel, EUAGGELION,* familiar to us from our verb "e*v*angelize." (When *u* is between two vowels, it is treated as a consonant, so we transcribe it *v*.) Then comes the hole, where once there was papyrus with the letters *GG*. (Since double *g* was nasalized, i.e., pronounced *ng*, we transcribe it that way, "*ng*," yielding "eva*n*gelize.") Just to the right of the hole, you can see (if you look hard) *ELION*. So we transcribe the first line of the title *PEUA[GG]ELION, The Gospel*.

The second line of the title, the bottom line of the papyrus page, has the letters *NI* in a dark patch you cannot read, then *OUDAS*. The *N* is the Coptic genitive preposition, meaning *of*. The *I* before the diphthong *OU* functions as a consonant, so we translate it *J*. We translate the diphthong *OU* as a single vowel *u*. And so there you have it: *Judas*. See, in just five minutes you have translated the title, *The Gospel of Judas*, and even learned a little about Coptic!

INTRODUCTION

# The Extravaganza of Easter 2006

Since the *Gospel of Judas* is a Gnostic tractate written in the middle of the second century, it does not add any new information about what happened in Jerusalem around 30 C.E. Though it is an important text for specialists in second-century Gnosticism, such as myself, it has been misrepresented so as to sensationalize it in order to make as large a profit on its investment as possible. Caveat emptor! Or, in plain English, Let the purchaser beware!

Hershel Shanks, who knows more about sensationalism than most of us, put the situation in perspective. His "First Person" essay, entitled "Sensationalizing Gnostic Christianity," has the byline, "Is All the Recent Hype About the Gospel of Judas Really Justified?" A second byline answers the question: "The idea that this new gospel might be an accurate historical report of the reason for Judas's betrayal of Jesus is arrant nonsense." He explains:

> For scholars, this recently released apocryphal gospel offers significant insights into the arcane world of Gnostic Christianity, a diverse movement centered in Egypt between the second and fourth centuries.... For the early church, the Gnostics were heretics.
>
> The *Gospel of Judas* is significant for another reason: It adds to our understanding of the development of early Christianity. As professor Elaine Pagels of Princeton University observed at the National Geographic Society's news conference, early Christianity was even more diverse in its variety

> of traditions than the Protestants, Catholics, Orthodox, Mormons, etc., are today.
>
> Yet neither of these reasons accounts for the immense public interest in the gospel. The *Gospel of Judas* elicits such intense public concern because we are led to believe that it may give us—contrary to the portrait of Judas in the canonical Gospels—the real story of Judas.
>
> Imagine a headline that read "New Text Illuminates Gnostic Christianity." That would be a true description of the *Gospel of Judas*. But that article would hardly make it into a major newspaper. Or how about this: "New Text Documents Diversity of Early Christianity"? That, too, would be an accurate description of the new gospel. That might even justify a brief article on the "Religion" page.

Shanks concludes:

> In sum, the way the *National Geographic* has played up this story makes it guilty of unjustified sensationalism. I realize that some may consider this a case of the pot calling the kettle black. If that be treason, however, make the most of it.[1]

The National Geographic Society placed its extravaganza during the Easter season, with a press conference in Washington, D.C., on April 6, a two-hour so-called documentary on its TV channel on Palm Sunday, April 9, and a photo essay by Andrew Cockburn, "The Judas Gospel," in the May 2006 issue of *National Geographic* magazine, all timed to be further sensationalized on May 19 by the première of the movie version of *The Da Vinci Code*.

Already on March 12, 2006, London's *The Mail on Sunday* scooped the other media with a front-page headline that screamed: "WORLD EXCLUSIVE: The Gospel of Judas Iscariot: 'Greatest Archaeological Discovery of All Time' Threat to 2000 Years of Christian Teaching." The page where the article by Ian Gallagher and Sharon Churcher appears had its own headline: "After 2,000 Years—the Voice of Judas." Its byline: "WORLD EXCLUSIVE:

Churches Braced for Explosive Publication of 'Lost Gospel' Which Could Threaten Very Basis of Christian Teaching." The article begins:

> The *Gospel of Judas*—said to be one of the greatest archaeological discoveries of modern times—is about to be published amid explosive controversy, *The Mail on Sunday* can reveal.

The later byline reads: "It was an opportunity to cause a sensation." The article explains:

> A Swiss arts foundation acquired the document in 2002....
>
> The foundation struck a deal with the internationally highly-respected *National Geographic* magazine to publish the translations. But the decision to do so just before the holiest week in the Christian calendar has prompted accusations of deliberate sensationalism.
>
> The unveiling of the text—and the publication at the same time of a book telling the story of the quest for the lost gospel—comes just a month before the release of the film version of The Da Vinci Code, the worldwide best-selling book which makes unfounded claims about Christ's life.
>
> National Geographic also plans to screen a two-hour film about the gospel on its satellite TV channel on April 9....
>
> Last night a high-ranking Church of England figure who is familiar with the project told *The Mail on Sunday*:... "But if they are planning to peddle it as an exciting new truth about Judas and to hype it as a new gospel, that will upset not only a lot of theologians but a lot of laymen and I think there will be a lot of cancelled subscriptions to *National Geographic*."

The much briefer follow-up article on April 2, 2006, is entitled "The Gospel of Judas 'Will Show That Resurrection Didn't Happen.'" It continued the sensationalism by reporting a claim that "the document has the potential to 'turn Christianity on its head.'" Although the *Gospel of Judas* has nothing in it to turn

Christianity on its head, this kind of propaganda does sell books and make money.

On April 7, 2006, Stephen Tomkins made a report entitled "Not So Secret Gospels" on *BBC News:*

> The *Da Vinci Code* has turned this 2nd-century tract from a talking point at theological conferences to a media event, perhaps even a blockbuster.

This publicity effort was intended to recuperate the payment to the Swiss owner (Shanks: "over $1 million") by means of high sales of the two books, *The Gospel of Judas: From Codex Tchacos,* edited by Rodolphe Kasser, Marvin Meyer, and Gregor Wurst, and *The Lost Gospel: The Quest for the Gospel of Judas Iscariot,* by Herbert Krosney, both published at Easter 2006. But the news media have seen through all this, and so the sensationalizing of the *Gospel of Judas* has met with scathing criticism.

In a *New Yorker* book review entitled "Jesus Laughed," Adam Gopnik describes the publication of National Geographic's *Gospel of Judas:* "The event feels uncomfortably hyped."[2] The *Pasadena Star-News* of April 15, 2006, headlined its article by Kelly Rush: "Revelation or Hoopla?"

Peter Steinfels wrote in the *New York Times* on April 15, 2006: "A Debate Flairs on Betrayal," with the byline: "Did Judas Betray Jesus, or Did the National Geographic Society and Assorted Scholars Betray Judas?" His thesis: "But there is a question whether calculated sensationalism and scholarly complicity in it were justifiable means to achieve these results." The essay's argument is as follows:

> The documentary broadcast by National Geographic was a breathless and familiar brew of pounding music and portentous statements: talk of "rehabilitating Judas" and a story "that could challenge our deepest beliefs," create a "crisis of faith" or turn "tradition on its head."

> The documentary featured dramatic re-enactments, some of which, like the attractive female martyr forced into a sizzling-hot iron chair, would have done Mel Gibson proud. Scenes re-enacting Judas's dealings with Jesus, first in the traditional four Gospels, then in the Gnostic version, are played by the same actors, so viewers might be forgiven if they thought the documentary was addressing "what happened around 30 A.D."

The poor girl frying to death (Saint Blandine) enlivens the National Geographic Society's "documentary," augments the sensationalism, sells books. All this is in terribly bad taste. She has absolutely nothing to do with the *Gospel of Judas,* but only with making money. I cannot help recalling the one-liner that brought the McCarthy hearings to a halt: "Have you no decency?"

The phoniness and blatant hypocrisy of it all become clear every time one compares theory with practice.

## THE MONEY

### Theory: Make a Nonprofit Gift

The *New York Times* had already published on April 13 an investigation by Barry Meier and John Noble Wilford entitled "How the Gospel of Judas Emerged." Its focus was on Frieda Tchacos, the Zürich antiquities dealer who purchased the manuscripts containing the *Gospel of Judas:*

> For her part, Ms. Tchacos Nussberger rejected any suggestion that she was trying to profit from the Gospel of Judas.
>
> "I went through hell and back, and I saved something for humanity," Ms. Tchacos Nussberger said in a telephone interview. "I would have given it for nothing to someone who would have saved it."

### Practice: Make As Much As You Can

If Tchacos "would have given it for nothing to someone who would have saved it," she had a good opportunity right at hand. Immediately after purchasing the four manuscripts that were involved, she deposited them for five months (April–August 2000[3]) with Yale University in order to have them identified. In view of Yale's impressive papyrus collection, she had high hopes of selling them to Yale for a handsome profit. "Mrs. Tchacos offered them to the Beinecke Library of Yale University for $750,000."[4] Yale also has an excellent tradition of papyrus conservation.[5] Stephen Emmel, who first saw the codex in Geneva on May 15, 1983, and said then that he could conserve it in about a month of work (see Chapter 1), was the papyrus conservator at Yale while doing his doctorate there. He once located a box of papyrus fragments in Yale's Beinecke Library, which he identified as part of Nag Hammadi Codex III, 144,15–146,24, all of which he promptly reassembled and published.[6] But Yale University decided not to buy for its papyrus collection what Tchacos offered, since its legal status was questionable.[7]

Tchacos could have offered the manuscripts to Yale as a gift on the condition that it conserve them and return them to Egypt. Yale would no doubt have been glad to accept them under such conditions. The codex would have been published a decade ago, without sensationalism, and returned safely to Egypt, where it would today be accessible in the newly renovated Coptic Museum both to the scholarly public at large and to interested tourists.

Instead, Tchacos sold all four manuscripts, which she had acquired for about $300,000, and of which the *Gospel of Judas* was only a small part, to Bruce Ferrini, an antiquities dealer of Akron, Ohio, for $2,500,000.[8] This hardly qualifies as "giving it for nothing to someone who would have saved it." Or, to quote the sanitized version:

> She was out of pocket a substantial sum, probably hundreds of thousands of dollars, and she believed the financial burden was too great for her to bear.[9]

This indication of her limited finances does not quite agree with her reputation among the illegal excavators themselves:

> Tchacos was powerful ... and had noteworthy means at her disposal.[10]

Or, to quote one of her London business colleagues:

> "She speaks all the languages, and does business on the highest level; millions and millions of pounds," says one London dealer.[11]

On December 15, 2000, Mario Jean Roberty, as Tchacos's lawyer, wrote Ferrini's lawyer recording an agreement Tchacos and Ferrini had just reached at a meeting in New York (see Chapter 2):

> The *Logos Project* intends to save and publish the *Gospel of Judas* and other related manuscripts for the benefit of historical truth and to generate the funds necessary for this task as well as for the compensation of the expenses and efforts incurred by the promoters, leaving them with a decent profit.

If Yale had paid what she asked, the markup would have been only two and a half times what she paid. But Ferrini offered over eight times what she paid. Clearly it was a lucrative business deal, covering "expenses," "efforts," and "a decent profit." Such a profit would obviously not be "too great for her to bear."

Ferrini was not even chosen because he would be the one "who would have saved it." Indeed, he was blamed for causing great damage to the papyri, by putting them in his deep freeze:

> Mario Roberty says: "Ferrini proudly told me that he had adopted this 'technique' in order to separate the pages 'with no harm to the manuscript'?! Every professional hearing about Ferrini's 'technique' was flabbergasted and shocked." The

> freezer was later judged to have contributed to the texts' steadily increasing deterioration.[12]

But Tchacos herself had already shown her disregard for their protection by taking them to Akron in the first place. When not permitted to take them as hand luggage, she checked the box containing them in the baggage compartment on the plane from New York to Akron:

> The Gospel of Judas and its accompanying texts were shoved into the luggage compartment of the plane. She had wanted to sleep, but she could only wonder what further damage was being done to the papyri.[13]

Everyone knows how luggage gets tossed around if it is checked. Clearly, all this does not reflect much concern for the fragility of papyrus. Obviously Tchacos was determined to sell the fragile manuscripts for a handsome profit, no matter what their condition when they arrived in Akron (see Chapter 2). Even Krosney points out: "Selling to Ferrini had been Frieda's decision and therefore her responsibility."[14]

When Ferrini not only expressed concern about whether the material left Egypt legally but, after agreeing to the purchase, defaulted on his payments, Tchacos recuperated as much of the material as Ferrini had not already sold. His report of that scene to Charles W. Hedrick does not reflect her great concern for the preservation of the papyrus (see Chapter 2):

> Whoever was selling it to him … became angry and slammed the codex down on the table and tiny pieces of papyrus flew all over the place. The seller picked up the codex and left angrily saying, "Well, maybe I will just burn it."

Tchacos took what was left back with her to Switzerland. There she sold it to the Maecenas Foundation for Ancient Art, run by her attorney Roberty, "for $1.5 million and a share of future profits," according to the *New York Times* article of April 13, 2006, entitled "How the Gospel of Judas Emerged." That article reported:

> And after she failed to profit from the sale of the gospel in the private market, she struck a deal with a foundation run by her lawyer that would let her make about as much as she would have made on that sale, and more.

Roberty proceeded to secure whatever profit could be made by selling exclusive and secretive publication rights to the National Geographic Society, after which the material would be returned to Egypt "eventually,"[15] "ultimately,"[16] "several years after its first publication in the West."[17] Gregor Wurst reported to me at the Sorbonne meeting in Paris on October 29, 2006, that he thought the agreement with Egypt to return the material included a deadline of around 2010 C.E. Why this long delay? Presumably to allow time for the final critical edition to be published by Rodolphe Kasser. He as usual gives for his part an upbeat prediction:

> Before the end of 2006, the *editio princeps* of all texts of Codex Tchacos is to be published. The edition will contain top-quality full-size color photographs of all the pages of this codex. These will be supplemented by the reproduction, also in color, of those fragments of papyrus (unfortunately very numerous) that, during the reasonable time granted by Maecenas to avoid delaying too long the publication of the already relatively legible written surfaces, have not yet been placed. These pieces will not be fully identified and placed in their place of origin without considerable future efforts. Thus, identified or not, no remnant of this famous codex will be excluded from its *editio princeps*.[18]

But on November 9, 2005, Roberty had told the French journalist Patrick Jean-Baptiste that this *editio princeps*, including the photographs, would be published along with the two other

National Geographic volumes at Easter 2006.[19] Yet on February 13–14, 2006, Roberty reported:

> It was painstaking puzzle work. It will probably be going on for some time ... because we had a few more fragments popping up very recently. So there will be—for a full publication of the codex—there will be a delay.[20]

Hence, the excuse is already provided for Kasser's not meeting any deadline in 2006. A side effect of this interminable delay is that it keeps other scholars from being able to study the originals or published photographs ("a full publication of the codex"), and to this extent maintains the monopoly as long as possible. Gregor Wurst conceded at the Paris meeting that the deadline of 2006 would not be met, but predicted the publication in 2007.

The Egyptian government in turn agreed not to prosecute Tchacos for her shady antiquities dealings in that country:

> Madame is to receive a whitewashing certificate that protects her from Egyptian persecution because of illegal art exports.[21]

This detail is omitted from the sanitized "official" version of the story in Krosney's book published by the National Geographic Society.

The National Geographic Society then obtained a grant from the Waitt Institute for Historic Discovery,[22] reported in the *New York Times* of April 7, 2003, as follows:

> Ted Waitt, founder and former chief executive of Gateway, said the Waitt Institute gave the geographic society a grant of more than $1 million for the restoration.

A "Letter to the Editor" by Paul Legutko of Lexington, Massachusetts, published in the *Boston Sunday Globe* of April 16, 2006, concluded:

> Judas Iscariot sold out Jesus Christ for 30 pieces of silver, according to the Canonical Gospels. It's ironic that this message seems to be recapitulated 2000 years later in the millions of dollars of money-grabbing over this (stolen) papyrus on the part of businesses, lawyers, art dealers, and even the National Geographic Society. Let's hope it turns out better for them than it did for Judas.

A "Letter to the Editor" by James Turner of Notre Dame, Indiana, published in the *National Geographic* of September 2006 read:

> No reputable scholar believes the Gospel of Judas can tell us what happened circa A.D. 30. Prior to N[ational] G[eographic] S[ociety]'s antics around this interesting but hardly revolutionary manuscript, I had believed the Society existed to bring knowledge to a wider public. Its mission instead seems to be pandering for cash.

## THE MONOPOLY

### Theory: Scholars Renounce Monopolistic Rights

At the Eighth International Congress of Coptic Studies in Paris, July 1, 2004, organized by the International Association for Coptic Studies, Rodolphe Kasser announced that the *Gospel of Judas* had been acquired by a Swiss foundation and he had been given exclusive rights to study, translate, and publish it.

I am not only Honorary President of the International Association for Coptic Studies, which organizes that congress every four years—I had founded that International Association for Coptic Studies itself by writing its constitution and convening a meeting of Coptic scholars in Cairo to adopt it! At that founding meeting on December 17, 1976, I proposed a resolution that was unanimously passed to prevent monopolies from taking place in the future (see Chapter 3).

The reason that this resolution seemed necessary at the time was because first French, then German monopolies had kept most of the Nag Hammadi Codices inaccessible for a quarter of a century. UNESCO had set up an "International Committee for the Nag Hammadi Codices" (of which I was elected Permanent Secretary) to break such monopolies by publishing a facsimile edition.[23] The last Nag Hammadi Codex to become accessible to everyone was Codex I, since it had been secretly taken out of Egypt and purchased by the C. G. Jung Institute in Zürich, which named it the Jung Codex. It was entrusted to very slow editors, led by none other than the same Rodolphe Kasser now in charge of the *Gospel of Judas*! He had delayed making the Jung Codex accessible to the rest of the scholarly community by returning it to Egypt until the last volume of his own voluminous *de luxe* edition finally appeared (1975)—it was only returned to Egypt twenty-three years after it had been acquired by the Jung Institute (1952–75). The resolution was unanimously approved in Cairo to prevent such monopolies as that of the Jung Codex, which Kasser had administered, from happening again. But it did happen again, the first chance he got (see Chapter 3).

Similarly on November 25, 1991, when the monopoly on the Dead Sea Scrolls was finally broken, the Society of Biblical Literature passed a comparable resolution to prevent any such monopoly from happening again.

It was hoped at the time that these scholarly consensuses would prevent such monopolies from occurring again. This is why I have been so shocked by, and opposed to, the new monopoly. It is not that I would myself want to get involved—I have completed my UNESCO assignment to break the Nag Hammadi monopoly and my own career has moved in another direction. But I think an important new discovery should be accessible to all coptologists, not just to a select few. The repeated efforts by Krosney in *The Lost Gospel* to trivialize the issue as petty jealousy on my part[24] are simply an attempt to obscure the basic scholarly policy that Kasser has been violating again and again.

## Practice: Scholars Accept Monopolistic Rights

Present in Cairo and voting at the meeting of the International Association for Coptic Studies in 1976 were over a hundred founding members, including Rodolphe Kasser and Marvin Meyer. Meyer was also present in Kansas City at the 1991 meeting of the Society of Biblical Literature when its resolution was passed. Yet Kasser has had access to the *Gospel of Judas* since July 24, 2001, without having given access to the membership of the International Association for Coptic Studies, to whom he made his announcement on July 1, 2004, or to the scholarly community at large, much less of course to an interested wider public. Meyer accepted access at least by August 2005, when he reported to colleagues that he knew a lot more about the *Gospel of Judas*, but was not free to divulge it. As it turns out, he had been secretly enlisted by the National Geographic Society to provide the English translation of the *Gospel of Judas*. Both Kasser and Meyer were doing precisely what the International Association for Coptic Studies had voted in 1976 not to do, and what the Society of Biblical Literature had voted in 1991 not to do.

I fear this may have affected their scholarly reputation among their colleagues. John D. Turner, the author of the standard book on the Sethian branch of Gnosticism, to which the *Gospel of Judas* is said to belong,[25] and the leading authority on Sethianism in the world today (indicated by the fact that he has been invited to lecture on Sethianism at the Sorbonne), comments on the official transcription and translation of the *Gospel of Judas*, made available at Easter 2006:

> It is painfully clear to me that we lack a decent transcription and, even worse, any sort of reliable photographic evidence. What we now have is a very provisional version riddled with problems (unnecessary and even impossible emendations and restorations, misunderstandings of syntax, etc.), and a translation that is just as unreliable.... To be sure, the Judas Gospel is an important addition to the Sethian corpus, but it

has not yet been properly assessed and discussed by experts....

What is more, it seems to me that even on the basis of what survives in the better sections, the text (and the characterization of Judas) has been grievously misinterpreted by its principal interpreters (or should I say "guardians"?), who have characterized Judas according to the profile they think he ought to have had in Gnostic thought (with its supposedly "inverse exegesis") rather than exactly how the text does characterize him. Rather than the thirteenth "spirit" (why not translate what the text actually says?), Judas is the 13th "demon," his star leads the way merely by raising him barely above the level of the [evil] archon, and, probably as in Zostrianos, the luminous cloud likewise raises him just above the thirteenth of the aeons controlled by the archon. Judas is not a Sethite! Instead, Meyer and Ehrman and others have read the text according to their own preconceived ideas ... (even without benefit of photographic evidence I myself have had to alter both text and translation in nearly 40 places).[26]

## JUDAS AND TCHACOS

### Theory: The Confidante of the Gnostic Judas

According to the New Testament, the resurrected Christ appeared to apostles after the resurrection. This practice invited Gnostics to claim for centuries that he was still appearing to them with esoteric teachings contrary to the doctrines of the mainline church. Hence Luke in his second volume, the Acts of the Apostles, perhaps sensing such a trend, may have tried to nip it in the bud by reporting that the resurrected Christ appeared for only forty days, after which he ascended into heaven. Centuries later, the Blessed Virgin Mary assumed this mediating role by appearing at Lourdes and other such holy shrines. But today it is the Gnostic Judas who has become the communicator with earthly believers. Frieda

Tchacos reported in the National Geographic "documentary," according to the *New York Times* article of April 13, 2006: "I think the circumstance of this manuscript coming to me was predestined.... I was guided by providence."[27] She must have experienced Judas's approval of her and thus legitimation of her actions devoted to his vindication, perhaps while he looked down from the "cloud of light" that the official translation says he entered, according to the *Gospel of Judas.* Krosney quotes Tchacos on her religious experience:

> I had a mission. Judas was asking me to do something for him. It's more than a mission, now that I think of it. I think I was chosen by Judas to rehabilitate him.[28]

Krosney quotes more of her "religiously inspired language":

> "Judas chose me to rehabilitate him," she said. "He was leading me, pulling the strings to put me on the right path. But the unworldly forces who had kept him in the dark for thousands of years were fighting his restitution.
>
> "It had started with the robbery and it continued, following me at every step. It was as if the genie had been released from the magic lamp of Aladdin. It was as if Judas were fighting on my side trying to protect me from the blows, resolving the problems as they arose, leading me through the labyrinth to the final salvation."[29]

It thus seemed quite appropriate that Tchacos named the codex containing the *Gospel of Judas* after herself, Codex Tchacos. But for those of us not lured into this neo-Gnostic sect, it all seems a bit silly.

The Swiss newspaper *Neue Zürcher Zeitung* asked me to write an article about the *Gospel of Judas* to be published on Maundy Thursday, April 13, 2006. I slanted it toward the Swiss audience. Hence it included the following:

> This is the second time that Zürich has succeeded in acquiring a manuscript with a Gnostic Gospel not found in the New Testament. Already on November 15, 1953, the C. G. Jung Institute of Zürich had a public celebration of its acquisition of a fourth-century Coptic codex containing "The Gospel of Truth." The Director of the Jung Institute, Dr. C. A. Meier, "baptized" the codex on that occasion the "Jung Codex." It is no doubt meant as a flash-back to that occasion that the newly acquired codex was named Codex Tchacos.
>
> Actually, Carl Jung himself had resisted the codex being named after him. On Oct. 27, 1953, he wrote Meier: "I never felt comfortable with the idea that the codex would be baptized in my name.... I do not want to be the middle point of the celebration, nor do I want the codex baptized in my name." Apparently Tchacos did not have such modesty, when she named her acquisition "Codex Tchacos."

Nonetheless, "'I am a dealer who is doing all the right things,' Tchacos said," according to an interview of April 12, 2006, with the *Los Angeles Times*.

### Practice: The Judas of the Antiquities Trade

The *Los Angeles Times* is the newspaper that has done the most thorough investigation of Tchacos's illicit trade in antiquities, since Los Angeles's prestigious Getty Museum has been directly involved. The headline of the article by Jason Felch and Ralph Frammelino published on April 13, 2006, reads: "Judas Gospel Figure Has Tainted Past." The byline reads: "A Dealer Credited with 'Rescuing' the Document Allegedly Played a Major Role in the Looting of Antiquities. She Received a Suspended Sentence." The article reports:

> She was arrested by Italian authorities in Cyprus on unrelated charges of trafficking in looted art. In an agreement with the Italian prosecutor, she received a suspended sen-

tence of 18 months and gave a lengthy statement about her knowledge of the antiquities trade.

The *New York Times* article of April 13, 2006, entitled "How the Gospel of Judas Emerged" reported:

> The art dealer was detained several years ago in an unrelated Italian antiquities smuggling investigation.
>
> She described her run-in with Italian officials as inconsequential.
>
> But the emerging details are raising concerns among some archaeologists and other scholars at a time of growing scrutiny of the dealers who sell antiquities and of the museums and collectors who buy them. The information also calls into question the completeness of National Geographic's depiction of some individuals like Ms. Tchacos Nussberger and its disclosure of all the financial relationships involved.

It would seem that Tchacos avoided serving time in Italy by ratting to the Italian authorities on her business associates, who then bore the brunt of the prosecution. The *Los Angeles Times* article of April 13, 2006, made public that:

> Tchacos' statement has played an important role in the ongoing criminal trial of Marion True, the J. Paul Getty Museum's former antiquities curator who is accused of trafficking in looted art. Tchacos' willingness to talk has led some dealers to call her the Judas of the antiquities trade.
>
> Records also show that Tchacos sold to the Getty fragments of two of the objects Italian authorities are requesting be returned. The Getty returned a third, a drinking cup known as the Onesimos kylix after the Greek painter, to Italy in 1999 after determining it had been looted from Cerveteri, an Etruscan necropolis north of Rome.
>
> True's co-defendant, Robert Hecht Jr., describes Tchacos as an aggressive competitor who "daringly went to Cerveteri

> and paid cash on the spot." The statement is in Hecht's journal, a key piece of evidence in the Italian investigation.

The article in the *Los Angeles Times* reports:

> "In the past, she was at the center of the looting in Italy," said Paolo Ferri, the Italian state prosecutor who has led an investigation of the illicit trade for 10 years.

The *Los Angeles Times* article goes on:

> In a short interview Wednesday, Tchacos said she was never convicted in the Italian case, which she called an "equivocal situation," and she retired from the antiquities trade in recent years because of changing attitudes about its propriety. "I am a dealer who is doing all the right things," Tchacos said.

We surely trust that this is confirmed as the outcome of the court proceedings.

This was followed up by the *Los Angeles Times* on June 17, 2006, with an article by Elisabetta Povoledo, "Accused Robber Leads Police to Ancient Tomb," which was followed the next day with a front-page article by Jason Felch and Ralph Frammolino, "Getty's List of Doubts Multiplied," with the byline, "A Museum Review Finds 350 Works Bought from Dealers Suspected of Trafficking in Looted Art. Italian Authorities Have Not Been Given Details." This was followed on June 20, 2006, with an article by Jason Felch, Tracy Wilkinson, and Ralph Frammolino, "Getty May Surrender 21 Works to Italy," with the byline "Trustees OK a Deal on the Disputed Antiquities, Sources Say. The Offer Could Be Made Today." The front-page headline on June 22, 2006, read: "Getty to Return Artworks to Italy." The byline of the article, by Tracy Wilkinson, Jason Felch, and Ralph Frammolino, reads: "In a Breakthrough Deal, the Museum Would Turn Over Some Allegedly Looted Antiquities. Rome Is to Lend Pieces of Comparable

Quality." One can only hope that this brings to a mutually agreeable solution a major scandal involving Tchacos and those from whom she purchased Etruscan antiquities on the scene at Cerveteri just north of Rome. The *Los Angeles Times,* especially its reporters Felch and Frammolino, who first exposed Tchacos's involvement, are to be commended for following this story to its apparently positive conclusion.

The article in the *Los Angeles Times* on April 13, 2006, also identified a similar charge against Tchacos in England:

> She is also being sued in an English court to recover $3 million from the sale of an Egyptian statue that is part of a bitter financial dispute between a London dealer and the estate of his late partner. Lawyers for the estate allege that the London dealer, now in bankruptcy, failed to tell court overseers about the sale that he ran through Tchacos' Basle [read: Zürich], Switzerland-based company, Galerie Nefer.

It is not known whether the London case has been resolved, and, if so, how.

The official version of the story by the National Geographic Society tells a lot about Tariq al Suwaysi, the partner of the Alexandria dealer with whom Tchacos was negotiating the purchase of the *Gospel of Judas:*

> Egyptian antiquities have also been funneled through Switzerland. In 2002, Egyptian and Swiss authorities signed a security agreement designed to stop illicit trafficking, and within a year, in 2003, Swiss authorities handed over to the Egyptian government two mummies, sarcophagi, and masks that were among nearly three hundred objects discovered in a duty-free customs warehouse in Geneva. A primary figure in the wave of Egyptian arrests that followed was Tariq al Suwaysi, the head of Egypt's National Democratic Party's Giza office, who for years had worked with some of Switzerland's best and most important dealers, including Nicolas Koutoulakis....

> Years later, as mentioned earlier, Tariq would be arrested and brought to trial as one of thirty-one people involved in a massive antiquities smuggling ring that allegedly removed nearly three hundred pharaonic, Coptic, and Islamic artifacts from Egypt to Switzerland. Convicted in 2003, he was sentenced to thirty-five years in prison.[30]

But omitted from this official, sanitized version of the story is the connection with the agreement to return the Codex Tchacos to Egypt. It was reported by Michel van Rijn, himself a retired antiquities dealer who relishes exposing his former colleagues:

> After all, Frieda was one of Tarek El-Sweissi's principal dealers, the latter, of course, sweating in a hot Egyptian cell for the next 30 years.[31]

Tchacos's attorney Roberty, who is the sole official of the Maecenas Foundation of Basel, which owns the *Gospel of Judas,* has specialized in defending dealers in antiquities who get into such legal difficulties, according to the article in the *Los Angeles Times* of April 13, 2006:

> Roberty has a long history of defending dealers in the antiquities trade, including three other dealers now implicated in the Italian case. "I had the pleasure or the bad luck of being successful 30 years ago in a case that got myself known in this small circle," he said.
>
> Asked about his relationship with many of the antiquities trade's central figures, Roberty said, "If you're specialized in murder cases, you have to deal with murder[er]s. It doesn't imply you're one yourself."

The National Geographic Society presented Tchacos as the heroine of the story. When the *Los Angeles Times* asked Roberty about this, he gave an ambivalent reply:

> Roberty defended National Geographic's depiction of Tchacos as a savior of an important archeological relic, saying "perhaps a few expressions may be overdone, but it is correct."
>
> "There is no contradiction between even a very successful ancient art dealer and a protector of cultural heritage," he added.

It is of course a bit consoling that Roberty can concede that "a few expressions may be overdone" in the National Geographic Society's portrayal of Tchacos as the heroine of the story. Yet it is a euphemistic version of the facts to present the accusation as if it were only that she is "a very successful ancient art dealer." The issue is whether she violated the international law protecting the countries whose cultural heritage is being looted by such "a very successful ancient art dealer," and whether she got off the hook by incriminating others involved in her transactions. It seems that this may in fact be her closest affinity to Judas Iscariot. She may not represent the Gnostic Judas of the *Gospel of Judas,* whom she claims communicated with her as his delegate on earth to vindicate him. Rather, she may represent the Bible's Judas, if she betrayed those closest to her, her business associates.

Tchacos's role in betraying her business associates in order to avoid serving a prison term in Italy has been presented in all its lurid details in a four-hundred-page book documenting the illegal excavation, smuggling, and profiteering that is in fact a very large scandal, *The Medici Conspiracy,* by Peter Watson and Cecilia Todeschini.[32] It was excerpted first by *U.S. News and World Report* on June 19, 2006, in its cover story by Thomas K. Grose entitled "Stealing History: Famous Museums, Brazen Thieves, and Priceless Antiquities," with the byline, "Cultural Treasures Are Being Looted—And Museums and Collectors Are Turning a Blind Eye." It was again excerpted in the Archaeological Institute of America's journal *Archaeology* in July/August 2006, in an article entitled "Raiding the Tomb Raiders: How Italy Cracked the Network of Looters, Smugglers, and Dealers Supplying

American Museums."[33] But the book itself contains much more. It takes nineteen lines in the index under "Tchacos-Nussberger, Frederique 'Frida'" to list all the references to her activities. Only the central facts of her betrayals to avoid imprisonment can be cited here:

> Frida Tchacos was interrogated in rather dramatic circumstances that came about partly by accident....
>
> Ferri [the Italian state prosecutor] issued an international warrant for Tchacos's arrest and initiated the legal process for her extradition to Italy. Now she couldn't travel—the minute she crossed any international border, she would be arrested and held.
>
> While the extradition process was working its way through the Swiss legal system, Ferri received a visit in Rome from Tchacos's lawyers, seeking agreement. After several hours of discussion, Ferri agreed that he would drop the charges against her *if* she complied with two demands. First, the real Artemis must be returned, and second, she must write a detailed memoir, setting out what she knew about the antiquities underworld in general, naming names and giving particulars about Medici's and Hecht's and Symes's operations....
>
> Tchacos agreed to Ferri's conditions.... At this point, Ferri rescinded his extradition request. But Tchacos ... never sent Ferri a memoir.... And so, although he withdrew the extradition request, he did not withdraw the international warrant for Tchacos's arrest.
>
> Therefore, when Tchacos—believing that there were no legal impediments hanging over her—next took a trip abroad, she was in for a surprise. She had a brother who lived in Cyprus, and in the second week of February 2002, she landed at Limassol airport. At passport control, she was recognized, arrested, and held. The Italians were informed, and she was kept in jail overnight, before being placed under house arrest at her brother's. It took three or four days before Ferri and two

of Conforti's senior men could get to Limassol, and the intervening period was clearly a distressing experience for her and may help explain why, during her interrogation, when it came, she was so cooperative. It may also have had something to do with the fact that Ferri, normally so mild-mannered, now saw his chance and, sensing Tchacos was vulnerable in Cyprus, agreed to hurry only if she agreed, in his words, to "amply cooperate." She agreed, he hurried, and she was interviewed over two days on February 17 and 18, 2002.

What he wanted from her was what he had originally asked for—a memoir, her view of the way the underworld really worked, and the part played in it by Medici, Hecht, Symes, and the others. She did not disappoint this time, immediately confirming the existence of the cordate....

Tchacos was astonishingly forthcoming. Perhaps it was her character, perhaps it was the fact that she was, at the time, under arrest in Cyprus.

Ferri's instincts about Tchacos's mood in Limassol were correct. While they were there together, they arrived at a deal.... He said the charges would be confined to offenses that carried penalties of two years or less (with a good chance that the prison terms would be suspended) and, more important, Tchacos would not be joined in the conspiracy charges that he was planning to bring against Medici, Hecht, Robin Symes, and perhaps Marion Treu.

Frida Tchacos agreed to this deal and, on September 17, 2002, she was convicted of handling stolen and smuggled goods, and of failing to notify the authorities of the antiquities that came her way. She was given one year and six months' imprisonment, suspended, and fined 1,000 euros (approximately $1,000).[34]

We can only hope that Ferri's case against "Medici, Hecht, Robin Symes, and perhaps Marion Treu" is being resolved as comfortably for them as it was for Frieda Tchacos herself. This, then, is what Tchacos has brushed off to the *New York Times* as "inconsequential." She had told the *Los Angeles Times* that the Italian case was an "equivocal situation," for she was never convicted. She had "retired from the antiquities trade in recent years only because of changing attitudes about its propriety." This sanitized version of the story is in line with her attorney's reference to her as "a very successful ancient art dealer and a protector of cultural heritage" and her own claim that she is "a dealer who is doing all the right things." There could hardly be anything more phony than this official version of the story.

## CONCLUSION

The radiant face of Tchacos in the pictures of her in the National Geographic Society's book *The Gospel of Judas* and in the *National Geographic* magazine's May 2006 issue, as well as again and again in the two-hour TV documentary on the National Geographic channel on April 9, 2006, makes it clear that she thought that the *Gospel of Judas* would make her famous. Instead, she has only succeeded in making herself infamous. She will go down in disgrace.

And what of those she enlisted in her money-making enterprise? What of the National Geographic Society's "calculated sensationalism" and the "assorted scholars" involved in the "scholarly complicity in it"?

1

# The *Gospel of Judas* Surfaces in Geneva

The *Gospel of Judas* has not been seen for many centuries, having been successfully suppressed by the orthodox church. But the veil of secrecy has been lifted by Rodolphe Kasser, who announced to the scholarly world the fact that it had surfaced and, incidentally, that he was editing it:

> On July 1, 2004, at 11:30 am the world finally hears more. In the Picard auditorium of a Paris research institute near the Seine, Kasser, the philological Nestor, climbs the platform of the "Eighth International Congress of Coptic Studies," to begin his 20-minute speech, long awaited by the scholarly world, on the topic that, at first glance, seemed harmless, "Un nouvel apocryphe copte" (A New Coptic Apocryphon).
>
> Already after a few sentences it becomes clear that Kasser will celebrate the discovery, as the "extremely seldom and wonderful resurrection" of its main document. It has to do with a work that made a sensation in the second century after Christ, but later again almost completely disappeared from the stage. It really has to do with the copy of the most condemned writing of antiquity: the *Gospel of Judas,* first attested by the church father Irenaeus of Lyon around 180.[1]

Kasser's Paris announcement has produced all too sensational German-language articles in journals for the nonscholarly public, first by Ralph Pöhner in the Swiss newsmagazine *FACTS,*[2] then a cover story by Roger Thiede in its German equivalent *FOCUS.*[3] This was then followed by Malcolm Macalister Hall's English-language exposé of the mutual attacks on the Internet by Roberty and Michel van Rijn.[4] Both Pöhner and Hall had interviewed me by phone from Zürich and London while preparing their articles, although my answers to their questions didn't seem to have much effect on what they wrote. The result is that these journalistic essays, which apparently first opened up the story to a wider public, function as a very entertaining, if not very enlightening, by-product of the otherwise sensational enough story of the *Gospel of Judas.*

The essay by Pöhner, entitled "Judas the Hero," begins, just below the title, with the summary:

> It is almost as old as the gospels of salvation of the New Testament—and shows a completely other view of the betrayer of Jesus. For centuries the "Gospel of Judas" was missing. Now the early Christian writing reappears. It is in Switzerland.

Pöhner quite rightly quotes scholars in the field to underline the importance of the *Gospel of Judas.* Ludwig Koenen, professor of classics at the University of Michigan, reported that "there was no doubt as to its authenticity"; "in my capacity I could judge that." From Stephen Emmel, professor of Coptic studies at the University of Münster, Germany: "Of extraordinary interest." From Peter Nagel, professor of church history at the University of Bonn, Germany: "Very, very valuable." And Charles Hedrick, professor of religious studies emeritus at Missouri State University, said: "It is always exciting when one discovers a lost Gospel. This one here will help us to complete the scintillating picture of Christianity in the second century."

Indeed, scholars assume that the *Gospel of Judas* was written somewhat more than a century after Jesus's death. The standard edition of the apocryphal New Testament books states:

> Dating: The *Gospel of Judas* was of course composed before 180, the date at which it is mentioned for the first time by Irenaeus in *adv. Haer.* If it is in fact a Cainite work, and if this sect—assuming it was an independent Gnostic group—was constituted in part, as has sometimes been asserted, in dependence on the doctrine of Marcion, the apocryphon can scarcely have been composed before the middle of the 2nd century. This would, however, be to build on weak arguments. At most we may be inclined to suspect a date between 130 and 170 or thereabouts.[5]

But the *Gospel of Judas* disappeared soon afterward and hasn't been seen again by academics until 1983.

## ORGANIZING THE GENEVA MEETING OF MAY 15, 1983

The University of Michigan is the American university with the strongest tradition of acquiring and editing papyrus manuscripts. And in 1975, Michigan reinforced this reputation by luring to its Classics Department from the German University of Cologne a distinguished expert with quite a track record of his own for acquiring and editing papyrus manuscripts, Ludwig Koenen. Perhaps he is best known for the Cologne Mani Codex, a miniature biography of the third-century Persian founder of the dualistic religion Manichaeism; the codex is today the star exhibit in the papyrus collection of the University of Cologne. It is so miniature that it can hardly be read with the naked eye and must have served more as an amulet to bring good luck than as a book to put on the shelf, much less to read.

Since Koenen had good connections both inside and outside Egypt for acquiring manuscripts, it is no coincidence that it is he who was invited to come to Geneva to meet with a Copt from Egypt and a Greek from Athens who had important manuscripts for sale.[6] Koenen had received a few photographs of very bad quality, presumably so that they could not be used for unauthorized publication, but good enough to indicate the importance of the papyrus manuscripts. He had been able to identify one as a Greek metrodological text (on how to measure things), in which he was primarily interested, and another as the book of Exodus in Greek, in which his Old Testament colleague David Noel Friedman was interested. So the two of them resolved to go to Geneva and negotiate the purchase. But a third was written in Coptic, which neither of them could read and which neither was interested in purchasing.

Koenen knew that I was working in Coptic, as the American representative on the International Committee for the Nag Hammadi Codices. Hence Koenen approached me about whether I would be interested in participating in the negotiations (and funding), so as to acquire the manuscripts in Geneva. He was going to Geneva in May 1983 to meet with the sellers and hoped to consummate a deal for their purchase while there.

I was not free to go to Geneva on a moment's notice, and the Institute for Antiquity and Christianity, of which I was director, did not have funds for such an acquisition, no matter how tempting it might be. But I did the best I could under the circumstances. I had earlier brought together a team of young American scholars to edit the Nag Hammadi Codices, and so I sent out an urgent appeal to them to see what they could do to make this venture possible.

The only member of our team who was able to offer any assistance was Harold W. Attridge of Southern Methodist University. Harry had been a Junior Fellow at Harvard, the highest distinction a graduate student there could receive. Then Harry moved to his first teaching position at the Perkins School of Theology at Southern Methodist University in Dallas, Texas. Harry later moved on to Notre Dame, where he became dean, and from there to Yale University, where he is currently dean of the Divinity School.

Harry secured a pledge from the acquisitions funds of the Bridwell Library at Perkins School of Theology, authorized by Deckerd Turner, the divinity librarian at the time, for the total budget for the year, $50,000. Harry reports that "Mr. Turner and Bridwell had a fund for the purchase of rare and theologically significant books and he was happy to collaborate with the effort to acquire the codices." Harry notified me promptly that this money could be made available for the Geneva venture.[7] It is interesting that the manuscripts would actually be seen by Harry years later when he was at Yale.

## WHAT STEPHEN EMMEL SAW IN GENEVA

Since I was not able to make the trip from California to Geneva to verify the value of the Coptic manuscript and negotiate its purchase, I thought the best I could do was to fund the trip for a former student of mine, Stephen Emmel, who was doing research at the time with Tito Orlandi, Italy's foremost Coptic scholar, in Rome, which was a less expensive "short" train trip to Geneva. I persuaded Steve to go to Geneva on my behalf.

Steve had become fascinated with Gnosticism when he was still in college and part of the student culture that grew out of resistance to the Vietnam War. Like most college students of the time, he knew all about taking trips through the heavens, but he determined that "thinking is the best way to travel." He came across Gnosticism in an introductory course on Judaism and Christianity in 1970 and then happened to get hold of Hans Jonas's *The Gnostic Religion,*[8] a book that made existential sense for him of the complicated mythology of Gnosticism, with its message of Gnostics escaping this evil world below by flying through the skies to the higher unknown God above.

Nothing would do but that Steve had to learn about these ancient "hippies," whose secrets were due to be revealed in the still unpublished Nag Hammadi Codices. Steve recalls:

> I became interested in Coptic history while I was a student at Syracuse University in the United States at the beginning of the 1970s. I was interested in philosophy and religion—all the philosophies and religions—as different ways in which human beings have searched for truth and the meaning of life. In an introductory university course about Judaism and

> Christianity, I discovered the ancient Gnosis or Gnosticism, and I learnt that most of the original ancient Gnostic sources were written in Coptic. The most important sources are the Nag Hammadi codices, which are ancient papyrus books written in Coptic. I was so interested in reading these books that I learnt Coptic, and came to Cairo in 1974 to work on them at the Coptic Museum with my university professor, James M. Robinson.

Steve found out that I was the person in America at the center of efforts to break the monopoly and get access to these new manuscripts, and so he came to study with me. That was just when I was about to go to Cairo for a sabbatical in order to reassemble the fragmentary leaves of the codices so that they could be photographed and published, which was the way that I had figured out to break the monopoly. He tagged along, and ended up the best conservator of papyrus anywhere! Steve stayed on in Cairo long after my sabbatical was over, to complete the work of assembling the fragments to restore the leaves.[9] And so he was still in Cairo at the right time to help me, from a distance, organize the First International Congress of Coptology in Cairo, where we founded the International Association for Coptic Studies.

Steve has advanced brilliantly throughout his career, ending up in the only permanent Chair of Coptic Studies in the world, at the University of Münster, Germany. The Institute for Egyptology and Coptology, where he works there, is in effect the Secretariat of the International Association for Coptic Studies he helped me found. He edits its newsletter and helps to organize its congresses every four years. Indeed, he was closely involved in organizing the most recent congress in Paris, in 2004, where the *Gospel of Judas* was first announced.

Steve took the train from Rome to Geneva, where he joined up with Koenen and Friedman. On May 15, 1983, they met in a hotel room with a Copt from Egypt, who spoke no English, and a Greek from Athens, John Perdios, who spoke English and functioned as translator.

Perdios had grown up in the international society of Cairo. But when the Egyptian revolution deposed King Farouk and created a socialist state, most of the well-to-do foreign colony left. Though Perdios now lived in Athens, he stayed in contact with his Coptic friend, for they had been classmates in Cairo. Obviously Perdios was functioning as the intermediary for the Coptic owner in the transaction.

Steve has recently described what went on:

> That was in 1983. At the time I did not know that it had to do with the *Gospel of Judas.* The codex contained three writings. I could identify on the spot the second text. I could also see the third part, a dialogue between Jesus and the disciples. I even read the name Judas. Only I did not see the line "The Gospel of Judas."

When asked why he did not see the title, he replied:

> The circumstances under which we had to work were very unfavorable. The examination took place in a hotel. We only had half an hour time, and were not permitted to take any photographs, or write anything. The papyrus leaves were very fragile. So I could peep in only here and there.[10]

Malcolm Macalister Hall, when reporting on the story, quoted Steve in considerably more detail:

> "We were given about half an hour to look into what were effectively three shoeboxes, with the papyri wrapped up in newspapers," says Emmel. "We weren't allowed to make any photographs, or take any notes. The people who had them knew really nothing about them except that they were valuable—and that they wanted money."
>
> The bundles included a mathematical treatise, and the Book of Exodus, both in Greek. Emmel saw that the Coptic manuscripts—in a single leather-bound volume with its back

cover missing—included *The First Apocalypse of James* and *The Letter of Peter to Philip* (both already known to scholars from a huge collection of ancient manuscripts which had been found in the 1940s, known as the Nag Hammadi Library). [A photograph of Codex Tchacos dated to 2001 shows the subscript title *Letter of Peter to Philip* (followed by the ankh symbol of life and a cross), no doubt much as Emmel saw it.[11]] But there was another manuscript too. It appeared to be a dialogue between Jesus and his disciples. Emmel saw the name Judas, but, because the papyrus was in such fragile condition and beginning to crumble, he could only lift each page slightly with his philatelist's tweezers, and could not see any title page. However, he deduced—correctly, as it turned out—that this was a previously unknown work of Gnostic literature, and unique. (An early sect within Christianity, the Gnostics were repeatedly denounced as heretics.)

To Emmel, the meeting had an air of cloak-and-dagger, and he suspected that the papyri had been smuggled. "The indication was that these were people who were not exactly working in bright daylight," he says. "I think there was no question but that this material should have still been in Egypt." And the price came as a shock.

"They were asking $3m [$3 million]—and they said that this was down from the original asking price of $10m. I don't know if that was true—I think this was just a way of saying $3m was a bargain. They were not interested in selling any of the items separately. And my budget from Southern Methodist was just $50,000. We were flabbergasted by this price."

Emmel says Professor Ludwig Koenen—the leader of the academic party—then went into the bathroom with the Egyptian, to negotiate. "When they came out I could see on Koenen's face it was a no-go," Emmel recalls. Banned from taking notes, he had all the while been desperately trying to commit to memory all the details of the texts he had seen. When the two sides then had a valedictory lunch together

> after the failed deal, Emmel made his excuses, slipped out to the lavatory, pulled a scrap of paper from his pocket and noted down everything he could recall. He never saw the manuscript again....
>
> Stephen Emmel agrees that this has been just another disaster for Coptology. "It is, but we're used to it," he says, resignedly. "Coptic manuscripts in general have not survived well. It's not anything new, but it's sad because if scientists could have taken that manuscript out of its shoebox in that hotel-room in Geneva in 1983 and worked on it, we would have had a very well-preserved manuscript. Now we've got another collection of fragments. We may never be able to restore it fully."[12]

The Dutch reporter Henk Schutten also quoted Steve in some detail:

> The meeting was extremely secretive, the manuscripts were smuggled out of Egypt, so much was clear. Questions about the origin were not appreciated.
>
> They were not experts. They believed that there were three manuscripts, but there were actually four. After a quick listing, we learned that they dated from about the fourth or the fifth century AD. Two manuscripts, a translation of the Book of Exodus and a mathematical essay, were written in Greek. They were packed in separate boxes just like some letters of Paul the Disciple also written in Coptic (old Egyptian).
>
> They were held together by a leather strap and the edges should have been intact back then. Its owners have not cared much for the find. Only half of the strap and part of the probable cover had been preserved and there were holes and tears in the pages.
>
> The numbers of the pages went up to sixty, while most papyrus-codices are at least twice as big. I suspected half of the manuscript to be missing.[13]

When asked what he thought when he saw the name Judas, Steve replied:

> The name was not decisive. Just as any knowledgeable person would have done, I assumed that it had to do with the namesake of Judas Iscariot, the disciple Judas Didymos Thomas. He occurs often in apocryphal Gospels, more often than Judas Iscariot. It is also for him that the *Gospel of Thomas* is named. If I had seen the title at the end, it would of course have immediately occurred to me that Iscariot was meant, especially since right above it, as the last sentence of the text, there stands: "Judas took some money and handed him over."[14]

Actually, Steve had edited the one Nag Hammadi tractate in which the name Judas frequently occurs, in a dialogue of the disciples with Jesus. He and everyone else assumes it refers to Judas Didymos Thomas, given its similarities to the *Gospel of Thomas* (Nag Hammadi Codex II,2) and the *Book of Thomas* (Nag Hammadi Codex II,7), where Judas Didymos Thomas is involved.[15] The sale price was $3 million, which was far more than the potential purchasers could produce. Perdios later reported to me that Friedman had said off-handedly that the owner should drop one zero from the asking price. Of course, when bargaining in the bazaar, it is not expected that one will pay the first asking price, but will negotiate down to a mutually agreeable price. This is the world the owner had always lived in and understood quite well. But it would be considered an insult for the first counteroffer to be only 10 percent of the asking price; such an offer intimates that the seller knows nothing of the value of his wares or is simply trying to milk the potential buyer. Hence, the owner was offended. The negotiations ended before they had really begun.[16] In any case, they would hardly have succeeded, since a tenth of the $3 million was probably as much or more than the purchasers would have been able to produce. In fact, Steve is reported to have said: "We could perhaps have paid a tenth."[17] There is some irony in the fact that this was the offer that was accepted seventeen years later! Yet the three codices were not acquired in 1983, and the three potential purchasers went away empty-handed.

Almost! Steve had been less involved in the negotiations themselves and had been able to focus instead on the Coptic codex. He was permitted to examine the Coptic leaves in enough detail to be able to decide that they were really all that was left of *two* Coptic codices. He was able to distinguish the second Coptic codex from the fact that it consisted of fragments put in the two boxes that held Greek texts, that it was of different dimensions from the main Coptic text, and that its writing area had been outlined in pink chalk. The existence of fragments of a fourth codex was kept secret from the sellers, since it looked as if they had set the asking price at the round figure of $1 million per codex. Obviously the potential purchasers did not want the price to jump to $4 million!

After the negotiations had failed, the parties nonetheless all went out for lunch together, which was when Steve excused himself to go to the bathroom and transcribe what his acute eye had seen and memory had retained of the Coptic material. He afterward wrote his notes in a confidential memorandum, which he sent to me. We did not want it made public at the time, lest it get back to the sellers and escalate still further the asking price. But its details can now be made public, since the purchase has been consummated, and nothing is to be gained by further confidentiality. His report is hence published for the first time at the conclusion of this chapter.

Steve identified three Coptic tractates, two of which are familiar from duplicates in the Nag Hammadi Codices: one was a copy of the *First Revelation of James* known from Nag Hammadi Codex V,*3*,[18] and one a copy of the *Letter of Peter to Philip* known from Nag Hammadi Codex VIII,*2*. There was no way to know whether there were more than three tractates. Of course Steve could not sort through the whole stack of fragile papyrus leaves with his "philatelist's tweezers," but had to "peep in only here and there." This comment is an important detail, since it indicates that journalists' statements referring to the number of leaves in the lot purchased by the Maecenas Foundation are no more than speculation.

Steve could only identify the third tractate, a previously unknown text, as a dialogue between Jesus and his disciples (a standard Gnostic literary genre), though he happened to observe the name Judas. This is what is now known as the *Gospel of Judas*. But he did not identify the Judas in question as Judas Iscariot. As he explained in the interview quoted above, the normal assumption would be that "Judas" referred to Didymos Judas Thomas, since he is listed as the author of two Nag Hammadi tractates. The *Gospel of Thomas* (NHC II,2) begins:

> These are the hidden sayings that the living Jesus spoke and Judas Thomas the Twin recorded.

This introduction seems to have been echoed at the beginning of the *Book of Thomas* (NHC II,7):

> The hidden sayings that the Savior spoke to Judas Thomas, which I, Mathaias, in turn recorded. I was walking, listening to them speak with each another. The Savior said, "Brother Thomas, while you are still in the world, listen to me and I shall reveal to you what you have thought about in your heart.
>
> Since it is being said that you are my twin and true friend, examine yourself and understand who you are, how you exist, and how you will come to be."

All this is clearly a play on the name Didymos Judas Thomas, with which the *Gospel of Thomas* begins. *Didymos* is the Greek word for "twin," and *Thomas* is the Semitic word for "twin." So both of these Nag Hammadi tractates are ascribed to a person named Judas and nicknamed "Twin."

In the Gospel of John (11:16; 20:24; 21:2), this Judas is simply named Thomas, with the added translation, "called the Twin," here using the Greek word *Didymos.* He is considered one of the inner circle, but is not identified as Jesus's brother. Nor is the nickname Twin explained. He is most familiar to us as the "doubting Thomas," due to his insistence that he touch Jesus's wounds before he will believe that it is the same person who was crucified (John 20:25, 27–28). So it would be logical for Steve to assume this new tractate was ascribed to Didymos Judas Thomas familiar from titles in the Nag Hammadi Codices, rather than to Judas Iscariot, the disciple who gave Jesus over.

## CODEX TCHACOS IS NOT FROM NAG HAMMADI

The very fact that two of the three tractates that are in the codex containing the *Gospel of Judas* are duplicates of Nag Hammadi tractates has misled some into thinking that this new codex, discovered only a few years before being shown in Geneva in 1983, is part of the Nag Hammadi discovery of 1945. But this is not the case, for a number of reasons.

It would be a misunderstanding of the collection of codices that were discovered near Nag Hammadi. Examination of distinguishing characteristics, such as the technique in manufacturing the leather covers, the different scribal hands involved in copying the codices, and the differences in Coptic dialect among the translations of tractates, shows that they tend to fall into four clusters. But there are no duplicates within a single cluster, only in different clusters. Hence if the codex with the *Gospel of Judas* had been part of the Nag Hammadi discovery, this one codex would have to be ruled a fifth separate cluster of tractates, only secondarily brought together with the Nag Hammadi Codices. But there is no reason to assume that such a fifth separate cluster of tractates was secondarily brought together with the Nag Hammadi Codices! In fact the only analogy points in a different direction.

There is already an instance of duplicates with Nag Hammadi tractates in a codex that we know was not part of the Nag Hammadi discovery. In 1896 a codex was discovered and deposited in

Berlin, named Papyrus Berolinensis 8502, which has duplicates of two Nag Hammadi tractates as well as two tractates not found in Nag Hammadi, the most famous of which is the *Gospel of Mary*.[19] So the existence of duplicate tractates does not mean that both copies came from the same discovery.

What the public does not realize is that Coptic manuscript discoveries are taking place in Egypt on an almost regular basis since the Nag Hammadi discovery, and no one has suggested that these come from Nag Hammadi.[20] The fact that the discovery that included the *Gospel of Judas* also involved a Greek mathematical text and a Greek copy of the Psalms as well as a Coptic copy of Pauline Letters does not suggest that these materials were part of the Nag Hammadi discovery.

Yet the idea that the *Gospel of Judas* was part of the Nag Hammadi discovery seems not to want to go away, since such a claim only heightens the sensationalism. So let me try to put it to rest once and for all.

Stephen C. Carlson reports:

> Roger Pearse of the Tertullian Project had put together a history of the discovery of the Nag Hammadi Library ("The Nag Hammadi discovery of manuscripts," July 30, 2003). Of possible relevance to the *Gospel of Judas* is this bit of information (**emphasis** added):
>
> The books were divided among the 7 camel-drivers present. According to 'Ali there were 13 (our 'codex XIII' was not included in the number, as it was inside codex VI). **Thus a codex was lost more or less at the site**. Seven lots were drawn up. Covers were removed and each consisted of a complete codex plus part of another. The other drivers, ignorant of the value and afraid of sorcery and Muhammad 'Ali, disclaimed any share, whereon he piled them all back together.[21]

This presentation, which is used by Carlson to suggest (boldface) that there is a missing Nag Hammadi codex, is an oversimplified summary of a report I made in 1979 that actually pointed in the opposite direction. So I need to quote my own presentation to straighten things out:

> Muhammad 'Ali decided to divide the codices on the spot among the seven camel drivers present. Evidence of only 12 codices survives today. What is called Codex XIII consists of only eight leaves, which were removed from the center of the codex in late antiquity, in order to separate out a tractate inscribed on them, and then laid inside the front cover of Codex VI. These leaves probably would not even have been noticed by the discoverers, much less considered a separate codex. Yet when pressed, Muhammad 'Ali maintained that the number of codices in the jar was not 12 but 13. Thus it is possible, though unconfirmed, that a quite fragmentary codex was completely lost at the cliff. Since the number of codices was fewer than enough for each camel driver to receive 2, Muhammad 'Ali prepared seven lots each consisting of a complete codex and parts of the others torn up for this purpose. Muhammad 'Ali has maintained that covers were abandoned at the cliff, which would account for the missing cover of Codex XII as well as for that of any unattested cover. The other camel drivers, ignorant of the value inherent in the codices and fearing both sorcery and Muhammad 'Ali, renounced their claims to a share. He then stacked the lots back together in a pile, unwound his white headdress, knotted them in it, and slung the whole bundle over his shoulder. Unhobbling his camel, he rode back to his home in al-Qasr, in the courtyard of which the animals were kept and bread baked in the large clay oven. Here he dumped the codices, loose leaves and fragments, on the ground among the straw that was lying by the oven to be burned. 'Umm Ahmad [his mother] has conceded that she burned much of the ripped-out papyrus and broken covers, perhaps parts of the covers of XI and XII, in the oven along with the straw.
>
> The removal of leaves from their cover at the cliff and the subsequent burning of some in the oven may be correlated to

some extent with the condition in which the material was first examined and recorded in detail. If another codex existed, no trace of it has been brought to light, since the surviving unplaced fragments either seem to have the same scribal hands as do the codices that survive, and hence, presumably, to have come from them, or are too small or preserve too little ink to provide a basis for conjecturing the existence of further codices.[22]

Muhammad 'Ali had heard me and others talk of thirteen codices, and so he would quite naturally speak of thirteen, not recalling what he had counted at the time (if he had counted at all—he was illiterate). In all probability he was just playing back what he had learned was the "correct" number. In any case, his report of what happened at the time of the discovery would not indicate that a previously unknown codex containing the *Gospel of Judas* survived to appear a generation later. Rather, his report would indicate that anything that has not reached its final destination in the Coptic Museum in Cairo was shredded at the cliff or burned in his mother's oven. There is no way that his report can be twisted into the suggestion that the *Gospel of Judas* was in a codex from the Nag Hammadi discovery. Subsequently, on reading my report, Roger Pearse has withdrawn his suggestion.

Henk Schutten interviewed the most famous Dutch Nag Hammadi expert and reported in an essay translated by Michel van Rijn:

> [Gilles] Quispel does not exclude that the Gospel of Judas has the same origin as the Nag Hammadi documents.

Quispel was the Dutch representative on the International Committee for the Nag Hammadi Codices, of which I was Permanent Secretary, and it is he who went to Belgium to take possession of Nag Hammadi Codex I on behalf of the Jung Institute of Zürich. But I have been through his archives, which he entrusted to me for preservation in the Nag Hammadi Archives I have collected, and can report that Quispel had no information on the present topic. There is nothing in them that would indicate any connection between the *Gospel of Judas* and the Nag Hammadi Codices.

Yet Schutten reports Quispel as saying:

> "Judging by its content, it is clearly a Gnostic document. There is a reference to Allogenes, also called Seth, the third son of Adam and Eve. In Jewish gnosis Seth is viewed as the Saviour." In many old documents from the first years of Christianity references to the *Gospel of Judas* can be found, says Quispel. But after being banned by the Church, the manuscript seemed to have disappeared from the face of the earth. Not surprising, according to Quispel: "Gnosis is the most persecuted religion in the world. Followers were put to death by the Catholic Church. He who possessed the manuscript risked his life." Religious historians assume that the *Gospel of Judas* has been written in the same period as the canonical gospels of Mark, Matthew, Luke and John. Because the Judas-manuscript is written in Coptic—the last stage of Old-Egyptian—it is assumed that this is a copy translated from Greek from the original text presumably from the first or second century. Is the Gospel written by Judas? That is a difficult question to answer for Quispel. "I doubt it very much, but you can never entirely exclude this option." An obvious conclusion is that this text is from an Early Christian Sect, called the Kainite....
>
> Till middle of last century what was known about old Gnostics was mainly based on documents of the Catholic Church that fought the doctrine with fire and brimstone. This changed when in 1945 farmers found an urn in Nag Hammadi in Upper-Egypt containing 12 books—or codices, written on papyrus and held together with a leather strap. The Nag Hammadi Codices consist of 52 documents, most of them with Gnostic intent. The most famous document out [of] this collection, the *Gospel of Thomas* [read: *Truth*], was

purchased by Professor Quist [van Rijn's play on the name Quispel] in 1952.

Just like the Gospel of Judas, the Nag Hammadi–documents ended up in the hands of money hungry art dealers, among them a Belgian dealer.... Quispel wrote to several sponsors when he heard of the discovery. With a cheque for 35,000 Swiss Francs in his pocket he finally got on the train to Brussels on May 10th, 1952. "A mere trifle, even in those days, but I did return to the Netherlands with the manuscript. Nowadays, these documents would be worth four to five million dollars." Quispel does not exclude that the Gospel of Judas has the same origin as the Nag Hammadi–documents. He remembers how in 1955 he visited Tano, a Cypriot dealer in Cairo with a large number of documents, upon request of Queen Juliana, who showed a lot of interest in the Gnostics. "The Egyptian authorities seized Tano's collection, but he wrote to me later on that he left for Geneva to offer some documents for sale that he was able to smuggle out of Egypt to Martin Bodmer, a rich Swiss. It would not surprise Quispel that the Gospel of Judas fell into the hands of Bodmer through the same Phokion Tano.

"Bodmer placed the documents in a Swiss foundation named after him. He hired a Swiss minister who taught himself Coptic to translate it. This minister, Rodolphe Kasser, is the man who is finalizing the translation of the Gospel of Judas."[23]

For Quispel to suggest that Tano sold the *Gospel of Judas* to Bodmer is utterly ridiculous. It has been put on display only recently in the Bibliothèque Bodmer near Geneva, having been conserved by its conservator in nearby Nyon. It had been offered for sale in Geneva a generation earlier (1983), and then wandered to New York, Yale University, Akron, Ohio, and perhaps elsewhere. But all of those travels would not have taken place if Tano had sold it to Bodmer! He would have promptly deposited it in the Bibliothèque Bodmer, just as he did his other acquisitions.

Quispel's pupil, a distinguished Dutch authority on Gnosticism, is Johannes van Oort. His more sober news release is also translated by Michel van Rijn, with the title "Gospel of Judas Not by Judas":

> The owner of the text, who only wants to make money from it, has carefully timed the publicity surrounding what is called the *Gospel of Judas*. That is the opinion of Prof. Hans van Oort, who specializes in Gnosticism, Manichaeism, Nag Hammadi and Augustine. He called a press conference on his own initiative, to counter "all the nonsense" being written at the moment about the *Gospel of Judas;* for example, that the Vatican has an interest in the document's not being published....
>
> Van Oort does not rule out that it involves the missing codex from the Nag Hammadi codices. What he does rule out is that Judas himself wrote it: "There is no reason whatsoever to assume that he did this. Nothing points to that."...
>
> Van Oort is one of the few people who knows the contents of the *Gospel of Judas*, but does not want any trouble with its owner, the Swiss Maecenas Foundation. "If I did, I would be killed."[24]

Yet I had first mentioned the discovery of the codex containing the *Gospel of Judas* in print precisely in order to make clear that it was not part of the Nag Hammadi discovery:

> There have emerged no cogent reasons to postulate that there were more [than thirteen Nag Hammadi codices]. For though a sizable part of a Fourth Century Gnostic codex was seen by Ludwig Koenen and Stephen Emmel in Europe in 1983, containing a different version of *The* (First) *Apocalypse of James* and a copy of *The Letter of Peter to Philip* (with this as its subscript title), as well as a previously unknown dialogue between Jesus and his disciples, it is associated provisionally with a different provenience than Nag Hammadi and should

> not, without some positive evidence to that effect, e.g., from physical traits or from the cartonnage, be identified as a Nag Hammadi codex.[25]

By "physical traits" I had in mind the handwriting, the technique in manufacturing the quire(s), and the leather cover. And by "the cartonnage" I had in mind references to places, dates, and names often found in the trash papyrus used to thicken and line the cover. No such supporting evidence has emerged. There is absolutely no reason to assume that the manuscript containing the *Gospel of Judas* was part of the Nag Hammadi discovery. The place where it is reported to have been discovered is much farther down the Nile, nearer where the Oxyrhynchus manuscripts (an enormous horde of ancient texts including many New Testament papyri) were discovered a century ago. And yet the association with Nag Hammadi is too good to let go of easily. Michel van Rijn comments, without any information to go on:

> The manuscript was dug up at [or] near Nag Hammadi, then illegally exported from Egypt and illegally imported in the US, where Frieda acquired it.[26]

## SCHOLARLY PUBLICATIONS ABOUT THE DISCOVERY

Though at first I had hesitated to publish anything about the discovery of this previously unknown Coptic manuscript, lest it get back somehow to the owner or his agent and they raise their asking price accordingly, Steve's report did have scholarly information that colleagues would of course be eager to know. I was particularly pleased that Steve had been able to read the title of the second tractate, the *Letter of Peter to Philip.* The copy in Nag Hammadi Codex VIII,2 has a title set off at its beginning that reads more fully: "The Letter of Peter Which He Sent to Philip." But I had, for purely practical reasons, abbreviated it, for use by scholars, to precisely the title that turned up on the new copy: "The Letter of Peter to Philip."

I passed on the information at the time to Hans-Gebhard Bethge, since he was writing a dissertation (at Humboldt University, Berlin, 1984) on the *Letter of Peter to Philip,* and he mentioned in print this second copy:

> Ep. Pet. Phil. however was also handed down outside the Nag Hammadi codices, but the text of the parallel version is so far not yet available for scholarly evaluation.

In a footnote he explained how he had heard about it:

> The first information about the existence of this text, which is in a papyrus codex along with a version of 1 Apoc. Jas. and a dialogue of Jesus with his disciples not identical with NCH III 5, was given by J. M. Robinson and S. Emmel at the Third International Congress of Coptic Studies in Warsaw in August 1984.[27]

At that time in Warsaw, we would never have dreamed that it would take twenty years, until the *Eighth* International Congress of Coptic Studies, in Paris, before we would learn on July 1, 2004, what the dialogue of Jesus with his disciples was: the *Gospel of Judas*!

My student Marvin Meyer, who was preparing our critical edition of the *Letter of Peter to Philip,* also included in it a reference to the duplicate copy in 1991:

> According to the reports of James M. Robinson and Stephen Emmel, a somewhat divergent Coptic text of the *Letter of Peter to Philip* is to be found in a papyrus codex which at the present time is neither published nor available for study.[28]

I had forwarded to Meyer in March 1991 what I could read from the blurred photographs that I had received from Koenen. Meyer published this very fragmentary transcription, parallel to the text of Nag Hammadi Codex VIII,2, 135,25–136,2. (Marv, like Harry

Attridge and Steve Emmel, reemerged a generation later as a major player in the story.)

It is striking that Rodolphe Kasser, when he announced on July 1, 2004, in Paris that he had been authorized to publish the manuscript of the *Gospel of Judas,* made no reference to these previously published bits of information about the codex, although he was aware of them. It is normally the scholarly way to begin with references to previous publications about such a new text. Surely he knew about them, for he was the Swiss representative on the International Committee for the Nag Hammadi Codices. Prior to the publication of each volume in *The Facsimile Edition of the Nag Hammadi Codices,* which was theoretically authorized and supervised by that committee, I sent each member a prepublication copy of what I had written for publication in the respective volume for review, and they all received complimentary copies of each volume as it was published (from the publisher, E. J. Brill). Furthermore, the places where Bethge and Meyer published their comments were the kinds of publications that, though too esoteric for the sellers to know about, were precisely the kinds of standard scholarly tools that were of course on Kasser's bookshelf.[29] But Kasser's presentation in Paris of a new manuscript discovery seemed more sensational by omitting any reference to its having already been mentioned in publications years ago. What was in fact the only new thing in Kasser's sensational speech about the codex was the title of the tractate, the *Gospel of Judas.*

## ONGOING EFFORTS TO FUND THE ACQUISITION

The experience of not being able to engender enough funds to negotiate successfully for the purchase of the manuscripts in 1983 made me realize that having contacts with wealthy patrons who collected such things might prove useful if ever I hoped to reopen these negotiations. So I was able to interest Martin Schøyen, a wealthy Norwegian collector of ancient manuscripts, in acquiring them.

In the late 1980s I was frequently passing through Athens, usually on my way to Egypt to work on the Nag Hammadi Codices. So I made a serious effort to track down the Athenian person whom Steve had met in Geneva. Naturally, I inquired of Koenen, for he had set up the Geneva meeting through this Athenian as the intermediary,[30] with whom he may well have had previous experience in acquiring manuscripts for the collection at Cologne. Koenen was kind enough to give me his name, John Perdios, and his phone number in Athens, at a travel agency operated by his brother. ("John" is of course just the anglicized form of his Greek name, Johannes. The "official" report uses the Greek nickname for Johannes, "Yannis" Perdios.)

I went to Athens, and he received me in his elegant home. His own specialty was buying and selling paintings of the nineteenth-century Bavarian tradition because, he explained, Greece had imported a royal family from Bavaria at the time, and imported along with the royal family were their Bavarian art and paintings. Perdios took me to dinner at the best outdoor restaurant in Athens to go over, in such a leisurely atmosphere, plans for acquiring the manuscripts. The outcome was that he agreed to meet Schøyen and me in New York along with the Coptic owner.

Perdios never divulged to me the name of the owner, perhaps lest the owner be charged by the Egyptian government with illegal excavation and exportation or Perdios be bypassed in favor of direct negotiations with the Coptic owner. Perdios would of course not want to be cut out of his share of the profit!

The "official" report has at the opening a "Who's Who in *The Lost Gospel,*"[31] where one finds "Hanna Asabil (pseudonym), antiquities dealer, Egypt." But the description of Hanna's residence in that report identifies him clearly for those who, like myself, have visited him there more than once. The report reads:

> Hanna, who originally came from Al Minya Province, had done well in Cairo. He was an able seller of precious items, though known in the marketplace for his high prices and a streak of stubbornness. It was said that he had bought several

> buildings in Cairo, including the multistory apartment house in which he lived in the well-to-do Heliopolis section northeast of the city. That he tried to sell items of antiquity out of his apartment is confirmed by dealers who dealt with him.
>
> Hanna Asabil's apartment was not ostentatious. Like many others in Cairo at the time, it was part of a series of dilapidated structures that conveyed a seedy elegance. Like much of the city, the building was in urgent need of renovation.
>
> Even though Hanna owned the entire building, the interior of his own apartment was not especially attractive or elegant. The narrow entrance was also a reception room. The living room was small, with a hard-cushioned sofa pushed against one wall. In front of the sofa was a rectangular table with a glass top, with ashtrays full of cigarette butts. A naked light bulb hung from the ceiling.[32]

I visited Riyad Jirjis Fam (and his son Nashi) in this apartment on January 15, 1980, and again on August 10, 1981.[33] My purpose was to interview them about the Bodmer Papyri, since I was writing an (unpublished) book on that topic.[34] I had identified, near Nag Hammadi, the site of that discovery (near Dishna) and had interviewed there those who had been involved. They had given me Riyad's name and Heliopolis address 37 Shari Abd Allah Abu al-Su'ud as the main middleman. Riyad proudly told me that he bought his Heliopolis "palace" and moved in already in 1961, though the building was only completed in 1963.

I inquired of Perdios why he proposed New York for the meeting. He said his brother lived there, and he would like to visit him. I assumed that the more basic reason was that the codices were there. He would have known that we would want to see them before committing ourselves, and indeed would want to take possession of them if the negotiations succeeded. Of course I could only conjecture that they might be in the custody of his brother or of someone in the large Coptic community in New Jersey. They are now reported to have been in a safety-deposit box in Citibank, Hicksville, Long Island, New York, to which Riyad had been taken by a Coptic priest from New Jersey. Michel van Rijn had reported:

> After Hannah and Koutoulakis worked out their differences, the gospel was sent to a cousin of Hannah in NY, without declaring it at customs.[35]

The "differences" between Hanna/Riyad and Koutoulakis were indeed very major, requiring a whole chapter in Krosney's book to narrate all the exciting/disgusting details.[36] The deposit of the manuscripts in New York required a more modest chapter.[37]

I proposed to Schøyen, and he agreed, that we meet on a date agreeable to the sellers. I had gone so far as to check out New York hotels! Thus, we were actively making preparations late in 1990 for the meeting. But just at this time Iraqi president Saddam Hussein decided he needed to annex Kuwait to expand his oil empire on the way to Saudi Arabia. President George H. W. Bush sent him an ultimatum to withdraw, with the threat that if he did not do so, the United States would intervene militarily in January. Thereupon I received word from Perdios that the Copt was not willing to abandon his family at the beginning of World War III. The trip had to be called off!

When I was in Europe a few years later I phoned Perdios, saying I could go quickly to Athens to see about setting up the New York meeting again. He said he would contact his Coptic friend when the friend next came from Middle Egypt to Cairo and would let me know. But I never heard from him again. The meeting never took place. But my interest in these elusive Coptic codices did not die.

French Canadian scholars at Laval University in Québec are publishing the French edition of the Nag Hammadi Codices, and I have functioned as a consultant for the Canada Council on their behalf. They have also received grants from the Canadian Bombardier Foundation. They thought that this foundation might also fund the acquisition of the new Coptic manuscripts that Steve Emmel had viewed in Geneva, making it possible for the Québec team to stay together and continue its work even after the completion of its edition of the Nag Hammadi Codices.

These scholars' funding from the Canada Council included a stipend for a visiting professor in Coptic to strengthen their own limited faculty resources. They had once inquired if I could recommend someone. I suggested one of the world's leading Coptic scholars, the German Wolf-Peter Funk, whom I expected to see shortly when I visited East Berlin. As it turned out, I was approaching Funk at a propitious time, and he expressed his willingness to go to Canada, where he has been ever since, as the authority on Coptic grammar in Laval's ongoing seminar as it prepares each volume for publication. But he has no permanent chair at the university, so that his future, after the completion of the Nag Hammadi project, is uncertain. It is understandable that the Laval team hoped that it could acquire the new Coptic manuscripts. I told members of the team how they could contact Perdios by phone, and one of them, the Norwegian Einar Thomassen, did phone him in September 2001, but nothing came of it. Of course by this time the manuscripts had long since been sold. Thus my efforts to acquire the new Gnostic manuscripts came to naught.

## KOUTALAKIS AND MIA

A German newsmagazine published an article by Roger Thiede that, despite his opening claim to the contrary, is a sensationalistic, and perhaps to some extent fictional, version of the efforts to sell the *Gospel of Judas:*

> The following story is true, even though on first glance it might seem to be a remake of John Huston's film "The Maltese Falcon."

His story begins:

> At the endless haggling over the coveted antiquity in the Swiss hotel room, there surface first of all: the unscrupulous

> jeweler Hannah from Cairo, who wants to hawk an anthology with three early Christian tractates in a foreign country, in a very stubborn way for exactly three million dollars, no cent less; further, as buyer, the art dealer who was a resident of Geneva, Nikolas Koutoulakis.

This would seem to be a false conflation of the meeting of May 15, 1983, with the confrontation in 1982 between Hanna/ Riyad and Koutoulakis. But then Thiede also provided otherwise unattested information about the provenience:

> The mysterious manuscript had survived 1600 years in a stone box in the desert sand of the Middle-Egyptian location Muh Zafat al-Minya.[38]

Krosney gives the location as follows:

> The burial cave was located across the river from Maghagha, not far from the village of Zarara in what is known as Middle Egypt.[39]

Then Thiede's story promptly turns sexy:

> Now, to be sure, its last hour threatens.
>
> For the pair of dealers have a falling out with each other. The cause is the indispensable *femme fatale,* who, as fits her genre, sees to it that there is chaos. Due to his lack of knowledge of human nature, Koutoulakis wants to entrust to his young love Mia detailed negotiations—promptly the lady attempts to get one over on him. In the counter-attack the furious sugar daddy forces his way into the apartment of the Egyptian. In the tumult the loot is ripped crosswise. Large parts land in Mia's purse, and then evaporate for a long time. One folio leaf is lost forever. The remainder Koutoulakis is able to secure. Later the Greek avenges himself on the Cairo opponent: Massive threats of murder had their effect.[40]

Krosney devotes much of his chapter entitled "The Robbery" to this young woman, whom he introduces somewhat ambiguously as follows:

> The well-known Geneva-based dealer Nicolas Koutoulakis often arrived in Cairo accompanied by two women who were his regular traveling companions. One was a red-haired beauty, the second a tall brunette. The redhead was a woman known sometimes as Mia, at other times as Effie, and she was known by some Egyptians as Fifi. She and Koutoulakis were understood to have an extremely close relationship. Though Greek, she hailed originally from Cairo and was considered by the Koutoulakis family as a Cairene native. Her Arabic was fluent, and Koutoulakis used her as a translator in his dealings with Hanna and other Egyptians.[41]

She surfaces later on in the story in disposing of the loot:

> Among those whom Koutoulakis called in his recovery effort was Dr. Jack Ogden, the distinguished London gem specialist....
>
> The person who had sent the necklace to Ogden was a redhead named Effie, Ogden said. She had come to London on several occasions to provide him with small items such as earrings or a tiny ring, which Ogden took on consignment. Some of these goods he assumed were bought by Effie in the souks of Cairo.
>
> Was the Effie who visited Ogden the same as the Effie or Mia who was a companion of Koutoulakis? That link makes sense because, according to one source, Effie's full first name was Efthimia. The name means "joy" in Greek. In popular Greek usage, she could be called either Effie—or Mia. In other words, judged only by the name, Effie and Mia could be one and the same person. As recounted by Ogden, Effie was a redhead. Manolis Koutoulakis, twenty-nine years of age at the time, agrees that the Effie his father knew was also a redhead.[42]

Michel van Rijn tells the story on his Web site briefly, though with even more detail, not to say humor:

> Egyptian jeweler Hannah received a stone box from a man who thought he'd come across something big. What he found was unbelievably huge: inside that box was the *Gospel of Judas.* Hannah hunted around for possible buyers, quite aware of its value, demanding US$3 million for it. Finally, Geneva-based Greek dealer Nikolas Koutoulakis sent his girlfriend Mia (or was it Effy?) to scope out the situation. Working behind her lover's back, she struck a private deal with Hannah, but too late. The Sneaky Greeky was leagues ahead of his two-timing wench of a girl, and robbed Hannah's home of all manuscripts including the pages of Judas's glory.
>
> He then smuggled them to Geneva, where they were offered for $3,000,000. In the madness of smuggling, theft and deception of sex and religion, Mia had ended up stealing a few of the pages. In the interim, Koutoulakis showed his papyri to fellow Greek antiquities dealer Frieda Tchakos, who was based in Zurich. This was in 1982.[43]

If the cliché is ever appropriate, then here: this is too good to be true! Yet this story is told in even more detail in the "official" text—which I leave for you to read for yourself.[44] But Thiede's story goes on:

> In spite of the clearly emaciated manuscript, Hannah is on the lookout further for clientele. Newly recruited evaluators from American elite *Unis* fly in. They should help transfer the discovery over into academic domains. Yet all transactions break down on the price. Even Yale is not willing to come up with such an exorbitant sum.[45]

The time when Yale had the manuscripts for identification and perhaps for purchase was much later (2000), and its reason for not acquiring the manuscripts was their questionable legal status.

"Yale was worried about possible legal issues and declined to buy them."[46] But Thiede, Pöhner, and van Rijn had obviously gotten a more or less correct version of what went on prior to 1983 even before it was officially published. One may well wonder whether anything can be done with their story other than enjoy it. But we pedantic scholars do look for bits and pieces of information even in such more or less fictional stories.

It is of course possible that efforts by Hanna/Riyad to sell to Koutoulakis took place, indeed went so far as to involve Frieda Tchacos, but when they broke down, Perdios approached Koenen on behalf of his friend. Yet the damage reported in connection with Mia/Fifi/Effie/Effy does not seem to be reflected in the eyewitness report by Steve Emmel in 1983. But really all that we can know with any certainty about the *Gospel of Judas* in Geneva is Steve's eyewitness report.

## EMMEL'S REPORT OF JUNE 1, 1983

### REPORT ON THE PAPYRUS MANUSCRIPTS OFFERED FOR SALE IN GENEVA, SWITZERLAND, MAY 15, 1983

The collection of papyri being offered for sale consists of four separate manuscripts, and possibly fragments of some others. A system of numeration and designations was agreed upon with the owner and his intermediary for referring to the four manuscripts, as follows:

1. "Exodus" (Greek)
2. "Coptic Apocalypses Codex" (Coptic)
3. "Letters of Paul" (Coptic)
4. "Metrodological Fragment" (Greek)

The material was being stored in three cardboard boxes lined with newspaper. Items 1, 2, and 4 were each in a separate box, with the fragments of item 3 mixed together with items 1 and 4. This report is concerned only with the Coptic items, mainly with item 2, briefly with item 3.

Item 3 is fragments of a papyrus codex from the 5th (possibly 4th) century A.D. containing at least some of the letters of St. Paul. The leaves are approximately 24 cm. tall and 16 cm. broad. The scribe outlined his writing area with pink chalk. His handwriting is cursive in style, as though somewhat quickly written. The pages are numbered above the center of a single column of writing, the highest page number observed being 115. There are some nearly complete leaves of the codex preserved, and many smaller fragments, which might be reassembled into at least a sizeable portion of the codex. There is also part of a leather binding (either the front or the back cover, including the spine, lined with scrap papyrus) which probably, though not certainly, belongs to this codex. The contents identified with certainty are Hebrews, Colossians, and 1 Thessalonians. The texts are in a nonstandard form of the Sahidic dialect.

Certainly the gem of the entire collection of four manuscripts is item 2, a papyrus codex from the 4th century A.D., approximately 30 cm. tall and 15 cm. broad, containing Gnostic texts. At the time that the codex was discovered, it was probably in good condition, with a leather binding and complete leaves with all four margins intact. But the codex has been badly handled; only half of the leather binding (probably the front cover) is now preserved and the leaves have suffered some breakage. The absence of half of the binding and the fact that page numbers run only into the 50's lead me to suppose that the back half of the codex may be missing; only closer study can prove or disprove this supposition. The texts are in a nonstandard form of Sahidic.

The codex was inscribed in a single column in a large and careful uncial hand. Page numbers were placed above the center of the column and decorated with short rows of diplés (>>>>) above and below. At least pp. 1–50 are represented by substantial fragments which, when reassembled, will make up complete leaves with all four margins intact. The portion of the leather binding preserved is lined with cartonnage, layers of scrap papyrus glued together to form a kind of cardboard. At least some of this cartonnage is inscribed, offering hope that the date and location of the manufacture of the codex can be determined with some precision once the cartonnage has been removed and studied.

The codex contains at least three different texts: (1) "The First Apocalypse of James," known already, though in a different version, from Nag Hammadi Codex (NHC) V; (2) "The Letter of Peter to Philip" known already from the NHC VIII (in the new manuscript this title, [in Coptic] TEPISTOLH MPETROS SHAFILIPPOS, is given as a subscript [cf. the superscript title, slightly different, in NHC VIII 132:10–11] accompanied by decorations to fill out the remainder of the page on which the text ends); and (3) a dialogue between Jesus and his disciples (at least "Judas" [i.e., presumably, Judas Thomas] is involved) similar in genre to "The Dialogue of the Savior" (NHC III) and "The Wisdom of Jesus Christ" (NHC III and the Berlin Gnostic codex [Papyrus Berolinensis 8502]).

The leaves and fragments of the codex will need to be conserved between panes of glass. I would recommend conservation measures patterned after those used to restore and conserve the Nag Hammadi Codices (see my article, "The Nag Hammadi Codices Editing Project: A Final Report," American Research Center in Egypt, Inc., *Newsletter* 104 [1978]: 10–32). Despite the breakage that has already occurred, and that which will inevitably occur between now and the proper conservation of the manuscript, I estimate that it would require about a month to reassemble the fragments of the manuscript and to arrange the reassembled leaves between panes of glass.

According to the owner, all four of the manuscripts in this collection were found near the village of Beni Masar, about 8 km. south of Oxyrhynchus (modern Behnasa). It is difficult to know how seriously to take such information. Study of the cartonnage in the two surviving covers will probably provide more certain information as to the provenance at least of the manufacture of the codices.

The owner asked $3,000,000 for the entire collection. He refused to consider lowering his price to within a reasonable range, claiming that he had already come down from $10,000,000 in negotiations with one previous prospective buyer. He also refused to discuss the prices of the four individual items separately. He would like to sell all four manuscripts together, but probably will sell them individually if necessary.

I strongly urge you to acquire this Gnostic codex. It is of the utmost scholarly value, comparable in every way to any one of the Nag Hammadi Codices. Like them as well, it is one of the oldest specimens of a book in codex form; the fact that part of the cover is also preserved is a remarkable stroke of luck. There is great danger of further deterioration of the manuscript as long as it is in the hands of the present owner. This unique item must be put as quickly as possible into the hands of a library or museum where it can be restored, published, and conserved.

Stephen Emmel
June 1, 1983

Riyad Jirjis Fam
37 Shari Abd Allah Abu al-Su'ud, Heliopolis

2

# The Peddling of the *Gospel of Judas*

In the previous chapter, the story by the Dutch-born, London-based Michel van Rijn on his "artnews" Web site ended with Geneva-based art dealer Nikolas Koutoulakis showing the papyrus manuscript of the *Gospel of Judas* to fellow antiquities dealer Frieda Tchacos in 1982. According to the "official" story, it was Perdios who inquired of Tchacos in Zürich "if Frieda possibly had a client for some valuable texts, giving her some photographs that had been taken previously."[1] But the actual acquisitions by Tchacos took place only in 1999–2000.

## THE SWISS PURCHASE, 1999–2000

Roger Thiede reported on the acquisition, making the point that Mia, Koutoulakis's devious girlfriend, was involved:

> First when the smart attorney Mario Jean Roberty, spokesman of the worldwide-active Basel "*Maecenas Stiftung für antike Kunst*" [Maecenas Foundation for Ancient Art], as well as his client, the business-woman Frieda Nussberger-Tchacos of the Zürich gallery Nefer, take over leading rolls, does the thing get rolling. In 1999 the purchase succeeds, with parts coming from Mia's direction.[2]

In typically Swiss bilingualism, Ralph Pöhner had given the first name of the Zürich businesswoman, in French, as Frédérique,[3] of which Frieda is a Swiss-German abbreviation or nickname. She was born of Greek parentage in the international community of Alexandria, Egypt. In that international community, French was the lingua franca, which would no doubt explain the French form of her first name as well as the fact that she went to Paris for her university education at the École du Louvre. She has a hyphenated last name, which in Switzerland is the proper way for married people to give their names: first the last name of the husband and then, after a hyphen, the maiden name of the wife. Thus, prior to her marriage, her name would seem to have been Frédérique (Frieda) Tchacos. Tchacos is a Greek name. (My Swiss friend and colleague at Harvard Divinity School, François Bovon, assures me that it is neither German nor Swiss dialect.) It is sometimes spelled with *k* (Tcha*k*os), instead of *c* (Tcha*c*os), with the *k* being of course the Greek kappa, though often transliterated, as here, with *c*.

Krosney gives more details. In 1999, Tchacos received a phone call from a Greek "with a rough village accent" who offered photos of a small ancient manuscript he had for sale. The photos had in the background Greek newspapers dated October 21, 1982, which made her think of the manuscripts offered in 1982. She sent the photos to Robert Babcock, curator of the Beinecke Library at Yale, who suggested the Coptic text must be part of what had been seen in Geneva on May 15, 1983. With this encouragement, she made the purchase for $25,000 from a certain Lyonis, Mia's boyfriend.[4]

Tchacos seems to have been just the right person for the job, as described by Malcolm Macalister Hall in his report:

> Behind the Maecenas Foundation façade, the manuscript's real owner is one of the biggest antiquities dealers, Frieda Tchacos (aka Frieda Nussberger). She declined, via Roberty, to be interviewed for this article, but is described by London dealers as "very shrewd, very low profile, very smart." Said to be of Greek parentage but brought up in Alexandria, she later moved to Switzerland and has run galleries in Paris and Geneva. "She speaks all the languages, and does business on

the highest level; millions and millions of pounds," says one London dealer.

Roberty says the reason Tchacos declines to discuss the manuscript is that, since publicity about the gospel in recent weeks in German and Swiss magazines, Christian fundamentalists have picketed her home in Switzerland, and daubed slogans on its surrounding walls.[5]

Tchacos no doubt speaks German and its Swiss dialect in Zürich and Basel, French in Paris and Geneva, Greek in Athens, Arabic in Cairo, and English in New York and on the National Geographic TV channel. It is indeed useful that "she speaks all the languages." Pöhner, a Swiss journalist of Zürich, reported with obvious pride:

> Finally in 1999 the Swiss interests take over the batch of documents from the Egyptian. "We have it from him," confirmed Roberty; who the man in Cairo was, the lawyer is not willing to reveal: "We want first to make sure that the Egyptian authorities do not take legal proceedings against him for exporting cultural materials."[6]

Actually, the acquisition of the bulk of the material from "the Egyptian" took place only in 2000. Van Rijn reported:

> In the summer of 1999, Frieda had come across some stolen papyrus that she thought to be Mia's. She then traveled to Cairo in November, where she discussed the purchase of the full manuscript with Hannah. Hannah had put the Gospel in a rusty safe-deposit box in a Citibank in Hicksville, New York. She flew out to see it and purchased it soon after for an unknown sum.[7]

Thiede also mentioned Hanna/ Riyad's parts as acquired only in 2000, when the "parts coming from Mia's direction" are united with the rest:

> In the year 2000 Frieda Nussberger achieved the reuniting of the treasure with those parts that Hannah had meanwhile deposited in the basement of the Citibank of Hicksville, New York.[8]

The "official" report gives the details of the meeting of Tchacos and Hanna/Riyad in New York.[9]

Roberty has clarified the awkward situation in which the Egyptians involved would find themselves:

> You see, the problem we have with Egypt (to whom the codex will be donated) is that their system of law is quite different from ours. There is not a real reliability. So we prefer, and in the publication many names of Egyptian nationals will be—not omitted—and we will use different names.

Asked whether the seller would be prosecuted under Egyptian law, he replied: "No. The statutes of limitation have already passed." But he explained that the problem lies elsewhere:

> People in the country may think these people have become extremely wealthy and there are many risks that we wouldn't want the people running into.
>
> All the real names will be deposited, so that on the scholarly level there will be full transparency.
>
> Legally speaking there are no risks. It is absolutely clean and transparent if it will be accepted as such, but in that country, with which I've had other experiences, you never exactly know how things are handled.
>
> If they stick to certain rules, it will mostly be harassment. Through the lapse of time most people have become very elderly, and I don't think they deserve being harassed much.[10]

## YALE UNIVERSITY

Tchacos turned to Yale University as a potential purchaser:

> At first it seemed unclear how one should proceed with the find. In the year 2000 the Zürich art dealer Frédérique Nussberger—client of Roberty—arrived with the documents at the Beinecke Library of Yale University. Again it comes to no settlement. "We renounced the purchase," says the curator of the library, Robert Babcock. "The reasons we do not discuss publicly." Only this much: "The genuineness was not the issue—we considered it to be authentic."[11]

Harry Attridge was involved in the assessment at Yale and submitted to me the following report:

> At Yale, the curator of ancient manuscripts in the Beinecke Library, Dr. Robert Babcock, invited Bentley Layton and me to have a look at the Coptic Codex and to give him our judgment about its probable significance. I believe that he was interested in acquiring the whole find. Since his area is Greek papyrology, he would have been in a position to make a judgment about the value and significance of the Greek material that was also part of the offering. I don't recall him discussing the price being asked for the materials—such discretion would be pretty standard—nor did he identify the seller or his agent. We had no contact with either seller or agent. We had brief access to the Coptic codex itself in offices of the Beinecke Library and were able to verify that it did indeed appear to be what we had heard about from Steve Emmel, a codex, probably of the 4th–5th century in a decent literary hand not unlike that of the Nag Hammadi codices. We did not have time to read or transcribe the texts in the codex, nor, to my recollection, did we discuss the possible identification of the text as a *Gospel of Judas*. I was not involved in the decision not to acquire the materials, which was made by the staff of the Beinecke, but I'm not sure at what level.

## TCHACOS AND FERRINI: CONTRACT OF SEPTEMBER 9, 2000

The manuscripts are next attested on September 9, 2000, where one finds on the Internet a contract signed on that date.[12] It is between "Frieda Nussberger Tchacos, whose address is Augustinergasse 14, 8001 Zurich, Switzerland (hereinafter referred to as 'Seller')" and "Nemo, LLC, whose address is 1080 Top of the Hill Road, Akron, Ohio (hereinafter referred to as 'Buyer')." The buyer can be identified as Bruce Ferrini. The purchase price, to be paid in installments without interest, is $2.5 million, half "on or before January 15, 2001" and the other half "on or before February 15, 2001." The contract states:

> The Manuscript was, in all regards, legally exported from the country of its origin and has been legally exported from and imported into all countries through which it has passed, including the United States.
>
> No person or entity is in possession of any copy, photograph, facsimile or reproduction by any means or in any medium of the Manuscript or the text thereof....
>
> Because Seller acquired and took delivery of the Manuscript in the United States, it does not possess and shall not be required to deliver hereafter any export or import licenses.[13]

The contract is signed by Bruce Ferrini, Pres., Nemo, LLC, as Buyer, and Frieda Nussberger Tchacos, as Seller.

## MARTIN SCHØYEN: SEPTEMBER 11, 2000

Ferrini promptly went to work to see if he could sell the manuscripts for more than he would have to pay for them, in order no doubt to have the cash in hand that he would need to make his payments. He offered them to one of his clients, Martin Schøyen, perhaps knowing that it is he who had earlier shown an interest in acquiring them. On September 11, 2000, he received the following response from Schøyen:

> The following prices were stipulated, and consented to by Hannah more or less, for the meeting in N.Y. 12th–13th Dec. 1990 (cancelled due to "Desert Storm"):
>
> | | | |
> |---|---|---|
> | 1. | Exodus, 4th c. More than 50ff. Greek | $365,000 |
> | 2. | 3 Gnostic texts, Coptic 25ff. +10? in fragments, 4th (incl. 1 cover) | 281,000 |
> | 3. | Letters of Paul (3 epistles), Coptic, ca. 400, 30ff. (incl. 1 cover & spine) | 252,000 |
> | 4. | Mathematical, 5th c. 12ff.? | 88,000 |
> | | | $986,000 |
>
> For no. 2 an addition was made of 10%, since 1 of the covers was preserved, and for no. 3 +15% for 1 cover & the spine of the binding (are these present?)...
>
> You should check whether everything is still present: 2 binding covers/spine about 12ff. Mathematical (distinctive cursive script) and Letters of Paul (part of Colossians, 1st Thessalonians and Hebrews).[14]

Schøyen had at the time made such calculations based on his familiarity with the antiquities market and sent them to me. But there was no response from the owner, so that his comment to Ferrini that the prices were "more or less consented to by Hannah" would have to be emphasized on the side of "less."[15] In effect, Schøyen was informing Ferrini what he considered a fair price. It did not come to enough for Ferrini to be able to pay Frieda her asking price, much less to make a profit.

Schøyen has been kind enough to send me further clarification:

> I could add to the account involving Ferrini, that I only gave him my evaluation as a help to him, not intending to buy myself, due to the bad provenance, but in the hope I could

convince him to deposit the papyri with the Institute for Antiquity and Christianity for conservation and publication, which I am sorry to say did not happen.

## CHARLES W. HEDRICK

Charlie Hedrick had been consulted by Ferrini from time to time about ancient manuscripts that Ferrini had access to in his business, asking Hedrick to identify them for him from photographs he would send. On February 6, 2001, Roberty e-mailed the following to van Rijn, having heard from him about the involvement of Hedrick in the present case:

> Charlie's contribution really surprises me. I had no idea of his theological background being as solid on such a particular subject. This kind as well as any other kind of contributions or revelations of facts I can't possibly be aware of, would make your update extremely more helpful—for the benefit of the cause ...!

I of course welcome Hedrick's education being called "solid," since, after all, I was his doctoral father! He is today Distinguished Emeritus Professor of Religious Studies at Missouri State University.

Hedrick received from Bruce Ferrini 164 "very dismal digital photographs," in which he could at least identify *James,* the title given to the *(First) Revelation of James,* and the title of the *Letter of Peter to Philip,*[16] which Steve Emmel had already identified in Geneva and which have been mentioned in the publicity about the *Gospel of Judas* as included in what has been returned to Switzerland.[17] He also received ten professionally made photographs and twenty-four taken with a regular camera. Hedrick transcribed and translated what he could from six pages that were more nearly legible. The difficulty was twofold: the papyrus itself was quite damaged and the top third of many leaves was now missing. Emmel had seen the pagination in the top margin, which was not visible in the photographs of Hedrick to help put them in their correct sequence. And also if the bottom of one page and the top of the next are extant, one can establish the sequence of leaves by following the train of thought, which unfortunately was no longer possible.

Hedrick circulated his transcriptions and translations to a number of colleagues who had worked together over the years on the Nag Hammadi Codices, Birger A. Pearson, John D. Turner, Douglas M. Parrott, Wolf-Peter Funk, Hans-Gebhard Bethge, and me, and received a series of suggestions for improving both the transcription and the translation. The outcome of this collaboration was a much improved transcription and German translation by the group in Berlin led by Bethge and a corresponding English translation by Stephen Patterson. It is much to be regretted that this familiar kind of collegial sharing and cooperation, characteristic of the study of Nag Hammadi by those not part of the Nag Hammadi monopolies, has not been shared, in the case of the *Gospel of Judas*, by those who had—a monopoly on it!

Hedrick published reports of his photographs of the *Gospel of Judas* in 2002 and 2003 in the scholarly journals *Bible Review* and *Journal of Early Christian Studies:*[18]

> In sum, in addition to the four canonical gospels, we have four complete noncanonicals, seven fragmentary, four known from quotations and two hypothetically recovered for a total of 21 gospels from the first two centuries, and we know that others existed in the early period. I am confident more of them will be found. For example, I have seen photos of several pages from a Coptic text entitled the *Gospel of Judas* that recently surfaced on the antiquities market.
>
> One of those gospels generally thought to have disappeared, the *Gospel of Judas* (known to Irenaeus toward the end of the second century), actually did survive in Coptic translation, and has been available on the antiquities market for several years.[19]

This too was picked up by the Swiss reporter Pöhner:

> In June 2002 the *Bible Review* reported about the photographs circulating on the manuscript market, as did in November 2003 the *Journal of Early Christian Studies.* It has to do with securing an important document for humanity. Already previously Michel van Rijn picked up the theme: The former art smuggler, who presents himself as a warrant officer, and illumines the cloudy side of the art market, reports on his web site that a *Gospel of Judas* is on the market. "Don't touch," he warns.[20]

Similarly, Thiede picked up the trail of Hedrick and indeed identified the fact that Hedrick himself had discovered and edited one of the noncanonical gospels that has appeared in recent times:

> Then rumors circulate in uni[versity] circles about the true content of the most voluminous part of the codex. Charles W. Hedrick, Professor at Southwest Missouri State University, goes public. Together with his colleague Paul Mirecki, he had become world famous in 1997 by making known "Papyrus Berolinensis 22220."[21] In the archives of the Egyptian Museum of the German capital the pair had dredged up remains of a Coptic Gospel fragment (see *FOCUS,* fascicle 14 of 1997), in Hedrick's numeration "E 34." Now the same scholar gave in evidence, in the scholarly journal *Bible Review,* that he had seen fotos of pages of a further, very important writing.
>
> "E 35" is for the first time spoken about publicly.[22]

## ROBERTY'S MEMORANDUM OF DECEMBER 15, 2000

The contract signed on September 9, 2000, by Ferrini and Tchacos was not implemented. On December 15, 2000, Roberty, as a Swiss attorney, wrote a memorandum[23] to a New York attorney, Eric R. Kaufman, who had been their host at a recent meeting of the two lawyers with "Frieda" and "Bruce," presumably their respective clients. The memorandum itemizes the agreements reached by "Frieda" and "Bruce" "under somewhat tensed circumstances" at that meeting. It begins by stating that the agreements of September 9, 2000, "have become obsolete."

Since, according to the memorandum, Bruce had "already disposed of" the Mathematical Treatise and Letters of Paul (some of whose fragments had been stored in the same box as the Mathematical Treatise), he would pay Frieda $300,000 for them by February 1, 2001. With regard to the rest of the manuscripts, a foundation would be created to carry out the "project":

> The entity which shall realize the Project shouldn't be a commercial entity but the *Logos Foundation* as officially recognized charitable trust of public utility to be established under Swiss Law soon.
>
> 11.... Moreover, the actual owner of the manuscripts [Frieda] intends to make a partial donation of the manuscripts to the Foundation whereby all rights to the manuscripts as well as deriving from the manuscripts shall be transferred to the *Logos Foundation* against assignment of totally 80% of the Foundation's future revenues from the commercialization of the manuscripts (i.e., from the exploitation of the deriving publishing rights etc. and ultimately—if legally admissible—from their sale).
>
> Bruce and Frieda are going to exchange the composite volume of at least three Coptic texts (*First Apocalypse of James, Epistle of Peter to Philip* and *Gospel of Judas*) as well as the Book of Exodus and the not expressly mentioned further fragments [of the Letters of Paul that had been in the box with Exodus?] with two checks emitted by Bruce of USD 1,250,000—each, the first due on January 15, 2001, and the second due on February 15, 2001.
>
> Immediately after the above described exchange has taken place, Frieda will set up the *Logos Foundation* in agreement with you and in accordance with the above described

> principles. She will then transfer the manuscripts to the Foundation entering into an agreement as described sub par. 11. above.
>
> Frieda will grant Bruce the option of acquiring half the rights assigned to her by the Foundation to the future revenues from the commercialization of the manuscripts against payment to her of USD 1,100,000 . . . (i.e., USD 750,000—corresponding to half the value of the composite volume plus USD 350,000—corresponding to half the value of the Book of Exodus) and against donation to the Foundation of the same amounts she will have donated herself by then. This option shall be valid and exercisable until June 30, 2001.

The purpose of the proposed Logos Foundation was stated as follows:

> The *Logos Project* intends to save and publish the *Gospel of Judas* and other related manuscripts for the benefit of historical truth and to generate the funds necessary for this task as well as for the compensation of the expenses and efforts incurred by the promoters, leaving them with a decent profit.

The agreement reached in New York also imposed the strictest secrecy, which seems to have been handed down at each stage of the project:

> It is clearly understood by all persons involved that nobody, not even Bruce and Frieda, but only the Foundation, will have the right to promulgate and commercialize any knowledge regarding, concerning or deriving from the manuscripts. Moreover, for the time being and until all legal aspects are clarified, it is in the best interest of the Project to maintain utmost secrecy about its existence.

This leaves only Roberty the freedom to discuss whatever he wants with whomever he wants, and he has apparently made great use of this freedom. Presumably the sensationalistic news reports published by Pöhner, Thiede, and Hall go back to Roberty.

Apparently Ferrini did not accept the offer to share in the income from the commercialization of the manuscripts to be owned by the new foundation. Subsequently, his name nowhere figures in connection with the foundation.

It is presumably the projected Logos Foundation that came to be part of the Maecenas Foundation, the current owner of the *Gospel of Judas*.

## BREAKING NEWS: "BRUCE ON THE LOOSE"

Michel van Rijn reports on what happened following the meeting in New York.[24] Van Rijn and Roberty had worked together cordially in earlier connections, and therefore van Rijn had notified Roberty of the news on the *Gospel of Judas* he was about to publish on his Web site. Van Rijn then published what was apparently Roberty's revised draft of what van Rijn had e-mailed him for approval, since it begins: "Michel, what do you think about the following text?"

> Crime against Humanity … Priceless and not replaceable *Gospel of Judas* embezzled by manuscript dealer Bruce P. Ferrini (http://www.ferrini.com)
>
> The mechanics:
>
> Last fall, Zurich based antiques dealer Frieda Chakos entrusts priceless papyrus manuscripts which had been in a Bank vault in New York for almost 20 years to the "safe" facilities of Akron/Ohio-based manuscript dealer Bruce P. Ferrini. She is approached by Ferrini through a middleman and doesn't have a clue that by this time Ferrini is already in deep financial troubles. The news had not hit the papers yet. Ferrini takes advantage of the secrecy of the art-market and offers to help Frieda 'in preserving these manuscripts for the benefit of mankind.'…

The papyrus manuscripts consist of

> a Gnostic codex in Sahidic dialect containing the lost *Gospel of Judas* known from history only through Saint Irenaeus (c. 140–202 AD), Bishop of Lyon, *The First Apocalypse of James* and *The Epistle of Peter to Philip*
> the *Book of Exodus* in Greek
> *Letters of Paul* in Sahidic dialect, and a
> *Mathematical Treatise* in Greek.

All these manuscripts are priceless historical documents, only comparable to major finds like the Nag Hammadi Library or the Dead Sea Scrolls from Qumran. They belong to mankind and shall be publicly preserved and studied. For this purpose, Frieda has set up a public foundation to which these manuscripts have been donated. But Ferrini wants to turn them into money for the satisfaction of his greedy ambitions and has therefore spirited the manuscripts away, to Japan.

Legal proceedings and criminal persecution [*sic*] are under way. This will take some time. As things develop, you will see how much more efficient I am with my DEVASTATING ART NEWS. Crimes against the most basic cultural interests of mankind must be persecuted by adequate means. Buyers beware, a maniac dealer is selling parts of our history. You buy? You touch? You will be prosecuted!

On February 5, 2001, Roberty again e-mailed van Rijn:

Let me quickly tell you what really has happened: Basically nothing. Last Monday night (Jan 29) Eric K[aufman] called several times and repeatedly confirmed he didn't know what this fuss was all about because his client was perfectly willing to return the manuscripts (exception for "The Mathematical Treatise" and "The Letters of Paul" which he has already sold and for which he should have paid $300,000 on Feb 1) as soon as [he] would be returning to Akron on Feb 14, back

> from the Palm Beach Antiques Fair (or from Japan?). Since these phone calls I (or Frieda) have received no further communication either from Eric or from the Italo-Sioux [Ferrini] himself. Tomorrow, we can check the bank for the arrival of $300,000 as promised!? Of course, I know Eric had been absent Tue and Wed and he knew I was going to Paris until Fri night.
>
> The point is, I would like to keep the pressure on B.F. until he really fulfills his (lawyer's) promise. Therefore, probably the best and only possible update on "Bruce on the Loose" is the naked truth: Thanks to "Devastating Art News" promising contacts have been established between the lawyers of the parties involved and hopefully B.F. will keep his (lawyer's) word and have the manuscripts returned by February 14/15, 2001.

Then on February 7, 2001, Roberty e-mailed van Rijn still another time:

> Now I know you don't only have a third ear but also a third eye: Yesterday, just before leaving for the meeting with Eric, I checked my mailbox and got your prophetical message about what Eric would be saying and proposing. You were right to the dot!
>
> I still don't quite get what Bruce really wants—besides trying to make the business of his life, i.e., selling manuscripts (letters of Paul and Mathematical Treatise) as well as some objects of art and exploiting and possibly selling the important manuscripts without ever having to pay for them. It's the precise attitude of a professional embezzler and thief....
>
> During our meeting, there were three major issues:
>
> who is passing information on to you
> the overdue payment of USD 300" [$300,000] for the manu[script]s already sold
> the refusal to return the other manu[script]s.

In order to figure out where the leak is, Eric suggested Bruce to feed three different, false infos to three different possible leaks. Watch out!

The overdue payment has been done because of a confusion with dealings Bruce has with Bill Veres. Bill claims Bruce [is] owing him money and pretends having paid Frieda on behalf of Bruce USD 90" [$90,000] (which is not true!) and Bruce claims Bill [is] owing him lots of money. Bill had introduced Bruce to Frieda and pretends to be his partner. At the same time he pretends feeling responsible towards Frieda for the mess she is in. For reasons completely independent of Bruce, Bill owes Frieda about USD 150" [$150,000]. All this confusion is basically bullshit and is being used by Bruce just to avoid payment. By the way, he pretends that the sales price obtained by Sam Fogg is not of USD 900" [$900,000] and that the sale was not to Thompson.

Because in your latest update you claim having been asked for assistance by the Egyptian authorities, Eric pretends Bruce being no longer able to return the manu[script]s without risking persecution [*sic*] under US law! This is pure bullshit again and he would have brought this same argument even if you had not mentioned the Egyptian authorities. From what I have learned and seen documented, I can affirm that following legal terms (the applicable Egyptian law being No. 215 of October 31, 1951) there is no possibility for a claim from that country. Of course, this does not foreclose some action out of purely political motives. . . .

We are now considering the remaining options. Possibly, there will be another meeting on Friday afternoon with Bruce present.

I'll keep you posted.

Apparently the Maecenas Foundation, whose purpose is to commercialize the *Gospel of Judas* and the other less sensational texts, had a rough start if it could not get hold of the manuscripts themselves. The "official" report narrates how they were finally recuperated, except that "thc mathcmatical treatise would be retained by Ferrini, for a purchase price of $100,000."[25]

## "BAD PROVENANCE": ILLEGAL EXCAVATION AND SMUGGLING

Michel van Rijn claims credit for exposing the illegal exportation of the *Gospel of Judas* from Egypt, which hence necessitated the agreement by the Maecenas Foundation to return it to Egypt after publication. But this did not take place automatically, as van Rijn explains with grim satisfaction:

> Zürich based dealer Frieda (Nussberger) Chakos, owner of the prestigious Gallery Nefer, is up to her old tricks again. Although she solemnly promised, after being exposed on my website, to return the illegally acquired, historically invaluable *Gospel of Judas* to Egypt, she is presently negotiating a possible sale to a US manuscript dealer. We are on the job as usual and will keep you posted. If Frieda will go forward, we will also dive into her past sales and rip the last bits of her already miserable reputation to pieces.[26]

Later, van Rijn follows up with his success story:

> In 2001 this portal first revealed the existence and the contents of the looted *Judas Gospel* as well as enough of the skullduggery in its recent history to make it unmarketable. The action on this portal forced the culprits who owned the long lost smuggled Gospel to restore it to its true country of origin, Egypt, and to look for other venues to capitalize on their illegally acquired treasure. This portal is used to not being credited in the media for the good work we do ... and we take consolation and soulage in the fact that as a result of our actions this historically important document will be returned to Egypt safe for posterity.

> Van Rijn prides himself on his art-world scoops, and it was on his website that news of the existence of an extraordinary document first broke—at least beyond the cabals of dealers, and the cloistered confines of the scholarly community. In 2001, he revealed that the long-lost *Gospel of Judas* Iscariot—not seen for at least 1,800 years—was being hawked around antiquities dealers on two, maybe three, continents. It wasn't quite the Dead Sea Scrolls, but not far off. Would this testament of Judas, the betrayer of Jesus, turn Christianity on its head? Van Rijn says it asserts that Judas worked in league with Jesus to betray him, thereby to ensure his crucifixion, martyrdom (and, for believers, his resurrection), and thus to lay the foundation for—and ensure the success of— Christianity. "Forget *The Da Vinci Code*," says van Rijn. "This is the real deal."[27]

The outcome, of course, has been a rupture in the good relations that had prevailed between van Rijn and Roberty (who had even functioned as van Rijn's representative), according to Malcolm Macalister Hall's report:

> But few allegiances last long in the quicksand of the antiquities market, and the two now have daggers drawn. "Van Rijn and Roberty—it's like Holmes and Moriarty; they're mortal enemies," says one major London dealer. In this feud, van Rijn has done all he can to discredit the provenance of the *Gospel of Judas*—all part of his plan, he says, to make it unsellable. He's now cock-a-hoop that the Maecenas Foundation has pledged to return the manuscript to Egypt—to the Coptic Museum in Cairo—after unsuccessful attempts to sell it and other papyri in the United States for some $2.5m. Van Rijn claims that his website postings over the last few years destroyed any possible deal.[28]

Roberty's memorandum of December 15, 2000, questioned the legal title and used what seems to have been a first draft of the pseudonym Hanna Asabil :

> In order to be able to pursue the Project responsibly, we first must ascertain that Mr. Hana A. Airian had obtained good legal and beneficial title to the manuscripts and that he had the right to sell these documents to Frieda.

Since no such legal title was forthcoming, this could have been used by Ferrini as a reason or excuse for not going forward, as Dutch journalist Henk Schutten has reported:

> The big question is why this manuscript remained hidden for such a long time after it was discovered. Almost no one wanted to get their fingers burned, according to Bruce Ferrini, an art dealer of Akron, Ohio. He himself was offered the documents in 2000 by Frieda Tchakos, a gallery owner in Geneva who bought the materials the year prior to that....
>
> The problem was the "bad provenance," its obscure origin. Tchakos and Roberty told Ferrini that farmers discovered the books in the mid-seventies in a stone box in Megaga, Upper-Egypt....
>
> Ferrini: "Frieda told me that the documents were obtained by a Greek trader, Nikolas Koutoulakis, who had supposedly stolen them from Hannah, an Egyptian jeweler. Koutoulakis smuggled them into Geneva. Frieda alleges that Hannah followed him by traveling to Geneva to reclaim the documents. A Coptic priest would have accompanied Hannah afterwards to New York, where the documents were held in a safe in Hicksville's Citibank. They remained there until the end of the nineties when they were purchased by Frieda."[29]

The "bad provenance" may well have been one reason that had prevented the agreement of September 19, 2000, from being implemented, since that agreement had stipulated that the title was clear.

The problem of smuggling may also help explain a cryptic comment by Thiede:

> Who finally paid what to whom, not even the expert on connections who lives in London, the 54-year-old Michel van Rijn, knows. His rude internet service "artnews" (Motto: "Hot Art Cold Cash") otherwise has its profile with constantly new exposure stories, as the "nemesis" of international art racketeers.
>
> Nonetheless his website suggests sufficiently that for Nussberger a juristic coup was successful. Many-years-long business dealings with an imprisoned art mafioso of the Nile scene should be forgiven and forgotten. Madame is to receive a whitewashing certificate that protects her from Egyptian prosecution because of illegal art exports.
>
> Whether, in order to achieve this, Nussberger or Maecenas had to deliver the promise to give her book back formally to Egypt? To be sure, corresponding commitments in a publication of the foundation are formulated in a very airy way.[30]

Similar reports are given by Michel van Rijn:

> Present "owner"—Zurich-based Frieda Nussberger Tchakos—struck a deal with the Egyptian government, under which she was absolved of looting that nation clean. But, unlike Judas, she held out for a bit more than 30 pieces of silver. After all, Frieda was one of Tarek El-Sweissi's [Egyptian official convicted in 2003 of smuggling ancient artifacts out of Egypt] principal dealers, the latter, of course, sweating in a hot Egyptian cell for the next 30 years.[31]

Even the sanitized "official" report confirms this unfortunate outcome:

> Egyptian antiquities have also been funneled through Switzerland. In 2002, Egyptian and Swiss authorities signed a security agreement designed to stop illicit trafficking.... A primary figure in the wave of Egyptian arrests that followed was Tariq al Suwaysi, the head of Egypt's National Demo-

> cratic Party's Giza office, who for years had worked with some of Switzerland's best and most important dealers, including Nicolas Koutoulakis....
>
> Years later, as mentioned earlier, Tariq would be arrested and brought to trial as one of thirty-one people involved in a massive antiquities smuggling ring that allegedly removed nearly three hundred pharaonic, Coptic, and Islamic artifacts from Egypt to Switzerland. Convicted in 2003, he was sentenced to thirty-five years in prison, a sentence that has been appealed.[32]

Thus van Rijn exposed the real reason for returning the material to Egypt, which does tend to put in question the lofty ideals. Tchacos wanted to be able to visit her native Egypt without the risk of imprisonment.

## COMMERCIALIZING THE *GOSPEL OF JUDAS*

The fact that the manuscript could not be sold for a profit, but rather has to be returned to Egypt, made the commercializing of the contents of the *Gospel of Judas* the chosen path to riches. Thiede explained:

> Clearly the Swiss now see their salvation in the rapid journalistic marketing of the codex. One lets it be known that the careful restoration has been turned over to the best experts. As scholarly editor, the dean of Coptic-Sahidic literature, the Geneva Professor Emeritus Rodolphe Kasser, the uncontested star of the discipline had been enlisted.[33]

It was apparently due to this strategy of making big money from sensationalizing the text, rather than selling the papyrus itself, that the matter had to be kept a secret until the moment of its publication. The suspense should not be broken by leaking the contents to the press, as Thiede takes satisfaction in reporting:

> Further inquiries pointless. For the rest, one stays covered. The Zürich art dealership Nefer at present no longer exists. Even friendly gallery people do not know where the ex-owner is hiding. But she still has the threads in hand. In any case, that is certified by experts who are commissioned as scholarly coworkers of the first edition, yet they cannot give information because of a prohibition to speak out.[34]

Thiede goes on:

> Precisely because the "new" text—due to its risky substance—is still unpublished, and Maecenas/Roberty likes to identify only the last page (circulating in the internet) as an original part of his manuscript, the discussion meanwhile overflows.[35]

By way of identifying Roberty, Thiede elaborates:

> The Judas manuscript belongs, after the transactions of the most recent past, to the Swiss "*Maecenas Stiftung für antike Kunst*." It supports archeological excavations and advises in museum construction. The institution is led by the Basel attorney Mario Jean Roberty, who appeared already in numerous cultural events. He was attorney of the Japanese Miho museum and contrived the transfer of antiquities back into Egypt. His restrictive politics on information with regard to the Judas book are severely criticized.[36]

## THE DETERIORATING CONDITION OF THE DISCOVERY

The convoluted story of the peddling of the *Gospel of Judas* was full of intrigue, greed, and drama, as the text was passed through many hands and across many borders. But such peregrinations have taken their toll on the ancient papyrus manuscript.

The size of the original fourth-century codex, the number of leaves it originally contained, is of course quite different from the number of leaves that survive today, though the two tend at times to be confused. Let's begin with the number of leaves that are thought to have survived, and only then turn to the number of leaves in the original codex. (Outsiders to the field need to be reminded that according to scholarly terminology two *pages* are on the front and back of one *leaf*).

Of course there are different ways to count the number of extant leaves in a very fragmentary codex. When does a *fragment* become honored with the designation of being a *leaf*? The policy might be, for example, that, if over half a leaf is extant, we should no longer call it a *fragment*, but rather a *leaf*. The online Coptic transcription of the *Gospel of Judas* states that on p. 41 lines 10–26 are "physically missing," and for the other side of that leaf, p. 42, it prints only parts of the first nine lines, with the comment "about 17 lines missing." The English translation has to do with the stars of each of the disciples, but such an interesting topic cannot be clearly deciphered, because the translation is of necessity so fragmentary.[37] If a word such as *Jesus*, or *Judas*, or *Allogenes* is legible, fine! But one is not often so lucky. So, is this a *fragment* or a *leaf*? In terms of what has survived, it may be more documentation for a leaf that did not survive than it is a surviving leaf in its own right. If the some thirty-two "leaves" in the Gnostic codex were all like this, we might as well forget it! Fortunately, some, indeed most, are much more nearly complete. But we must be aware of the problem inherent in a simple list of how many "leaves" are extant.

Any estimate had to be based on Steve Emmel's report cited in Chapter 1:

> The absence of half of the binding and the fact that page numbers run only into the 50's lead me to suppose that the back half of the codex may be missing; only closer study can prove or disprove this supposition.... Page numbers were placed above the center of the column and decorated with short rows of diplés above and below. At least pp. 1–50 are represented by substantial fragments which, when reassembled, will make up complete leaves with all four margins intact.

Schutten reports Emmel as saying:

> The numbers of the pages went up to sixty, while most papyrus codices are at least twice as big. I suspected half of the manuscript to be missing.[38]

Emmel was of course thinking of the Nag Hammadi Codices, where a good number of them have over one hundred pages.

Ferrini indicated that by his time some leaves had been removed from the lot for individual sale, so that Emmel's estimate of 1983 does not apply to the present state of the manuscript:

> Ferrini suspects that in the meantime several single pages of the manuscript were put on the market. "When I saw the work for the first time in 1999 [2000], only 25 pages remained intact, so at least half of them were missing. I cannot be absolutely sure if the manuscript was found incomplete or if its writing was never finished. But from time to time new pages would appear. Five or six different documents in total without page numbers, it was just a mess."[39]

There is also the report of Mia being responsible for some loss. Recall what Thiede had said:

> Large parts land in Mia's purse, and then evaporate for a long time. One folio leaf is lost forever.

Van Rijn paraphrased: "Mia had ended up stealing a few of the pages."

Hedrick reported an alarming detail about fragments:

> He [Ferrini] did tell me that he had paid for the codex and then when the provenance was in question that he called his money back in and returned the codex to whoever was selling it to him,... and the individual became angry and slammed the codex down on the table and tiny pieces of pa-

> pyrus flew all over the place. The seller picked up the codex and left angrily saying, "Well, maybe I will just burn it."[40]

Hedrick later clarified this important detail:

> My understanding is that the person who slammed the book on the table was not Frieda, but no names were used. Frieda would not have threatened to burn the book when her price was not met, I do not think.[41]

I agree with Hedrick that Frieda is far too good a businessperson to burn something worth big money. But she may also be a good enough businessperson to have made such dramatic statements during ongoing negotiations! After all, it was she who was in Akron carrying on the final unsuccessful negotiations.

Regarding page numbers at the top of leaves, Hedrick reported from his photographs:

> I do not have the top of the last page of Judas and hence I do not have a page number.... There is a top of which I can read "60."[42]

But the number of extant *leaves* could well be fewer that half the highest *page* number that was observed. Hedrick reported:

> At one point I heard that there were only 50 pages in the entire codex (per Ferrini).[43]

This statement from Hedrick may serve to correct the report of Schutten, quoted above, that Ferrini said there were only twenty-five pages left. This is probably to be understood as the frequent confusion between *leaf*, a piece of papyrus with two sides and hence two *pages* of a book, and *page*, which refers to only one side of a *leaf*. Ferrini may have counted twenty-five *leaves* and correctly inferred that this meant fifty *pages*, which he reported to Hedrick.

And yet Schutten continued his report on Ferrini by quoting: "So at least half of them were missing." This suggests that Schutten took Ferrini to be speaking, after all, of pages rather than leaves, from fifty pages down to twenty-five pages. This could be a confusion with Emmel's report. Schutten had reported Emmel's saying that "the pages went up to sixty" but that Emmel suspected "half of the manuscript to be missing." Of course Emmel meant that the codex may well have had 120 pages originally, but that only half, "up to sixty," were still extant. Schutten may have reconciled the two reports as best he could, but inaccurately. Of course this remains speculation. All that seems clear is that Ferrini thought the total seen by Emmel had shrunk appreciably.

Hedrick reported on what he could see on the photographs he received from Ferrini:

> You must think in terms of jumbled mess. There is only one stack (not two if you had a neat book and the book were opened with some leaves on left and right). The top with the page number has leaves behind it, but because of the breaks in the stack (the breaks seem to go completely through the stack) and because of the jumbled character of the stack, it is not possible to tell which top goes with which of the two pieces of papyrus in the two bottom breaks. The text cannot be read from my poor digital photographs except for the occasional letter, and reading fibers is impossible. There are definitely tops, however.[44]

He clarified still further:

> There is only one stack of leaves one on top of the other. I see three breaks in the stack. One about two-thirds of the way up and then the top third has a break. There are tops of some pages in the stack and the Coptic page number 60 is clearly distinct. (I found no other page numbers.)[45]

Of course Hedrick's parenthetic comment that "the breaks seem to go completely through the stack" suggests the kind of wrenching experience associated with Mia, when the personages in the story more or less fought over the codex and may well have broken it literally in two (or more) pieces!

Hedrick was contacted about the photographs in his possession by a law firm representing Tchacos and Roberty.[46] Then Hedrick was asked by Kasser to turn over his photographs to him, in hopes of finding there material that he was missing in the papyri themselves, and of course to ensure the monopoly. Hedrick reported:

> Kasser was talking about material missing completely from the material he had. He specifically asked me about three bottoms of pages he identified among the photographs I sent him that he did not have among the extant papyrus material in his possession. I suspected, however, he was also concerned about tops of pages.[47]

Hedrick did supply Kasser with copies of the photographs he had. The critical edition of Codex Tchacos reports in a footnote: "The lower part of this page (ll. 10–26) is physically missing. Thus far, the editors have had access only to photographic evidence of poor quality for a lower part of a page, which might represent the missing portion of page 41. Only the last lines are clearly legible."

## SIXTY-TWO EXTANT PAGES?

Pöhner wrote, "The book contains 62 pages."[48] Thiede published a photograph of the page with the subscript title *The Gospel of Judas* clearly visible, with the caption for the photograph:

> In the manuscript of p. 62 at the end, placed one under the other the designation of the title: "Gospel" and "Judas." The foto circulating in the worldwide Web shows, according to the information of the owner of the codex, the last page of the manuscript that is in his possession.[49]

Then Hedrick's provisional draft translation of that page is translated into German, with this caption:

> Not all letters of p. 62 are to be deciphered; text according to C. Hedrick.[50]

Why did Thiede think that it was "p. 62"? Or, putting the question more correctly (since it is actually p. 58): Where does the figure 62 come from? Possibly, if he took literally the comment "one folio leaf is lost forever," then he might assume that two more pages than those seen by Emmel would have originally been involved. If, then, he took literally Schutten's version of Emmel's memory, "up to sixty," rather than Emmel's written report, "at least pp. 1–50 are represented by substantial fragments," he could postulate that there were, when Emmel saw them, in fact sixty pages. Adding the two pages already lost in the fray yields a total of sixty-two pages. If, then, the title *Gospel of Judas* is on the last page, that last page would be p. 62. *Voila!* The incorrect pagination listed by Pöhner and Thiede! And then they seem to assume that this page number can apply as well to the number of extant pages.

Such a calculation would of course not have been made by a careful scholar. Emmel did not literally count sixty pages. The tattered papyrus leaves were too fragile for him to thumb through and count thirty leaves. Did someone else actually count the sixty-two pages? Or did Pöhner just assume that two pages had been removed, on the basis of the story that Thiede tells, and add two to Schutten's comment "up to sixty"? This may be only a garbled version of Emmel's report to Schutten, but in any case Emmel did not mean to be exact. He is a very exacting person and would have made an exact statement if he had had an exact figure.

Of course anything seemed possible, when one had no concrete information. Yet the page number "60," much less an invented pagination "62," does not inform us about the number of leaves that were extant when Emmel saw them, or are extant today. According to the latest reports, one leaf (pp. 31–32) may be completely lost as well as whatever may have originally been in the codex after p. 66. A fragment with the number 108 is reported to be extant, but fragments may be all that survives of any latter parts of the codex.

## THE AMOUNT OF LOSS SINCE 1983

The exact amount that has been lost since the codex was first seen by Emmel on May 15, 1983, is unclear. A few years ago Roberty is reported to have been rather pessimistic:

> Roberty hopes passionately that one day another copy of the *Gospel of Judas* will turn up, because the copy as owned by the Maecenas Foundation is only 65 to 70 percent complete. "We assume that some fragments are still wandering around on the market here and there, but I am afraid that a quarter of the manuscript has been lost forever."[51]

Henk Schutten reported that Michel van Rijn helped search for the missing fragments and in the process made up with Roberty:

> But lately they settled their disagreements. Van Rijn even conducted some research for the Maecenas Foundation regarding the missing fragments of the *Gospel of Judas,* and successfully, so he said. "Roberty offered me to act as project consultant," says van Rijn: "I was offered 50,000 pounds and a share in the foundation. My name would also be mentioned as one of the discoverers of the manuscript."[52]

This much Roberty has confirmed:

> Mario Roberty confirms that Michel van Rijn did some work for the Maecenas Foundation. "Van Rijn would provide us with further information about the lost fragments of the *Gospel of Judas.* He received a payment of 50,000 pounds."[53]

Later on, in his interview with Stacy Meichtry on February 13–14, 2006, Roberty provided more details of the damage, but also a more encouraging estimate of what has survived:

> You will see it's in awful shape.... Initial estimates, when you looked at it, were just desperate.
>
> It was painstaking puzzle work. It will probably be going on for some time.
>
> Each page is put under glass. It's incredibly brittle and in bad shape. I marveled myself to see how they were able to work on such material.

As to the original sequence, Roberty conceded:

> Not received in original sequence, but they are confident to have the right order now. Small fragments that couldn't be precisely attributed ...

As to it having page numbers, Roberty reports:

> Yes it does, but just on the upper part. The whole is cut into parts, so the lower parts cannot be attributed in their page numbering to the upper parts. This has to be done following the fiber structure and also the content.

With regard to fragments, Roberty reports:

> There were some souvenir hunters laying their hands on it. Partially reclaimed.

The reference to some fragments being "partially reclaimed" is intriguing, especially since others had spoken of some fragments being secondarily reunited with the whole, in which connection van Rijn had claimed some credit. But there seems also to have been a quite recent acquisition of fragments, for Roberty, in his interview of February 13–14, 2006, has justified a delay in the publication of the critical edition as follows:

> ... because we had a few more fragments popping up very recently. So there will be—for a full publication of the codex—there will be a delay.[54]

Roberty provides a final encouraging report of what has been brought together: "85 percent of the main text." That is, after all, considerably better than his earlier report. Things seem to have turned out better than he had feared. But apparently some of the thirty-two leaves that are extant are very fragmentary. Pp. 1/2, 5/6, 7/8, 41/42, 63/64, and 65/66 are more than half missing, and pp. 31/32 are completely missing.

## THE FOUR TRACTATES IN CODEX TCHACOS

Emmel identified three tractates in the codex. Since he could not thumb through all the leaves, looking for tractate titles and the like, he had no way of knowing that there was another tractate in the codex that he had not noticed. That last tractate is now given the title the *Book of Allogenes,* or in translation, the *Book of the Stranger*. It is another previously unknown Gnostic text.

The table of contents of the codex is as follows: pp. 1–9 is the *Letter of Peter to Philip;* pp. 10–31 is the *First Revelation of James* (the subscript title is simply *James*); pp. 33–58 is the *Gospel of Judas;* pp. 59–66(ff.?) the other previously unknown tractate, the *Book of Allogenes,* or the *Book of the Stranger*.

The first two are duplicates of Nag Hammadi tractates. A comparison of the length of these two with their parallels in the Nag Hammadi collection shows that they are similar in length. The *Letter of Peter to Philip* (VIII,2: 132,10–140,27) is just over nine pages long, corresponding to the nine pages it occupies in Codex Tchacos. The *First Revelation of James* (V,*3*:24,10–44,10) is twenty-one pages long, compared to its twenty-two pages in Codex Tchacos.

Such minor fluctuations in the number of pages do not tell us much about the relative length of the two copies of parallel tractates. The amount of text found on a given page varies, depending on the dimensions of the leaves, the amount of empty papyrus taken up in margins, the size of the scribe's lettering, the space between the lines, and so on. But since Codex Tchacos is comparable in size to Nag Hammadi codices (Steve Emmel: "approximately 30 cm. tall and 15 cm. broad),"[55] the rough comparison is useful. In one instance of duplicates in the Nag Hammadi library (*Secret Book of John*) there is a shorter edition and a longer edition. The duplicate copies of the *First Revelation of James* do seem to diverge that much one from the other.

Of course the actual wording of different copies of the same Coptic text does vary. The duplicates that occur within the Nag Hammadi collection itself tend to be diverging translations from the original Greek texts, which themselves may not have been identical. One translation may be more correct than the other. Scribal errors in the transmission of the Greek original and of the Coptic translation in one of the duplicates vary from those of the other. Yet when one copy retains text that is lost in a hole in the other copy, that hole may be filled by referring to the fully extant copy, so that they supplement each other very usefully in this regard. Hence duplicate copies of the same text are far from redundant, but were very important in reconstructing Nag Hammadi tractates. The transcriptions and translations of the two Nag Hammadi tractates that now have duplicates from Codex Tchacos can be improved greatly with the help of Codex Tchacos.

In the case of the previously unknown *Book of Allogenes,* or *Book of the Stranger,* the eight pages it takes up in Codex Tchacos are for the time being all that can be said regarding its length. But the bottom of p. 66 is very fragmentary and seems to lack a formal ending of a tractate, so this tractate may continue for an unknown amount of space within the last part of the codex that is lost. The report of a fragment with the number 108 is of course tantalizing. But there may be completely unknown tractates at the end of the codex that are lost.

The length of the *Gospel of Judas* as known to Irenaeus and Epiphanius is unknown, except for Epiphanius's comment that it was "a short work." In his time, a book would have been more the size of a canonical Gospel. Of course there were much longer works, such as the Nag Hammadi tractates *Tripartite Tractate* (I,5), 88 pages, and *Zostrianos* (VIII,*1*), 132 pages. But in the Nag Hammadi library they are more the exception than the rule. The 26-page long *Gospel of Judas* in Codex Tchacos could qualify as "a short work." But one cannot be certain that its length is the same as the length of the *Gospel of Judas* to which Irenaeus and Epiphanius refer.

The critical edition of Codex Tchacos is now predicted to appear a year after the "official" publication of Easter 2006! Hence the new translation of the *Gospel of Judas* and of the *Book of the Stranger* as well as perhaps information relevant to the Nag Hammadi copies of the *Letter of Peter to Philip* and the *First Revelation of James,* in whatever ways the duplicates in Codex Tchacos make that possible, may become promptly available.[56]

With the *Gospel of Judas* lost for more than eighteen hundred years, the story of its discovery and marketing has proven to be very colorful, replete with smugglers, black-market antiquities dealers, religious scholars, backstabbing partners, and greedy entrepreneurs meeting secretly over the course of two decades across the borders of two or three continents. But what has this long-lost and then found *Gospel of Judas* revealed to us? Does it exonerate the historical Judas? Does it turn Christianity on its head, as sensational reports have claimed? Of course not! But let us turn to these questions in the next chapter, as I try to explain what is involved in the conserving and editing of such ancient manuscripts and then the meaning and significance of this remarkable discovery.

3

# The Publication and Significance of the *Gospel of Judas*

Mario Jean Roberty had mentioned in his memorandum of December 15, 2000, to Eric R. Kaufman:

> The whole conservation process preferably is to be conducted in a highly reputable private institution disposing of the necessary secure facilities (e.g., the Bodmer Foundation in Celigny) by outside professionals. This should guarantee the best possible control. The exploration and evaluation of such institution will be the first task to be carried out by the Foundation.[1]

## THE BIBLIOTHÈQUE BODMER

The Bibliothèque Bodmer, in Celigny, a suburb just outside Geneva, is of course an appropriate place, the most appropriate place in Switzerland, for such a manuscript to be stored, conserved, and edited. In fact, it is where priceless third-century papyrus copies of the Gospels of Luke and John in Greek are housed ($\mathfrak{P}^{66}$ and $\mathfrak{P}^{75}$). It was created to be a repository for the many manuscripts and rare books acquired by its founder, the distinguished Swiss man of letters (and vice president of the International Red Cross) Martin Bodmer. A number of the manuscripts he acquired are in Coptic.[2] Years ago, a young pastor, Rodolphe

Kasser, was employed to edit them. It would hence be very convenient, once he was chosen to edit the *Gospel of Judas,* for him to work again for the Bibliothèque Bodmer, as he had in his youth. He lives within convenient commuting distance.

I can tell you about Kasser's famous Paris speech of July 1, 2004, for I was there. In the brief time for discussion following Kasser's presentation to a French-language section (from which most participants not familiar with French were hence absent), I was the only one to comment. My brief remarks included the fact that the manuscript had been seen in 1983 by Stephen Emmel, who had organized the congress, but to whom Kasser had made no reference, and that the discovery had already been announced to the scholarly world in publications as early as 1984. I then mentioned the fact that Hedrick had been circulating photographs of the *Gospel of Judas,* which Kasser should consult in case they had text that had subsequently been lost. This had been the case with the Nag Hammadi Codices, where photographs I secured from Jean Doresse did in fact in some instances supply subsequently lost text. I had, just the day before, turned over to Emmel the photographs I myself had received from Ludwig Koenen in 1983. Kasser did in fact subsequently contact Hedrick and Emmel. The "Sigla" of the critical edition for the *Gospel of Judas* lists "Hedrick—Older photographic evidence and preliminary transcriptions provided by Ch. W. Hedrick, Missouri, U.S.A." This siglum is used at 40,15; 55,17; 56,17; 59,19; 60,17; 61,13.14.25; 62,23. It is therefore a disappointment to see that my well-intended helpful comments seem to have rubbed Kasser the wrong way, to judge by the pejorative language in the "official" publications. Perhaps the problem was that my comments seemed (quite rightly) to put Kasser's claim to exclusive knowledge of a completely unknown text in question.

Rodolphe Kasser's name as editor provided Michel van Rijn an opportunity to make a humorous pun, no matter how inappropriate it may be:

> Rodolphe is not to be confused with the red-nosed reindeer. This one's as brown-nosed as they come.

As if this pun is not bad enough, van Rijn, himself Dutch, thought of the German word for cash register: "Kasse." He could not resist using it as a play on words with "Kasser":

> They await its publication (with, of course, full transcription) from Frieda's payrolled Rodolphe 'Cash' Kasse (oops, I mean Kasser).... Cash-&-Kasser is hoping to publish the manuscript ...[3]

It's only fortunate that Kasser's last name isn't "Golden"! But to think of Kasser as having a "money-bag" mentality is very inappropriate, as I know firsthand. Kasser and I worked together year after year, a couple of weeks each time, at the Coptic Museum in Cairo reassembling the fragments of the Nag Hammadi Codices into publishable leaves. We worked seven days a week, from the time the museum opened in the morning until it closed at two in the afternoon. We stayed at the same hotel, the Garden City House, a cheap *pensione* run by an amicable Italian woman named Scarzella. Her establishment was frequented by archeologists and scholars to such an extent that every day she posted the list of those staying there, so that we could know who was there and visit with one another. Kasser and I thus had our very modest meals together. I never saw him making costly expenditures or showing any interest in money. He was much more the shy, scholarly recluse.

I only regret that he seems never to have forgiven me for pressuring him to return the Jung Codex (Nag Hammadi Codex I) to Egypt so that it could be included in *The Facsimile Edition of the Nag Hammadi Codices* being published by UNESCO, with myself responsible for getting the job done in my capacity as Permanent Secretary of UNESCO's International Committee for the Nag Hammadi Codices. No doubt it was my exposure of that monopoly that led to his bitterness.[4] The "official" report refers to it as my "broadside against Kasser."[5] The "official" report awards me the dubious distinction of being the only academic repeatedly criticized. This is no doubt because Krosney describes me as "one of Professor Kasser's longtime rivals.... The two ... remained estranged."[6] Yet when I was a Visiting Professor at the University of Geneva in 1992, where Kasser taught, he and his wife attended my first lecture and we went out to dinner together, so I hoped that the tension between us was behind us. I did note that when I was awarded an honorary doctorate by the same university in 2003 he did not attend the ceremony.

## THE NATIONAL GEOGRAPHIC SOCIETY

Michel van Rijn commented on his Web site in December 2004:

> NATIONAL GEOGRAPHIC THOUGHT THEIR BIGGEST COMPETITORS WERE THE DISCOVERY CHANNEL ... BUT IT'S US!
>
> This weekend National Geographic will film and photograph the Gospel's fragmentary pages in a vault in Switzerland. But of what value is their "world exclusive" if they are unaware of the diggers, smugglers, art-dealers, governments and bankers alike [who] are backstabbing one another for ownership of the Gospel.[7]

This would seem to be the first disclosure of the involvement of the National Geographic Society in the saga of the *Gospel of Judas,* though what it had in mind with its photographs was not made clear, and van Rijn's passing comment went largely unnoticed at the time. The cloak of secrecy surrounding the discovery and publication of the *Gospel of Judas* seems to have prevailed, until it was more formally broken by me, in a presentation at the annual meeting of the Society of Biblical Literature in Philadelphia on November 20, 2005.

## UTMOST SECRECY

In the memorandum sent by Mario Jean Roberty to Eric R. Kaufman on December 15, 2000, item 18 specified, as we have seen:

> It is clearly understood by all persons involved that nobody, not even Bruce and Frieda but only the Foundation, will have the right to promulgate and commercialize any knowledge regarding, concerning or deriving from the manuscripts. Moreover, for the time being and until all legal aspects are clarified, it is in the best interest of the Project to maintain utmost secrecy about its existence.[8]

This policy of utmost secrecy has been criticized repeatedly as inappropriate in the scholarly community.

Marvin Meyer reported in August 2005 that he knew much more about what is going on regarding the *Gospel of Judas,* but had been obliged to sign a document promising not to divulge what he knows. Indeed, on October 30, 2005, in preparing my report on what I could learn about the *Gospel of Judas* to be presented on November 20, 2005, at the annual meeting of the Society of Biblical Literature in Philadelphia,[9] I asked him by e-mail if he could provide me with even minimal information about the source of his information. To quote in full his e-mailed reply: "I'm sorry—but I must say, no comment."

But then I had a stroke of good fortune. I received a phone call from Paris, from the scientific journalist Patrick Jean-Baptiste, who was writing for the French monthly *Sciences et Avenir.*[10] He interviewed me by phone on November 9, 2005, after having just talked by phone the same day with Mario Roberty of the Maecenas Foundation. At my request, he e-mailed me what he had learned from Roberty. Thus he provided very up-to-date information for my presentation:

> The Maecenas Foundation (Mario Roberty and Frieda Nussberger-Tchacos) had signed a very good agreement with National Geographic for the intellectual exploitation of the *Gospel of Judas*. (Actually, I do not [know] how much NG [National Geographic] paid, but I heard nearly a million $ !!!)
>
> The negotiations with Bruce Ferrini failed because the lawyers of this merchant from Akron, Ohio, advised him not to sign the partnership Roberty and Tchacos offered him (the first offer was of 2 million $, the second less).
>
> So, next year around Easter, Roberty told me, will be broadcast a documentary film about the *Gospel of Judas* and [they will] publish an article in *NG* [*National Geographic*] magazine.
>
> Also, three books will be published by NG [National Geographic]. The first one: a big book with pictures of the gospel and 3 language translations (English, French, German) and commentaries by Rodolphe Kasser, Gregor Wurst, Marvin Meyer and François Godard. The second book, more journalistic, will be written by an American producer/journalist named Herb Krosney—it will be about the story of the documents. The third book, a popularized version of the Gospel, will be written by Kasser and also a certain Bart Ehrman.[11]

This report at the Society of Biblical Literature (SBL) convention, in a panel that included not only me but also Marvin Meyer on the platform, created something of a sensation, as one might well imagine.

Jean-Baptiste was thus the first to publish the specifics of the project of the National Geographic Society as follows:

> Today, no longer does anyone have access to this text. An ad hoc foundation, the Maecenas Foundation based in Basel, Switzerland, owns it and has just negotiated a wonderful contract of exclusivity with the National Geographic Society. In theory, nothing is to leak out before Easter 2006, date of the diffusion of a grand documentary film and of the publication

> of three books. As to the announcement of the Maecenas Foundation, according to which the codex will then be restored to the Egyptians, this is not able to make one forget that at the beginning it was quite simply stolen, then exported illegally.[12]

He also published the names of those involved, as follows:

> "This codex will be published completely translated in English, German, and French, with all the photographic material, in the form of a handsome book destined for specialists," rejoices Mario Roberty, the director of the Maecenas Foundation for Ancient Art, Basel, who retains the Gospel. "This work will be co-signed by the Professor Rodolphe Kasser, to whom we have confided the manuscript in 2002 [first shown to him on July 24, 2001], as well as the Professors Gregor Wurst, François Godard and Marvin Meyer."[13]

At the founding meeting of the International Association for Coptic Studies in Cairo on December 17, 1976, I proposed a resolution that was unanimously passed. To quote the minutes:

> A resolution was adopted to ask the Board to contact the responsible authorities of the collections of every kind of Coptic source materials in order to reach agreement with them as to free access, at stated conditions, for all the members, and the best possible facilities for their study. The International Association for Coptic Studies went on record as opposing giving or receiving exclusive publication rights, after approving an amendment offered by Prof. Kasser to the effect that a period of grace of twelve months from the date of this resolution be approved for editors presently in the course of preparing an edition.

This resolution seemed necessary because of monopolies that had kept the Nag Hammadi Codices inaccessible for more than two decades. The last Nag Hammadi Codex to become accessible was Codex I, which had been taken out of Egypt and acquired by the Jung Institute in Zürich, which named it the Jung Codex.

At a celebration of the fiftieth anniversary of the discovery of the Nag Hammadi Codices, I made a formal address[14] at the annual meeting of the Society of Biblical Literature in which I stated:

> The publication of the complete facsimile edition, just eight years after first getting access to the papyri themselves, has set an obvious standard for avoiding or overcoming monopolies in other manuscript discoveries. After all, we, though outsiders to the field, had shown that where there is a will there is a way. For the impossibilities ticked off by the insiders usually turned out to be excuses to justify their own self-interest, excuses that could readily be overcome if one really wanted to.
>
> For example: The last bit of the Nag Hammadi monopoly had been the Jung Codex (Codex I), since it was not in Cairo, where we had achieved open access, but in a bank vault in Zürich belonging to the heirs of Carl Gustaf Jung. The heirs were the owners, but had agreed to return the codex to Cairo when the team of editors no longer needed it for their transcription. The spokesman for the editors, Rodolphe Kasser, was on our technical subcommittee [at the Coptic Museum in Cairo], and would still have unlimited access to it in Cairo, had it been returned. But then so could the rest of us! So he maintained that the heirs were not willing to return it because they knew it was worth a lot of money. But then the spokesman for the heirs told me that the Jung family was ready to return it whenever the editors said they no longer needed it in Zürich. He even agreed to write the editors to inquire if he could return it. Thereupon he informed me that all who had responded (a postal strike had prevented the French from responding) had agreed to return it, except ... Rodolphe Kasser! Only when Kasser had sent the last volume

of their edition to the publisher and thus insured that it would be the *editio princeps* did he agree to the return of the codex to Egypt.[15]

The most obvious comparison to the Nag Hammadi publication experience has been the abysmal publication record of the Dead Sea Scrolls, since both discoveries took place at about the same time and hence have all along been compared in various regards.

At the annual meeting of the Society of Biblical Literature (that year, 1991, in Kansas City, just a week after *A Facsimile Edition of the Dead Sea Scrolls,* which I co-edited, had appeared),[16] SBL president Helmut Koester convened a special, called meeting of the society at nine o'clock on the last evening, 25 November. The chair of the research and publications committee [the same Harold Attridge who has played such a central role regarding the *Gospel of Judas*] read a resolution that had just been officially adopted by SBL:[17]

> *Recommendation to those who own or control ancient written materials:* Those who own or control ancient written materials should allow all scholars to have access to them. If the condition of the written materials requires that access to them be restricted, arrangements should be made for a facsimile reproduction that will be accessible to all scholars. Although the owners or those in control may choose to authorize one scholar or preferably a team of scholars to prepare an official edition of any given ancient written materials, such authorization should neither preclude access to the written materials by other scholars nor hinder other scholars from publishing their own studies, translations, or editions of the written materials.
>
> *Obligations entailed by specially authorized editions:* Scholars who are given special authorization to work on official editions of ancient written materials should cooperate with the owners or those in control of the written materials to ensure publication of the edition in an

expeditious manner, and they should facilitate access to the written materials by all scholars. If the owners or those in control grant to specially authorized editors any privileges that are unavailable to other scholars, these privileges should by no means include exclusive access to the written materials or facsimile reproduction of them. Furthermore, the owners or those in control should set a reasonable deadline for completion of the envisaged edition (not more than five years after the special authorization is granted).

When the resolution had been read, Emanuel Tov, then head of the Dead Sea Scrolls project, himself arose and announced that all restrictions on free access to the Dead Sea Scrolls had been officially lifted. You might as well unlock the barn door once the horse is stolen.

I hope and trust, and in fact am convinced, that we have all learned a lesson from this sad tale, for which we all bear some collective responsibility, and that in the case of future important manuscript discoveries a much more enlightened policy will be followed.[18] The Nag Hammadi experience deserves some credit for providing positive incentives to such a better future, in helping to change the ethos for handling important new manuscript discoveries.

In the case of the *Gospel of Judas* and the other texts involved in the same discovery, the volume published at Easter 2006[19] contains a first translation of only that one of the four tractates in Codex Tchacos (much less of the other three documents Tchacos purchased), and does not include its Coptic transcription and photographs. This is a decisive difference! The Coptic transcription made available on the National Geographic Web site was intended to prevent others from publishing their own translations, as the lawyers of the National Geographic have made all too clear (see the Preface above).

There are rumors to the effect that my opposition to the monopolizing of Codex Tchacos by Kasser was motivated by jealousy at my not being given access to it to publish. Nothing could be farther from the truth. I sent my student Stephen Emmel to Geneva on May 15, 1983, when it was offered for sale; if that sale had succeeded, the codex would have gone to Southern Methodist University, which pledged the money, where it would have been published by Harold Attridge after conservation by Emmel. If a few years later Martin Schøyen and I had been able to buy it in New York, the codex would have gone to Norway and the same two persons would no doubt have been entrusted with the conservation and publication. If a few years later the French-language Nag Hammadi team from the University of Laval had made the acquisition, after I put it in contact with the owner's agent, the codex would have gone to Québec and been edited by that team. In none of my initiatives would I myself have been involved at all. My only concern was to facilitate the acquisition and publication of the codex by responsible persons, persons whom I could count on to conform to the policies of sharing such important texts with their coptological colleagues (including Kasser) during the process. By this time I myself was working full-time on the sayings Gospel Q and had no desire to get back into the conservation and publication of Coptic papyri.[20]

## STEVE EMMEL TO THE RESCUE

I asked Steve Emmel if what I was planning to say in this book about his interest in Gnosticism and his resultant interest in the Nag Hammadi Codices and the Coptic language was all correct. To my surprise, in his reply (from Cairo, Egypt, where he has been studying Shenoute manuscripts) he casually, almost sheepishly, added that as of February 16, 2006, he had joined, with some reluctance, the National Geographic Society's "Codex Project Advisory Panel." He hoped in this way to see to it that the Coptic text is made available to the public at the same time that the English translation is published.

I'm simply delighted that Steve has become an insider in what is going on. It gives me hope that things will be done right.

Roberty reports that fragments are still being placed and thus the conservation has not been completed, much less the *editio princeps* with the Coptic transcription and photographs. But as Emmel brought the publication of the Nag Hammadi Codices almost single-handedly to a successful completion after the Technical Subcommittee of UNESCO's International Committee for the Nag Hammadi Codices had ceased to function, I know firsthand that no one would be a better addition to the team at this eleventh hour.

One may recall how Emmel recommended in his memorandum of June 1, 1983, the conservation of the newly discovered Coptic Gnostic codex:

> The leaves and fragments of the codex will need to be conserved between panes of glass. I would recommend conservation measures patterned after those used to restore and conserve the Nag Hammadi Codices (see my article, "The Nag Hammadi Codices Editing Project: A Final Report," American Research Center in Egypt, Inc., *Newsletter* 104 [1978]: 10–32). Despite the breakage that has already occurred, and that which will inevitably occur between now and the proper conservation of the manuscript, I estimate that it would require about a month to reassemble the fragments of the manuscript and to arrange the reassembled leaves between panes of glass.

As I read this, I could almost see Steve drooling at the mouth, he was so eager to get his hands on the material and conserve it properly before more damage was done to it. That did not happen in 1983. But now, a generation later, Herr Professor Dr. Emmel may have the chance he has been waiting for so very long. I see light at the end of the tunnel!

It should be pointed out that this final verification of the accurate placements of fragments on the leaves, indeed the completion of the reassembling of a very fragmentary papyrus codex, is precisely one of Emmel's specialties. As he mentioned in the paragraph just quoted from his memorandum, he did write the "Final Report" on "The Nag Hammadi Codices Editing Project." The much more detailed itemization of all he did to bring that project to its successful conclusion is in the final volume of *The Facsimile Edition of the Nag Hammadi Codices,* somewhat innocently entitled *Introduction*. There, after introductory chapters I wrote, is an extensive section of *corrigenda* composed for all intents and purposes by Steve.[21] All thirteen Nag Hammadi Codices had been published in facsimile volumes as rapidly as we could, so as to break, codex after codex, the monopoly on this discovery and make it available to everyone. But that meant that inevitably there were slight improvements and additions that could be added to those volumes, especially in the ongoing placement of fragments.

Let's take, for example, an instance of what we called an "island" placement, where a fragment does not actually touch the fragmentary leaf to which it belongs. All too often what is involved is a small fragment with only a single letter legible on it. Who cares if it is placed a centimeter out of its correct position? Well, anyone trying to edit that text cares! Where it is placed, in the volume of *The Facsimile Edition* that has already appeared, has been a pain for everyone working on the text. What is missing in the line on which it occurs seems to be easily and convincingly reconstructed, except for one detail: that letter on the little fragment does not fit in the otherwise convincing reconstruction of that line! If only we didn't have that letter to cope with—but now we don't, thanks to the little note in the *corrigenda* that it is to be raised (or lowered) a centimeter. That means it is no longer in that line, but in the line just above (or below). That may sound to you like a circular argument: if you don't like it where it is, just get rid of it! But Steve would rather die than commit such a sin! Rather, he had traced the horizontal fiber pattern on the body of that leaf across the gap and onto the small fragment and had seen that the fiber pattern did not fit. But by raising (or lowering) the fragment precisely one centimeter, the horizontal fiber pattern does work! So that is why he changed the position in the *corrigenda*. And then, after the prose description of the minor improvement, there is a photograph of just the relevant lines with the fragment in its correct position. Steve had opened the sealed Plexiglas container where that leaf had been conserved, loosened with a drop of water the sliver of transparent tape holding down that fragment (not Scotch tape, but special tape manufactured just for this purpose), and moved the fragment precisely one centimeter up (or down). Then, with a sliver of transparent tape, he reattached it to the lower pane of Plexiglas and resealed the two panes together. And that is how you will find it if you visit the newly renovated Coptic Museum today!

This may be what has been going on at the Bibliothèque Bodmer near Geneva, before Roberty considered the conservation task achieved to the extent possible, which means before Kasser published the final transcription, translation, and photographs in the *editio princeps*.

## HOW A PAPYRUS CONSERVATION LAB FUNCTIONS

Of course I have not been given access to the conservation laboratory at Nyon near Geneva, where the work of reassembling the fragmentary leaves of the codex containing the *Gospel of Judas* has actually been taking place. It has been carried on by the Bibliothèque Bodmer's conservator, Florence Darbre, aided by Gregor Wurst with the help of new computer technology (Adobe). But I once organized such a lab, in which both Kasser and Emmel worked! As Permanent Secretary of the International Committee for the Nag Hammadi Codices, I enlisted a Technical Subcommittee to work for several years, a week or so at a time, in the Coptic Museum in Cairo, doing precisely this same kind of work of placing fragments on tattered papyrus leaves and thus preparing the codices for photography and publication. As a result, I know firsthand what has to be done. I even know how Kasser works in such a situation, since he and I worked side by side in the Coptic Museum, after I enlisted him as a member of the Technical Subcommittee. So I can with some justification imagine what has been going on, I think with more reliability than any outsider could.

Kasser proved to be a very conscientious, laborious, punctilious, scrupulous, meticulous, exacting technical worker with papyrus, from the time the museum opened in the morning until it closed in the afternoon. There is no doubt that he knows from personal experience how to do the work that needs to be done in conserving the codex that contains the *Gospel of Judas*. But he also has the responsibility for transcribing, translating, and publishing the text in the *editio princeps,* with its introductions, notes, and indices of Coptic words, Greek loanwords, and proper names. He really does not have time to do the actual physical placement of the fragments as well. Indeed, the Parkinson's disease with which he has come to be afflicted means that he no longer has the steady hand to do such detailed work. But he has enlisted the conservator of the Bibliothèque Bodmer, Florence Darbre, to do this for him.

Since I worked with Kasser in Cairo doing this same kind of task, I know the procedure that he must be implementing there. First of all, there are four different tractates in the codex. The first task may have been to sort the fragments, to determine to which tractate each fragment belongs. This could be relatively easy, since there are duplicates of two of the tractates in the Nag Hammadi Codices. Fortunately, the critical editions of the Nag Hammadi Codices include indices. One could readily look up in these indices any words that are legible on the fragments of the new codex and determine if the fragment in question belongs to one or the other of these two previously known tractates. But in actual practice it is not all that simple. The Coptic translations in the new codex are apparently different translations from those used in the Nag Hammadi Codices, or the Greek from which they were translated differs, or both. Especially the second tractate, *James,* diverges considerably from its Nag Hammadi parallel, the *(First) Revelation of James.* As a result, a fragment may belong to one of those tractates but not be identifiable as such, because it involves a slight variation in wording. It is hence not certain that every fragment that cannot be placed in this way in one of the two previously known tractates belongs, by the process of elimination, to the *Gospel of Judas* or the *Book of Allogenes* (*Book of the Stranger*).

The easiest fragment placements are of course those that occur when one fragment (or fragmentary leaf) has the letters of part of a word, another fragment (or fragmentary leaf) has the other letters of that same word, and the two fit together nicely, as in a jigsaw puzzle. But one is not usually so lucky! There are many "island placements," where a fragment does not actually touch the fragmentary leaf to which it belongs, but it can be identified by the postulated flow of the lettering of the text. But this involves a higher degree of uncertainty.

Of course even the most "certain" placement must be verified by the continuity of fibers from one piece to the other. The fiber patterns serve as the "fingerprints" of papyrus, since no two sheets of papyrus have exactly the same pattern of papyrus strips. This flow of fibers on a papyrus leaf or fragment, horizontal on one side and vertical on the other, confirms that the placement of a fragment is correct. Sometimes an identification can be made on the basis of the fibers, even though there is no recognizable continuity of lettering, and even if the two fragments do not actually touch and fit into each other's edges.

When a fragment is thus "placed," it is taken out of the mass of unidentified fragments and put together with the leaf or other fragment with which it belongs. They are put between panes of glass in their correct positioning in relation to each other, awaiting, it is hoped, additional fragments to be placed on that same leaf. Thus, bit by bit, a leaf grows, sometimes beginning quite humbly with one medium-sized fragment or only with a couple of small fragments that belong together into, it is hoped, ultimately a much fuller leaf. But even if it remains so minimal, it is still evidence of a leaf in the original codex, deserving to be counted in the determination of the number of leaves that originally made up the codex, even if, for all practical purposes, that leaf is lost.

Such a leaf is pp. 65/66, where fragments are too small to do more than document that there once was such a leaf, and pp. 63/64 is not much better. The leaf of pp. 31/32 is completely missing, so that one could even speculate if it ever existed, since a tractate ends on p. 30 and another begins on p. 33.

The comments of Roberty in the interview of February 13–14, 2006, are hence very understandable:

> It was painstaking puzzle work. It will probably be going on for some time ... because we had a few more fragments popping up very recently. So there will be—for a full publication of the codex—there will be a delay.

Actually the initial translation by Kasser, Meyer, and Wurst reports in an endnote:

> A new fragment was placed on the top of pages 57 and 58 of Codex Tchacos as this book went to press. The new readings are in the present translation, but the fragment is not visible in the photograph of the Gospel of Judas on page vi.[22]

Furthermore the *National Geographic* article reports: "Latest find: A new piece of the gospel has emerged. See it and learn what it says at ngm.com/gospel."[23] At that Web site one learns that this fragment was "found in New York," with the hope of more to come. It was placed at the bottom of p. 37. Presumably the other side of the fragment provided the translation for the bottom part of p. 38. At both places the translation is relatively complete.

Publication was planned for the week after Easter, then hastily shifted to just before Easter, only two months after admitting that fragment placement "will probably be going on for some time," causing "a delay." Of course, Kasser knew how much time such work takes when he promised in his speech of July 1, 2004, to publish the *editio princeps* in 2005. The English handout read: "The publication is scheduled for 2005." No one expected him to meet that deadline. But then the National Geographic Society required a 2006 deadline of the week after Easter (April 16, 2006), to profit most from the fact that Easter is always the occasion for a Christian focus in the newsmagazines, not to mention the release of the film version of *The Da Vinci Code* (May 17, 2006). The team was enlarged and focus was shifted away from a complete *editio princeps* that would include the Coptic transcription as well as the French, German, and English translations, plus introductions, indices and photographs, to what is only a preliminary popularizing translation with notes. Roberty has already provided the excuse for not meeting the promised deadlines with a definitive work. Kasser could have provided these explanations from the very beginning, but may have been required to agree to meet a 2005 deadline in order to get the assignment for himself. Once he had the assignment and the work was well under way, one deadline extension after the other would be understandable and, for some of us, predictable.

## THE SIGNIFICANCE OF THE *GOSPEL OF JUDAS*

So what will be the significance of the *Gospel of Judas*? In his interview by the German news magazine *FOCUS* Steve Emmel made some reasonable speculations:

> Emmel: Naturally the text awakens, because of its pretended author, the interest on the most varied sides. How interesting it will ultimately be, we do not yet know. Certainly it was not written by Judas Iscariot himself (*laughs*)....
>
> *Focus:* It has to do with a pseudepigraph....
>
> Emmel: ... Exactly, a genre that contains fictional ascriptions to apostolic authors. Decisive is whether the text provides a new perspective on the early history of Christianity. Up until now, one cannot speak of that. The people who previously owned the codex always thought only about money. Also the current owners are out for sensation. I still doubt, though, that the text proves to be so terribly exciting. There are hundreds of unpublished Coptic manuscripts, only none have such sensational a title.
>
> *Focus:* Is the delay in publication a scandal?

Emmel: . . . At least I would not work that way. I would have produced a provisional edition. Normally experts exchange texts one with another. Here it is apparently the goal to stay covered so that once it appears everyone will immediately buy the book. One understands: He who has access to an especially interesting text will perhaps always want to win something from it: money, fame, honor, or whatever.

*Focus:* For a long time there are attempts to define in a new way the relation of heresy and orthodoxy, in early Christianity, for example, in the sense that the Gnostic "heresy" presented perhaps the original part of Christianity. Will the *Gospel of Judas* play a role here?

Emmel: There are people who believe that, or want to believe it. The topic could become exciting—if the new text were to prove once for all that in the beginning Christianity was completely different. For 2000 years the church has invested a great deal in the orthodox form of its history. It uses a historical myth to support faith. Scholars have said for a long time that the history must have taken place differently. But what really happened back then is debated. Also the Gospels of the Bible were probably not written by eyewitnesses. Most probably we will never learn who Jesus was or whether there ever was such a person. The new material no doubt shows only, still another time, that early Christianity is to be seen very diversely. Much is unclear as to what counted then as genuine, heretical or orthodox.

*Focus:* What religious thought lurks behind the *Gospel of Judas*?

Emmel: The most interesting thing will be whether a theologically thought-out reason for the betrayal of Judas is named. We already know sources according to which Judas is a hero in a certain sense, since without him the Christian salvation history could not have taken its course.

*Focus:* A conscious blasphemy is excluded?

Emmel: Not necessarily. The authors of these texts were partly very smart people who found the simple faith a bit laughable. It can be that it had to do with putting orthodox concepts intentionally on their head. That belongs to the spirit of the second century, in which the doctrine of Gnosticism reached its peak.[24]

There has been much speculation on what the discovery of the *Gospel of Judas* would mean for the Roman Catholic Church. Pöhner wrote:

> The name alone—*Gospel of Judas*!—may inflame theses of conspiracy and provoke speculation as to whether the Pope now needs to tremble and the Vatican is shaken in its foundations.[25]

But Hedrick convinced him that this is hardly probable:

> What the text really signifies theologically is another question. "I doubt," says Charles W. Hedrick, "that the leaders of organized Christianity will waste a second thought on it, once the excitement about its discovery has once passed."[26]

Thiede has also picked up on this potential sensation:

> Internet authors, in the style of Dan Brown's super-seller critical of Rome, *The Da Vinci Code,* have long since fabricated stories about the "unheard of shock waves" of the text, which will soon "shake" the Catholic Church "in its foundations." The public prepares itself to be able possibly to buy the original text of an ancient "Anti-Bible," which presents the pre-Easter events in the year of Jesus' death (or, if one prefers, only in early church history) in a completely different light from what the orthodox presentations have to offer.[27]

Yet it is not simply a matter of scholars being able to choose whichever they prefer, "pre-Easter events in the year of Jesus' death" or something "in early church history." They do not have the choice between what their research convinces them is historically accurate and what is just sensational. The *Gospel of Judas* is a second-century apocryphal Gospel that tells us about the Gnostics of the mid-second century, not about what happened in 30 C.E.!

Even Henk Schutten published a newspaper report in *Het Parool* entitled "Is There a Copy in the Vatican," for which he interviewed Roberty:

> Roberty does not rule out at all that the Vatican owns a copy of their own all this time, securely locked away. "In those days the Church decided for political reasons to include the Gospels of Luke, Mark, Matthew and John in the Bible. The other gospels were banned. It is highly logical that the Catholic Church would have kept a copy of the forbidden gospels. Sadly, the Vatican does not want to clarify further. Their policy has been the same for years: 'No further comment.'"

In the early centuries, there was no such thing as the Vatican, much less a Vatican library. But even if the church had had a copy, which is of course pure speculation, would it have been retained through all the centuries—when the capital of the Roman Empire moved to Constantinople, when Rome was captured by the Goths, when the Vatican moved to Avignon, France, when the old basilica was replaced by the present cathedral? It is very, very, unlikely that a copy is safely hidden away in the Vatican archives, and if it were, it would be highly unlikely that anyone on the staff at the Vatican knows that it is. Such speculation is simply invented to heighten the sensationalism while discrediting the Roman Catholic Church.

Stephen C. Carlson tried to put this issue to rest once for all, but apparently without success:

The Australian *Daily Telegraph* now has an article about it: "Controversial gospel to be translated" (Mar. 30, 2005). The news article relies heavily on a person from a certain Maecenas Foundation in Basel, Switzerland, which seems to be involved in exploiting this document....

Another aspect of the news article is no news: "'We do not want to reveal the exceptional side of what we have,' Mr. Roberty said,"—except that "the Judas Iscariot text called into question some of the political principles of Christian doctrine."

Nevertheless, that did not prevent the article having its *Da Vinci Code* moment:

The Roman Catholic Church limited the recognized gospels to the four in A.D. 325, under the guidance of the first Christian Roman emperor, Constantine. Thirty other texts—some of which have been uncovered—were sidelined because "they were difficult to reconcile with what Constantine wanted as a political doctrine," according to Mr. Roberty.

Not this canard again. The canonization of the New Testament was a long process that began well before Constantine and ended decisively decades after him....

Given how Mr. Roberty is quoted, it is not clear whether he is fully responsible for this historical nonsense.[28]

A newspaper in Turin, Italy, *La Stampa,* reported on January 11, 2006, that some sources said the apocryphal manuscript would lead to a favorable reevaluation of Judas. This was picked up January 12, 2006, by the London *Times* in an article written by Richard Owen with the headline "Judas the Misunderstood" and the subtitle "Vatican Moves to Clear Reviled Disciple's Name." It says Monsignor Walter Brandmüller, president of the Pontifical Committee for Historical Science, is leading a campaign "aimed at persuading believers to look kindly at a man reviled for 2,000 years." The next day, January 13, 2006, the same paper had an article written by Ben MacIntyre entitled "Blamed, Framed or Defamed. Three Good Reasons to Free the Judas

One." This essay is clearly a spoof, formulated as Judas's defense attorney's final appeal to the jury to acquit him. There is a similar article the same day, January 13, 2006, in the London *Guardian* written by John Crace entitled "Judas Iscariot: His Life and Good Works":

> Reports emanating from the Vatican suggest that the Catholic Church may be about to rehabilitate the reputation of Judas, the apostle commonly held to have betrayed Jesus. Scholars now suggest that, in fact, Judas was merely "fulfilling his part in God's plan." Below, we pre-empt the possible rewriting of the gospel.

Thereupon follows a rewriting of the canonical story, which is ridiculous, or infuriating, or both, and concludes:

> Jesus blessed him. "I forgive you now, but it will take everyone else 2,000 years." And so it came to pass.

On January 16, 2006, the *Toronto Star* published an article written by Rosie DiManno entitled "Judas Reborn: Are We Ready to Rethink the Fink?" It retraces the same steps as the other newspaper articles of the preceding days, only to end: "It's scheduled for publication at Easter. Nice timing."

But Monsignor Brandmüller told the Catholic news agency of Rome, ZENIT: "I have not talked with the *Times*. I can't imagine where this idea came from.... This news has no foundation." He went on to explain:

> In regard to the manuscript, it must be emphasized that the apocryphal gospels belong in the main to a special literary genre, a sort of religious novel that cannot be considered as a documentary source for the historical figure of Judas.

When it was suggested that the rehabilitation of Judas would favor the dialogue with Jews, Monsignor Brandmüller replied:

> The dialogue between the Holy See and the Jews continues profitably on other bases, as Benedict XVI mentioned in his visit to the Synagogue of Cologne, in the summer of 2005 during World Youth Day, and as he stressed last Monday in his meeting with the chief rabbi of Rome.

In an interview late in January 2006 with Stacy Meichtry, the Vatican correspondent of the Religious News Service, Monsignor Brandmüller is even more explicit:

> This gospel is apocryphal—a kind of historical fiction. Religiously and theologically it is of no interest. But it helps to illustrate the literary scene of ancient Christianity ... for thought that is non-religious and non-theological. It is a literary work, not a religious or theological text. With all probability, the author knew that. He knew what he was writing.
>
> There is no campaign, no movement to rehabilitate the traitor of Jesus. The reports are absolutely false.... One has to admit that the figure of Judas has always been a mystery. As a result he has stirred much speculation and attempts to interpret his betrayal. But an accepted explanation does not exist. The mystery remains. He remains a figure on the margins.
>
> We welcome the publication of a critical edition like we welcome the study of any text of ancient literature.
>
> A fan club, a group, never existed. Someone (an individual) probably went to work writing a novel on Judas.
>
> Much could depend on the critical study of the text itself. Some small finding could emerge, but I don't believe so. It is a product of religious fantasy. Usually these apocryphal gospels originate from a desire to know details beyond that which we read in the gospels.

Thus the Roman Catholic Church has maintained its calm, reaffirming its traditional position and refusing to be drawn into a discussion one way or the other that could only serve the sensationalists.

Actually, this dimension of the story had already been anticipated, if you will, even before the *Gospel of Judas* became the sensation that it now threatens to become. A novel was published in 2000 entitled, of all things, the *Gospel of Judas: A Novel.* In it, a priest in Rome, Father Leo Newman, receives fragments of a first-century scroll (of course) found near the Dead Sea (of course), which he is to decipher. It is an account of Jesus's life apparently written by Judas even before the canonical Gospels, explaining that Jesus did not rise from the dead. Father Leo realizes it could blow apart the foundation of Christianity and of his own life as a believing priest. So when he is called upon to validate and interpret the fragments, everything comes apart.

This book, apparently written without knowledge of the ancient Coptic papyrus manuscript of the *Gospel of Judas,* does in substance what some would expect (want?) the real *Gospel of Judas* to effect. But amazon.com lists one hundred new and used copies available from 49 cents.

Pöhner cannot help concluding his story on his own secular note:

> A fictional story. In our unchristian time the text appears as a weighty historical document, though its religious power will have limits. Yet perhaps it can arouse our fantasy: What, if the view of that Judas priest had prevailed? What significance would then loyalty have for us, what would betrayal be? What was the lie?[29]

Of course the publication of the translation of the *Gospel of Judas* has brought to an end this anticlerical tempest in a teapot, just as the publication of the long-withheld parts of the Dead Sea Scrolls and the Nag Hammadi Codices did.

In the case of the Dead Sea Scrolls, a sensational effort was undertaken to use the scrolls to discredit the Roman Catholic Church. Robert W. Eisenman, a Jewish scholar at Long Beach State University, had launched the theory that the unpublished fragments were being withheld by the Roman Catholic Church, lest their contents completely disprove the validity of Christianity. He claimed that the founder of the community that produced the Dead Sea Scrolls was none other than Jesus's brother James! In this case James, and presumably his brother Jesus, would, just as did the Teacher of Righteousness in the Dead Sea Scrolls (whom Eisenman identified as James), advocate very strict adherence to Judaism. This would mean that Paul's departure from Judaism and hence the church of today, following Paul's lead, are illegitimate! But this theory breaks down for a series of very solid scholarly reasons.[30] As a result, Eisenman did not have an academic following. But he was somehow able to secure, out of Israel, a copy of the monopolized photographs of the unpublished fragments of the Dead Sea Scrolls.

Then he enlisted my aid, since he knew of me as a monopoly breaker in the case of the Nag Hammadi Codices, to help him get them published. So we worked together as odd bedfellows, he to prove his sensationalist theory, I to disprove it.[31] Now that the fragments in question have been available for over a decade, Eisenman's sensationalistic theory has simply disappeared from the media. The Dead Sea Scrolls, which are of great significance to scholars in the field, have been left to them, Jewish and Christian scholars alike, to be studied carefully and soberly, free of that kind of sensationalism.

In the case of the Nag Hammadi Codices, the sensationalist was Jean Doresse, a French graduate student who made his reputation by being the first to publicize the material in Cairo.[32] He arranged an interview with the French-language newspaper of Cairo, which published his sensational report:

> According to the specialists consulted, it has to do with one of the most extraordinary discoveries preserved until now by the soil of Egypt, surpassing in scientific interest such spectacular discoveries as the tomb of Tut-Ankh-Amon.[33]

Here again, once the Nag Hammadi Codices were published and fully available to the public with the publication of *The Nag*

*Hammadi Library in English,* the sensationalism in the news media disappeared and serious scholarship took over. Of course the Nag Hammadi Codices are of great importance for reconstructing early Christian history. But sensationalism only serves to discredit discoveries of such importance as the Dead Sea Scrolls and the Nag Hammadi Codices.

It will no doubt be the same in the case of the *Gospel of Judas*. Now that it has become available, one finds that it does not shed light on what happened during Jesus's trip to Jerusalem (which is what the sensationalists imply), but rather sheds light on a second-century Gnostic sect. This is important for scholars, but not for the lay public. But by the time the sensationalism dies down, the Maecenas Foundation will, no doubt, as the memorandum of December 15, 2000, stipulated, have achieved its first objective:

> The promoters of the Project have incurred and will incur substantial expenses of money and time in order to realize the Project. It is a clear understanding that they shall be fully compensated and shall make a decent profit.

They can then turn the *Gospel of Judas* over to the scholarly community to achieve the other objective stated there:

> On the other hand, it is understood that this Project leads into a dimension far beyond a commercial transaction. The manuscripts involved being of potential importance to a major part of mankind imposes an approach substantially different to an ordinary business transaction.

So let us close this narration of the (mis)handling of the *Gospel of Judas* since its discovery on that happy note! In what follows, we turn to the *Gospel of Judas* itself.

4

# The Judas of the New Testament

Judas Iscariot is, if not the most famous, then surely the most infamous, of the inner circle of Jesus's disciples. He was one of the twelve apostles who stuck with him through thick and thin to the bitter end, until it became time to deny him three times before the cock crows twice, or tuck one's tail between one's legs and run for life back to Galilee, or, if you must, betray him. Is Judas just fulfilling biblical prophecy, implementing the plan of God for Jesus to die for our sins, doing what Jesus told him to do? Why else does he identify Jesus to the Jewish authorities with a kiss—just for thirty pieces of silver? What do the Gospels inside the New Testament—and then what does the *Gospel of Judas* outside the New Testament—tell us about all this?

## JEWISH AND GENTILE CONFESSIONS

In order to be able to understand the presentation of Judas in the Gospels of the New Testament, it is first necessary to understand the Gospels themselves as products of their own time, serving the purposes of churches in the last third of the first century. They were not primarily historical records, but rather were Christian witnesses to Jesus, "Gospels," "Good News." They were written for evangelizing rather than simply to inform. The Evangelists worked hard to formulate the traditions they recorded in such a way as to convey the evangelizing point they had in mind. Since most of what we know about Judas is found in these Gospels, we must first become familiar with this evangelizing procedure of the Evangelists, before we can move back behind them half a century to talk about the historical Judas himself.

Jesus's own "public ministry" was largely confined to Jews, and his disciples were Jews. Those who had the Pentecost experience of receiving the Spirit after Easter were Jews from all over the ancient world. They had gathered in Jerusalem to celebrate a Jewish festival. And Judas was a part of this very Jewish context out of which Christianity was born.

Judaism was (and is) a very impressive ethical monotheistic religion, appealing not only to Jews, but also to Gentiles. Gentiles admired the high ethical standards of Jewish communities and appreciated the form of worship they practiced throughout the Roman Empire: a religious service without the outdated trappings of a temple with animal sacrifice (confined to the temple in Jerusalem), but rather with an edifying, uplifting reading from their holy scriptures in Hebrew, followed by its interpretation in the everyday language of the audience. Gentiles liked to attend these services in Jewish *synagogues,* a Greek word that means "assemblies." But few of them were actually willing to convert to Judaism, to become Jews, "proselytes," by undergoing circumcision and accepting strict conformity to the Jewish lifestyle. Judaism meant abstaining from much of the desirable social life of their community! They preferred to attend the synagogue on the Sabbath, but live their normal lives the rest of the week. These Gentiles who attended the synagogue were called "God-fearers," but not "Jews."

In the Jewish synagogues where Paul preached, these God-fearers were those who were most sympathetic to his message, for he offered them precisely what they wanted from Judaism: the high ethical ideal without animal sacrifice or outdated restrictions on their social relations. Baptism was much better than circumcision! And so the gentile Christian church blossomed, far surpassing in numbers what was left of Jesus's disciples in Galilee, the withering Jewish Christian church.

Barnabas had enlisted for his gentile Christian mission in Antioch the most prominent convert from Judaism since Easter: the

Pharisee Paul, from Tarsus on the southern coast of modern Turkey, a Jew raised out there in the gentile world (Acts 11:25–26). Paul and Barnabas took Titus, a gentile convert to Christianity, with them to Jerusalem to convince the "pillars" of the Jewish Christian church there that this Gentile, though uncircumcised, should be recognized as a fully accredited Christian (Gal. 2:3). The Jerusalem church conceded the point (Acts 15:19–21) and reached a working arrangement with Paul and Barnabas: the original disciples would continue their mission limited to Jews, but gave the right hand of fellowship to Paul and Barnabas to continue converting uncircumcised Gentiles (Gal. 2:7–9). Paul in turn agreed to make a collection in gentile churches for the poor of the Jerusalem church (Gal. 2:10; Acts 11:29–30).

This fine ecumenical solution ratified by the Jerusalem Council proved difficult to implement back in the mixed congregation of Antioch, where Paul and Barnabas had in practice given up their Jewish custom of eating only among Jews to retain their ceremonial purity. Instead, they ate together with all members of their mixed congregation. The Lord's Supper could not be segregated! Even Peter, there for a visit from Jerusalem, went along with this tolerant Christian practice. But Jesus's brother James, who by then had taken over the leadership of the church in Jerusalem (Acts 15:13), sent delegates to Antioch to insist that Jewish Christians should eat only at a table with Jews, to retain their ceremonial purity, even if the congregation included Gentiles (Gal. 2:12). So Peter himself withdrew to a Jews-only table, and even Barnabas went along with this segregation (Gal. 2:11–13). But Paul stood his ground, denouncing this reliance on Jewish purity as a condition for salvation (Gal. 2:14–21), and from then on did his missionary work without the support of the church of Antioch or of Jewish Christianity.

From Paul's time on, this alienation between the Jewish and gentile branches of Christianity only got worse. The ecumenicity of the Jerusalem Council gave way to the dominance of the more numerous and prosperous gentile Christian church, which "returned the favor" by rejecting the small Jewish Christian church as heretical.

By the fourth century, Epiphanius, bishop of Salamis on Cyprus, wrote against the Jewish Christians, calling them heretical sects of "Ebionites" and "Nazarenes." The first term means "the poor," the second "from Nazareth" (Matt. 2:23). Both were originally names for Jesus and his disciples! All these Jewish Christians were doing was continuing their Jewish lifestyle, as had Jesus, while being Christians as well. Surely we would not call them heretics today!

## JEWISH AND GENTILE GOSPELS

In the generation after Paul, each side collected its treasured recollections of Jesus into Gospels, the Jewish Christians into their sayings Gospel Q, and the gentile Christians into their narrative Gospel Mark. One main reason that the sayings Gospel Q did not become a book within the New Testament is that the New Testament is the book of the gentile Christian church, not the book of the Jewish Christian church. We know about the sayings Gospel Q only because, as a last expression of ecumenicity, both confessions decided to merge both the sayings Gospel Q and the narrative Gospel Mark into a single Gospel, each from its own perspective, of course. Matthew did it from the perspective of the Jewish Christian church, Luke from the perspective of the gentile Christian church. So it is possible to reconstruct rather accurately the sayings Gospel Q, though no manuscripts have survived, once it ceased to be copied by the gentile Christian church.

The sayings Gospel Q made no reference at all to Judas, but the narrative Gospel of Mark, followed by the other Gospels in the New Testament, presented the familiar picture of Judas leading the Jewish authorities to the Garden of Gethsemane to arrest Jesus. It is precisely this familiar story that needs to be reexamined in the context of the emergence of the *Gospel of Judas.* But first we must familiarize ourselves with Judas in the Gospels of the New Testament themselves, from which both our quite understandably hostile feelings about Judas and an emerging more tolerant attitude toward Judas are derived. We begin with the first gentile Christian Gospel, the Gospel of Mark.

## THE GENTILE NARRATIVE GOSPEL OF MARK

Mark presents the inner circle of Jesus's disciples as being very ignorant about who Jesus was and what he was trying to do. You really have to wonder why they followed him at all—or you have to wonder why Mark portrayed them that way! So let's see how he did portray them, and try to figure out why.

After telling the parable of the sower, which even I can understand, Jesus asked the disciples with amazement:

> Do you not understand this parable? Then how will you understand all the parables? (4:13)

A whole chapter of parables follows, which Jesus has to explain rather pedantically to them:

> With many such parables he spoke the word to them, as they were able to hear it; he did not speak to them except in parables, but he explained everything in private to his disciples. (4:33–34)

Yet the disciples seem still in the dark:

> He said to them, "Why are you afraid? Have you still no faith?" And they were filled with great awe and said to one another, "Who then is this, that even the wind and the sea obey him?" (4:40–41)

They still don't seem to understand who Jesus is.

When the disciples in the boat saw Jesus walking on the water toward the boat,

> they all saw him and were terrified. But immediately he spoke to them and said, "Take heart, it is I; do not be afraid." Then he got into the boat with them and the wind ceased. And they were utterly astounded, for they did not understand about the loaves, but their hearts were hardened. (6:50–52)

Looking back on the feedings of the multitudes, Jesus asks:

> "Why are you talking about having no bread? Do you still not perceive or understand? Are your hearts hardened? Do you have eyes, and fail to see? Do you have ears, and fail to hear? And do you not remember? When I broke the five loaves for the five thousand, how many baskets full of broken pieces did you collect?" They said to him, "Twelve." "And the seven for the four thousand, how many baskets full of broken pieces did you collect?" And they said to him, "Seven." Then he said to them, "Do you not yet understand?" (8:17–21)

It is not surprising that Jesus knows just how unreliable the inner circle is:

> And Jesus said to them, "You will all become deserters; for it is written, 'I will strike the shepherd, and the sheep will be scattered.'" (14:27)

How many of this inner circle of the Twelve does Mark portray as being with him at the end, at the foot of the cross? None! Jesus knew quite well that none would die with him, but that they would do a quick retreat to Galilee, as Jesus told the faithful women at the tomb:

> But go, tell his disciples and Peter that he is going ahead of you to Galilee; there you will see him, just as he told you. (16:7)

In the Garden of Gethsemane, the inner circle had been out of it completely:

> He came and found them sleeping; and he said to Peter, "Simon, are you asleep? Could you not keep awake one hour? Keep awake and pray that you may not come into the time of trial; the spirit indeed is willing, but the flesh is weak." And

> again he went away and prayed, saying the same words. And once more he came and found them sleeping, for their eyes were very heavy; and they did not know what to say to him. He came a third time and said to them, "Are you still sleeping and taking your rest? Enough! The hour has come; the Son of Man is given over into the hands of sinners. Get up, let us be going. See, the one giving me over is at hand." (14:37–42)

With this, the antihero Judas walks across the stage. But, as our survey of Mark's presentation of the inner circle indicates, none of them is really much better according to Mark than is Judas! Some have thought that such a scoundrel as Judas could not possibly have been chosen by Jesus as one of the Twelve and admitted into the innermost circle. But, from Mark's point of view, he fitted right in!

At least Peter should be presented favorably, since after all it is he who is the rock on which the church is built. But not in Mark—that is Matthew's effort to clean up Peter's act (Matt. 16:18)! In Mark, Peter's confession to Jesus at Caesarea Philippi, "You are the Messiah" (8:29), takes a turn for the worse:

> Then he [Jesus] began to teach them that the Son of Man must undergo great suffering, and be rejected by the elders, the chief priests, and the scribes, and be killed, and after three days rise again. He said all this quite openly. And Peter took him aside and began to rebuke him. But turning and looking at his disciples, he rebuked Peter and said, "Get behind me, Satan! For you are setting your mind not on divine things but on human things." (8:31–33)

Peter, not as the rock, but as Satan? What is going on? "Get behind me, Satan!" might fit Judas, but to refer to Peter?

On the Mount of Olives, Jesus had predicted that Peter would deny him:

> Peter said to him, "Even though all become deserters, I will not." Jesus said to him, "Truly I tell you, this day, this very night, before the cock crows twice, you will deny me three times." But he said vehemently, "Even though I must die with you, I will not deny you." And all of them said the same. (14:29–31)

So did Peter stick by him to the bitter end? Not according to Mark! Instead, Mark tells us:

> "All of them deserted him and fled." (14:50)

When Jesus was being interrogated by the high priest, Peter followed him "at a distance" (14:54). Then Peter copped out completely:

> While Peter was below in the courtyard, one of the servant-girls of the high priest came by. When she saw Peter warming himself, she stared at him and said, "You also were with Jesus, the man from Nazareth." But he denied it, saying, "I do not know or understand what you are talking about." And he went out into the forecourt. Then the cock crowed. And the servant-girl, on seeing him, began again to say to the bystanders, "This man is one of them." But again he denied it. Then after a little while the bystanders again said to Peter, "Certainly you are one of them; for you are a Galilean." But he began to curse, and he swore an oath, "I do not know this man you are talking about." At that moment the cock crowed for the second time. Then Peter remembered that Jesus had said to him, "Before the cock crows twice, you will deny me three times." And he broke down and wept. (14:66–72)

Judging by the way Mark presents Peter, it would not have been surprising if Peter, like Judas, had gone out and killed himself, for both publicly let Jesus down. Instead, Peter lived to see a better day—but not Judas!

The greatest cathedral in the world was built over the site where Peter is thought to have been buried. But Mark would not have contributed a penny to the massive fund-raising effort involved! Fortunately, that took place long after Mark's time.

Jesus's family hardly comes off much better in Mark than do the apostles. There is no infancy narrative in Mark, so the whole Christmas story is missing. Instead, Jesus's family is ashamed of him, convinced that he is out of his mind, so they try to get him out of the public eye. Right after Mark's list of the twelve apostles, culminating in "Judas Iscariot, who gave him over" (3:19), Mark continues:

> Then he went home; and the crowd came together again, so that they could not even eat. When his family heard it, they went out to restrain him, for they were saying, "He has gone out of his mind."... Then his mother and his brothers came; and standing outside, they sent to him and called him. A crowd was sitting around him; and they said to him, "Your mother and your brothers and sisters are outside, asking for you." And he replied, "Who are my mother and my brothers?" And looking at those who sat around him, he said, "Here are my mother and my brothers! Whoever does the will of God is my brother and sister and mother." (3:19–21, 31–35)

The "holy family"? Hardly in Mark! Does Mark present Judas as all that much worse than Jesus's family? The same put-down is applied to Jesus's hometown, Nazareth (Mark 6:1–6).

Judas Iscariot fits all too well into Mark's portrayal not only of the twelve apostles, especially Peter, but also of Jesus's family and hometown! What is going on here?

Mark was the first Evangelist of the thriving gentile Christian church, as it became increasingly alienated from the Jewish Christian church built by Jesus's original disciples. Put into that context, it is less surprising that Mark so decidedly puts down the Twelve and Jesus's family. One can only recall the strained relations reflected already by Paul (Gal. 1:15–19; 2:1–14).

Should one expect the Gospel of the gentile church to be more favorable than was Paul toward Peter ("Cephas"), whom Paul "opposed to his face, because he stood self-condemned" (Gal. 2:11), and toward the "circumcision faction" (2:12), "this hypocrisy" (2:13), those who were "not acting consistently with the truth of the gospel" (2:14), not to speak of the "false believers" (2:4) who opposed Paul in Jerusalem? After all, Paul had warned explicitly against any gospel other than his own (1:6–9).

One would actually expect a gentile Christian Gospel to be anything but enthusiastic about those whom Paul put down so decidedly! The portrayal in Paul's Letter to the Galatians of the Twelve ("Cephas and John"), specifically Peter ("Cephas") and Jesus's family ("James"), fits perfectly the negative portrayal of the Twelve, Peter, and Jesus's family in the gentile Gospel of Mark. One should not expect it to be otherwise. But then the question has to be raised as to whether these Markan portrayals do full justice to these persons, or whether they are the victims of Paul's, and Mark's, theology. And what does this, then, suggest about Mark's portrayal of another one of the Twelve, Judas Iscariot?

The Gospel of Mark has been characterized as "a passion narrative with a long introduction." What this characterization has in mind is the way in which Mark seems to have his focus on the cross long before the actual crucifixion story itself. Already very early on, the plot to kill Jesus is brought into the story:

> The Pharisees went out and immediately conspired with the Herodians against him, how to destroy him. (3:6)

Then, the second half of Mark is dominated by Jesus again and again predicting his crucifixion in all too much detail even for Peter, as we have seen:

> Then he began to teach them that the Son of Man must undergo great suffering, and be rejected by the elders, the chief priests, and the scribes, and be killed, and after three days rise again. He said all this quite openly. (8:31–32)

Then on the descent from the Mount of Transfiguration, Jesus casually mentions his resurrection to Peter, James, and John, who had been with him there:

> As they were coming down the mountain, he ordered them to tell no one about what they had seen, until after the Son of Man had risen from the dead. So they kept the matter to themselves, questioning what this rising from the dead could mean. (9:9–10)

Had he not just told them that three days after he was killed he would rise again?

Shortly thereafter, there is a second detailed prediction of Good Friday and Easter:

> He was teaching his disciples, saying to them, "The Son of Man is to be given over into human hands, and they will kill him, and three days after being killed, he will rise again." But they did not understand what he was saying and were afraid to ask him. (9:31–32)

Then, a third time, Jesus describes in even more detail what is going to happen:

> He took the twelve aside again and began to tell them what was to happen to him, saying, "See, we are going up to Jerusalem, and the Son of Man will be handed over to the chief priests and the scribes, and they will condemn him to death; then they will hand him over to the Gentiles; they will mock him, and spit upon him, and flog him, and kill him; and after three days he will rise again." (10:32–34)

For all practical purposes, this is a rather detailed summary of Mark's passion and resurrection narratives (Mark 15–16). Indeed, it is generally recognized that such a detailed prediction was not made by the historical Jesus himself, but rather was formulated by the Evangelist and put on Jesus's tongue.

Even the Pauline gospel, limited to preaching only "Christ crucified" (1 Cor. 1:23; 2:2), "dying for our sins in accordance with the scriptures" (1 Cor. 15:3), "an atonement by his blood" (Rom. 3:25) crops up once in Mark on Jesus's tongue:

> For the Son of Man came not to be served but to serve, and to give his life a ransom for many. (10:45)

After all these allusions to the crucifixion, not to speak of detailed narrations, the Markan Jesus could quite understandably mention at the Last Supper: "The Son of Man goes as it is written of him" (14:21). And Judas would only have to be a bit smarter than Peter and the other apostles to know that it was the will of God that Jesus "die for our sins in accordance with the scriptures" (1 Cor. 15:3), that is to say, "as it is written of him."

In view of Mark's portrayal of Jesus's death as the fulfillment of prophecy and as being the will of God of which Jesus and the Twelve were fully aware, with Jesus acquiescing to God's will even to the point of death, it is really surprising not that Judas gave Jesus over to the authorities to kill him as part of the plan of God, but that Mark can even present this in a reproachful way:

> And when they had taken their places and were eating, Jesus said, "Truly I tell you, one of you will give me over, one who is eating with me." They began to be distressed and to say to him one after another, "Surely, not I?" He said to them, "It is one of the twelve, one who is dipping bread into the bowl with me. For the Son of Man goes as it is written of him, but woe to that one by whom the Son of Man is given over! It would have been better for that one not to have been born." (14:18–21)

But then, according to Mark, if Judas Iscariot had never been born, how would the scripture have been fulfilled, how would the will of God have been done, how would Jesus have "died for our sins in accordance with the scriptures" (1 Cor. 15:3)? Why pronounce a woe on Judas, who is only doing what he was born to do—what God and therefore Jesus want him to do?

Mark explains that the Jewish authorities want to kill Jesus, but need to find a way to arrest him privately:

> The chief priests and the scribes were looking for a way to arrest Jesus by stealth and kill him; for they said, "Not during the festival, or there may be a riot among the people." (14:1–2)

Jesus picks this up to mock them at the arrest—and to emphasize that all they are doing is fulfilling the scriptures:

> "Have you come out with swords and clubs to arrest me as though I were a bandit? Day after day I was with you in the temple teaching, and you did not arrest me. But let the scriptures be fulfilled." All of them deserted him and fled. (14:48–50)

Thus Judas is aiding the Jewish authorities' arrest of Jesus in order to kill him. This cannot be, from Mark's point of view, just an innocent referral to the religious authorities for them to hear what Jesus has to say, such as is appropriate on any and every issue that arises within Judaism (see below). Their intention is not to interview Jesus to learn who he is and what he is trying to do, whereupon they might agree with him and release him. They only want to "arrest Jesus by stealth and kill him" (14:2). This had been their intention from the very beginning, when the Pharisees and Herodians conspired together "how to destroy him" (3:6). So, from Mark's point of view, Judas is at best a party to the crime. Mark doesn't whitewash the scene by presenting Judas Iscariot as just doing the will of God and so the will of Jesus.

The Gospel of Mark presents in graphic detail the scene in the Garden of Gethsemane, where Judas plays the central role:

> Immediately, while he was still speaking, Judas, one of the twelve, arrived and with him there was a crowd with swords

> and clubs, from the chief priests, the scribes, and the elders. Now the one who gave him over had given them a sign, saying, "The one I will kiss is the man; arrest him and lead him away under guard." So when he came, he went up to him at once and said, "Rabbi!" and kissed him. Then they laid hands on him and arrested him. (14:43–45)

It is of course this text that is primarily responsible for the "bad press" Judas Iscariot has received ever since.

## THE JEWISH SAYINGS GOSPEL Q

The Jewish Christian church of the first generation spoke primarily Aramaic, of which no written texts have survived. After all, most of the original disciples were illiterate! But, fortunately, somewhere along the way they did translate Jesus's sayings into Greek, no doubt for use in their mission among Greek-speaking Jews. They even brought them together into a small collection of Jesus's sayings. So I have spent the last two decades reconstructing that collection, with a group of scholars I brought together for this purpose.[1] Let me explain.

*The Critical Edition of Q,* which we published in 2000, presents the written text of sayings ascribed to Jesus. It is not a book that exists today in its own right in the New Testament. Instead, it lurks just below the surface and has to be reconstructed. This is how: both Matthew and Luke had copies of the sayings Gospel Q, and used it, together with the Gospel of Mark, in composing their Gospels as a kind of "ecumenical" gesture. So when Matthew and Luke have the same saying of Jesus, but it is not in Mark, they must have gotten it from this other source. Scholars a century ago nicknamed this other source "Q," the first letter of the German word meaning "source," *Quelle.* Today we refer to it as the sayings Gospel Q, to distinguish it from the four narrative Gospels with which we are familiar from the New Testament: Matthew, Mark, Luke, and John.

Since Q itself does not have chapter and verse numbers, we make use of Luke's chapter and verse numbers when quoting Q. This is because Luke follows Q's sequence more faithfully than does Matthew. Since there is no birth narrative in Q, the text of Q begins at Luke 3 with John the Baptist. So the first chapter of Q is called Q 3. Q material is scattered through Matthew and Luke, but ends just before the passion narrative in Luke 22. So the last chapter of Q is Q 22.

Since the sayings Gospel Q was composed for use in the actual continuation of Jesus's own message by his disciples, it does not look back on Jesus's public ministry as a past reality to be described; rather, it is a collection of sayings still to be proclaimed. What is important is not who said what to whom, and where and when, as in a narrative Gospel, but that these sayings are decisive for you—your fate hangs on hearkening to them! It is perhaps for this reason that it does not mention by name those who carry on the message. None of the Twelve is mentioned by name, not even Peter—and not Judas!

## THE JEWISH CHURCH'S ECUMENICAL GOSPEL OF MATTHEW

The Gospel of Matthew seems to have been written when the remaining vestiges of the Jewish church using Q merged into the much larger gentile church using Mark. The merging of the Gospels of the two communions was a kind of ecumenical gesture attesting to the hoped-for harmonizing of the two confessions.

Matthew supplements the Markan record about Judas in significant ways. Mark had ascribed the initiative for the bribe to the chief priests (14:11). But in Matthew, Judas actually asks the chief priests to offer him a bribe: "What will you give me if I give him over to you?" (26:15). And Matthew focuses on Judas at the Last Supper when it comes to identifying who will give Jesus over:

> Judas, who gave him over, said, "Surely not I, Rabbi?" He replied, "You have said so." (26:25)

This is not fully explicit, but nonetheless readers get the message: Judas will do it.

It is quite significant that Matthew presents Judas here as addressing Jesus as "Rabbi" rather than the Greek translation "Lord" normally used in the Gospels. Of course it may very well be that in the Aramaic used at the Last Supper, and elsewhere, Jesus was in fact addressed as "Rabbi." At that time the term did not yet have the specialized modern meaning of Jewish clergy, but was just a Jewish term of respect for a religious leader.

But there seems to be a clear aversion to "Rabbi" or "Rabbouni" on the part of Matthew and Luke: once when Mark uses "Rabbouni" of Jesus (10:51), both Matthew and Luke read "Lord" (Matt. 9:28; Luke 18:41). Another time when Mark presents Peter addressing Jesus in the transfiguration story as "Rabbi" (9:5), Matthew and Luke read "Lord" (Matt. 17:4; Luke 9:33). In still another Markan instance of Peter addressing Jesus as "Rabbi" (11:21), Matthew omits the address (21:20), and Luke omits the whole incident.

It is only when Mark presents Judas addressing Jesus as "Rabbi" (14:45) that Matthew retains "Rabbi" (26:49); Luke omits here the address completely (22:47). In fact, Luke never uses "Rabbi" anywhere. His is the Gospel most emphatically addressed to Gentiles! But Matthew actually inserts a second instance of Judas addressing Jesus as "Rabbi" where there is no parallel at all in the other Gospels (Matt. 26:25). This is obviously because Matthew has disowned Judas. Such a form of address on the part of Judas merely documents his status as an unworthy disciple.

Actually, Matthew explicitly rejects the use of "Rabbi" by arguing that teachers of the Law and Pharisees seek to be so addressed out of pride:

> They do all their deeds to be seen by others; for they make their phylacteries broad and their fringes long. They love to have the place of honor at banquets and the best seats in the

> synagogues, and to be greeted with respect in the marketplaces, and to have people call them rabbi. (23:5–7)

It is hence to be avoided in addressing each other:

> But you are not to be called rabbi, for you have one teacher, and you are all brothers. (23:8)

So Matthew emphasizes that it is Judas who calls Jesus "Rabbi"!

When Judas actually kisses Jesus in the Garden of Gethsemane to identify him to the Jewish authorities, Matthew has Jesus add: "Friend, do what you are here to do" (26:50). This is almost an exoneration of Judas for the identifying kiss! The irony of the scene is that Jesus addresses him as "friend," an extremely rare term on Jesus's lips!

Then Matthew, alone among the Gospels, reports the remorse of Judas. He returns the money to the chief priests and elders, saying: "I have sinned in giving over innocent blood" (27:4). Then, when they shrug their shoulders, Judas, "throwing down the pieces of silver in the temple, departed; and he went and hanged himself" (27:5).

Matthew, as a Jewish Gospel, would of course have every reason to present a more favorable view of the Jewish disciples of Jesus than do Paul and Mark. After all, it was Matthew who rescued Peter from being Satan to let him be the rock:

> And I tell you, you are Peter, and on this rock I will build my church, and the gates of Hades will not prevail against it. I will give you the keys of the kingdom of heaven, and whatever you bind on earth will be bound in heaven, and whatever you loose on earth will be loosed in heaven. (16:18–19)

To be sure, Matthew retains Peter's opposition to the idea of the passion, and lets Peter still receive the rebuke "Satan." But Matthew did flesh out the dialogue to make it less shocking and more understandable:

> And Peter took him aside and began to rebuke him, saying, "God forbid it, Lord! This must never happen to you." But he turned and said to Peter, "Get behind me, Satan! You are a stumbling block to me; for you are setting your mind not on divine things but on human things." (16:22–23)

Here the Markan criticism is retained, but put in a context that mitigates it somewhat. This is the point of adding Peter's very understandable comment: "God forbid it, Lord! This must never happen to you." And Jesus's explanation justifies his rebuke: "You are a stumbling block to me."

Matthew had every reason to clear Peter's name, since after all Peter is, of course after Jesus, the hero of his Gospel. If Mark might have been the first to cast a stone at Peter, Matthew would have been the first to lay the cornerstone of the cathedral of St. Peter in Rome.

## THE GENTILE CHURCH'S ECUMENICAL GOSPEL OF LUKE

Luke presented the public ministry of Jesus as a sort of idealized time, a period not only quite different from the time before Jesus's public ministry, but also quite different from Luke's own time long after it.

We are quite familiar with Luke's way of presenting the beginnings of the church after Easter as a wonderful time, but a time that did not continue down into his present. In Luke's book of Acts, the beginning of the church is idealized, portraying a kind of voluntary sharing of all goods and funds, almost a kind of Christian communism. However, this was no longer the practice in Luke's own time. It was just the way things were done at the beginning of the church, which he looked back on with admiration and nostalgia, but not as a way of life to follow now. It was not a time to imitate.

Luke presented Jesus's public ministry in a similar way, as an idealized time in the past that does not really apply to the present.

Luke reports that after failing in the temptation, the devil left Jesus "until an opportune time" (4:13). The devil found that opportune time just before the passion narrative, when Satan reappeared just in time to enter Judas (22:3) and to tempt Peter (22:31). The period of the devil's absence, corresponding to the public ministry of Jesus, is for Luke an unrepeatable idyllic, paradise-like period of time, much like the idealized beginning of the Christian church.

This idealized time, free of the devil, corresponds very closely to the limits of Q in Luke. Q begins at Luke 3:2, with John the Baptist, and goes through Luke 22:30, just before the passion narrative. Indeed, the idyllic period of time ends in the very next verse after Q ends. Immediately after quoting the conclusion of Q in 22:30, Luke presents Satan reemerging to tempt Peter and give Jesus over in 22:31. Then Luke revokes quite explicitly the mission instructions of Q that had been quoted in 10:1–16. Those mission instructions had stated:

> Carry no purse, nor knapsack, nor sandals, nor stick, and greet no one on the road. (Q 10:4)

Just listen to Luke revoking these mission instructions, to get ready for the passion narrative:

> He said to them, "When I sent you out without a purse, bag, or sandals, did you lack anything?" They said, "No, not a thing." He said to them, "But now, the one who has a purse must take it, and likewise a bag. And the one who has no sword must sell his cloak and buy one. For I tell you, this scripture must be fulfilled in me, 'And he was counted among the lawless'; and indeed what is written about me is being fulfilled." They said, "Lord, look, here are two swords." He replied, "It is enough." (22:35–38)

In this way Luke prepares for Mark's immediately following report of the arrest:

> But one of those who stood near drew his sword and struck the slave of the high priest, cutting off his ear. (Mark 14:47)

So, by rearming the disciples, Luke has closed down the epoch of Q, wonderful though it may have seemed, and reentered the "real world" of push and shove. With Q safely behind him, Luke can proceed to follow Mark through the passion narrative and move on into the gentile church's mission practices, which Luke exemplified in the book of Acts in his portrayal of Paul moving about in a rather business-like way throughout the whole Hellenistic world.

This periodizing of history into an idealized past and a realistic present did not require Luke to omit the mission instructions of Q, though they were now outdated and formally abrogated by Jesus himself. Rather, Luke preserved them in their most archaic form (10:1–16). He had not been required to update them, as had Matthew, to conform to current practice. Matthew, clinging longer to the older procedures, had to make the adjustments called for by the passage of time. Most prominently, Matthew justified, by appealing to Jesus's instructions, a mission limited to Jews, a Jewish mission carried out to the exclusion of Gentiles and Samaritans, probably almost up until Matthew's own time:

> Go nowhere among the Gentiles, and enter no town of the Samaritans, but go rather to the lost sheep of the house of Israel.... When they persecute you in one town, flee to the next; for truly I tell you, you will not have gone through all the towns of Israel before the Son of Man comes. (10:5b–6, 23)

It is this Jews-only mission that one must presuppose was still being carried out by the Jerusalem church at the time James sent delegates to Antioch to enforce the segregated policy at the Lord's Supper, which Paul had so strenuously opposed.

In the Gospel of Luke, Jesus does not say to Peter, "Get behind me, Satan!" This scene would come right after Luke 9:22, to be parallel to Mark 8:33, but is completely missing. In Luke, Satan had tried to get hold of Peter, but Jesus protected him:

> Simon, Simon, listen! Satan has demanded to sift all of you like wheat, but I have prayed for you that your own faith may not fail, and you, when you have turned back, strengthen your brothers. (22:31–32)

But Satan has instead gotten a grip on Judas:

> Then Satan entered into Judas called Iscariot, who was one of the twelve; he went away and conferred with the chief priests and officers of the temple police about how he might give him over to them. They were greatly pleased and agreed to give him money. So he consented and began to look for an opportunity to give him over to them when no crowd was present. (22:3–6)

One would think that Judas, into whom Satan had entered, would have been the most obvious candidate for an exorcism such as Jesus performed most dramatically for an epileptic boy (Mark 9:17–29). Even the disciples had become adept at exorcism. Luke reports their return from the mission of the seventy as follows:

> The seventy returned with joy, saying, "Lord, in your name even the demons submit to us!" He said to them, "I watched Satan fall from heaven like a flash of lightning." (Luke 10:17–18)

The best-known disciple from whom Jesus had cast out a demon, or, more precisely, seven demons, is of course Mary Magdalene:

> The twelve were with him, as well as some women who had been cured of evil spirits and infirmities: Mary, called Magdalene, from whom seven demons had gone out, and Joanna, the wife of Herod's steward Chuza, and Susanna, and many others, who provided for them out of their resources. (Luke 8:1–3)

It is difficult to imagine Judas really being possessed by a demon, or even by Satan, and Jesus or one of the apostles not freeing him of that possession. Put otherwise, Luke's talk of Satan entering Judas sounds more like Luke's put-down than a historical fact. Judas wasn't really a demoniac.

Luke modifies only in small details the Markan report of Jesus speaking of the one who would give him over:

> But see, the one who gives me over is with me, and his hand is on the table. For the Son of Man is going as it has been determined, but woe to that one by whom he is given over! (22:21–22)

Just whose hand is on the table is not made clear,[2] but it replaces Mark's reference to someone who dips into the dish with Jesus, which is where John clearly identifies Judas (John 13:26). Luke then adds, after Jesus said that one at the table with him would give him over:

> Then they began to ask one another, which one of them it could be who would do this. (22:23)

But rather than following this up by pointing to Judas, as does Matthew (26:25), Luke instead inserts here a scene about true greatness found earlier in Mark (Mark 10:41–45): the disciples argue about which of them was to be regarded as greatest (Luke 22:24–30), triggered in Mark by the request of James and John for places on each side of Jesus in his glory (Mark 10:38–40). This was so awkward that Matthew transfers it to a request by their mother (Matt. 20:20–23), and Luke omits it completely, only to insert the ensuing discussion of true greatness into the Last Supper rather than going on to identify Judas as the one who would give Jesus over.

In the Garden of Gethsemane, Luke adds the fact that Judas was *leading* the crowd (22:47). As Judas comes to kiss Jesus, Jesus recognizes this act as the sign to the Jewish authorities:

> Judas, is it with a kiss that you are giving over the Son of Man? (22:48)

Judas promptly disappears from the scene; instead, one finds the Markan story of a disciple cutting off the right ear of a slave of the high priest, whereupon Luke has Jesus reproach the unnamed disciple:

> But Jesus said, "No more of this!" And he touched his ear and healed him. (22:51)

Such an act of kindness to a person who had come to arrest him is worthy of Pope John Paul II forgiving the person who tried to assassinate him. Indeed, at the crucifixion only Luke presents Jesus saying:

> Father, forgive them; for they do not know what they are doing. (23:34)

Just where this leaves Judas is not made clear. For Luke, Judas did not commit suicide, but he did pay the price for what he did:

> Now this man acquired a field with the reward of his wickedness; and falling headlong, he burst open in the middle and all his bowels gushed out. (Acts 1:18)

## THE GOSPEL OF JOHN

It is decidedly the Gospel of John that bears most of the responsibility for discrediting Judas completely. Here is the way he does it:

> "But among you there are some who do not believe." For Jesus knew from the first who were the ones that did not believe, and who was the one that would give him over. And he said, "For this reason I have told you that no one can come to me unless it is granted by the Father."

> Because of this many of his disciples turned back and no longer went about with him. So Jesus asked the twelve, "Do you also wish to go away?" Simon Peter answered him, "Lord, to whom can we go? You have the words of eternal life. We have come to believe and know that you are the Holy One of God." Jesus answered them, "Did I not choose you, the twelve? Yet one of you is a devil." He was speaking of Judas son of Simon Iscariot, for he, though one of the twelve, was going to give him over. (6:64–71)

The frequent question as to why Jesus would have included Judas in his inner circle is thus most acute in the Gospel of John. If Jesus knew "from the first" that Judas would give him over, he must have included him for that very purpose!

Just as Luke had changed Peter's being called Satan (Mark 8:33) into Judas's being possessed by Satan (Luke 22:3), just so John presents Judas as possessed by Satan. He smuggles this "detail" into the story much earlier than at the Last Supper.

The scene is of Jesus at the home of Simon the leper in Bethany (Mark 14:3–9) or, as Luke has it, at the home of Simon the Pharisee much earlier, in Galilee (Luke 7:36). A woman (in Luke 7:37, a prostitute), carrying an alabaster jar of very costly ointment of nard, pours it over his head (in Luke 7:38, his feet), whereupon those present (in Luke 7:39, the Pharisee) are indignant at the waste. If one can thus see how Luke changes a story in the home of a leper into something that fits better his polemic against the Pharisees, it should come as no surprise to find that John transforms much the same story to serve his purposes as a polemic against Judas.

John takes the familiar story of Jesus in the home of Mary and Martha (Luke 10:38–42), where Mary is praised for her attentive listening to Jesus, rather than just serving him at table, and turns it into a polemic against—Judas:

> Six days before the Passover Jesus came to Bethany, the home of Lazarus, whom he had raised from the dead. There they

> gave a dinner for him. Martha served, and Lazarus was one of those at the table with him. Mary took a pound of costly perfume made of pure nard, anointed Jesus's feet, and wiped them with her hair. The house was filled with the fragrance of the perfume. But Judas Iscariot, one of his disciples (the one who was about to give him over), said, "Why was this perfume not sold for three hundred denarii and the money given to the poor?" (He said this not because he cared about the poor, but because he was a thief; he kept the common purse and used to steal what was put in it.) Jesus said, "Leave her alone. She bought it so that she might keep it for the day of my burial. You always have the poor with you, but you do not always have me." (12:1–8)

Here it is quite obvious that John, as did Luke, takes a story from the tradition about Jesus and, by changing the characters and plot, makes it serve his polemical purposes. This should then make it equally clear that the damning of Judas, as the keeper of the moneybags who only pretends to care for the poor so as to steal money from Jesus and the other disciples, is more probably a creation of John than a historical fact. At the Last Supper John needs only to mention that the devil had already inspired Judas to give him over (13:2). Even more pointedly John writes that Satan entered Judas when Jesus gave him bread he had dipped into the dish (13:27).

The Gospel of John has Jesus identify Judas as the one to give him over already at the beginning of the parting discourse held at the Last Supper:

> Jesus knew that his hour had come to depart from this world and go to the Father. Having loved his own who were in the world, he loved them to the end. The devil had already put it into the heart of Judas son of Simon Iscariot to give him over. And during supper Jesus ... got up from the table, took off his outer robe, and tied a towel around himself. Then he poured water into a basin and began to wash the disciples' feet and

> to wipe them with the towel that was tied around him.... Jesus said to him [Simon Peter], "One who has bathed does not need to wash, except for the feet, but is entirely clean. And you are clean, though not all of you." For he knew who was to give him over. ...
>
> "I am not speaking of all of you; I know whom I have chosen. But it is to fulfill the scripture, 'The one who ate my bread has lifted his heel against me.' I tell you this now, before it occurs, so that when it does occur, you may believe that I am he."...
>
> After saying this Jesus was troubled in spirit, and declared, "Very truly, I tell you, one of you will give me over." The disciples looked at one another, uncertain of whom he was speaking. One of his disciples—the one whom Jesus loved—was reclining next to him; Simon Peter therefore motioned to him to ask Jesus of whom he was speaking. So while reclining next to Jesus, he asked him, "Lord, who is it?" Jesus answered, "It is the one to whom I give this piece of bread when I have dipped it in the dish." So when he had dipped the piece of bread, he gave it to Judas son of Simon Iscariot. After he received the piece of bread, Satan entered into him. Jesus said to him, "Do quickly what you are going to do." Now no one at the table knew why he said this to him. Some thought that, because Judas had the common purse, Jesus was telling him, "Buy what we need for the festival"; or, that he should give something to the poor. So, after receiving the piece of bread, he immediately went out. And it was night. (13:1–5, 10–11, 18–19, 21–30)

In the so-called high priestly prayer with which Jesus's parting discourse concludes, there is a flashback to Judas:

> While I was with them, I protected them in your name that you have given me. I guarded them, and not one of them was lost except the son of destruction, so that the scripture might be fulfilled. (17:12)

The final scene of Judas in the Gospel of John is at Jesus's arrest:

> After Jesus had spoken these words, he went out with his disciples across the Kidron valley to a place where there was a garden, which he and his disciples entered. Now Judas, who gave him over, also knew the place, because Jesus often met there with his disciples. So Judas brought a detachment of soldiers together with police from the chief priests and the Pharisees, and they came there with lanterns and torches and weapons. Then Jesus, knowing all that was to happen to him, came forward and asked them, "Whom are you looking for?" They answered, "Jesus of Nazareth." Jesus replied, "I am he." Judas, who gave him over, was standing with them. When Jesus said to them, "I am he," they stepped back and fell to the ground. Again he asked them, "Whom are you looking for?" And they said, "Jesus of Nazareth." Jesus answered, "I told you that I am he. So if you are looking for me, let these men go." This was to fulfill the word that he had spoken, "I did not lose a single one of those whom you gave me." Then Simon Peter, who had a sword, drew it, struck the high priest's slave, and cut off his right ear. The slave's name was Malchus. Jesus said to Peter, "Put your sword back into its sheath. Am I not to drink the cup that the Father has given me?" So the soldiers, their officer, and the Jewish police arrested Jesus and bound him. (18:1–12)

Here Judas plays his indispensable role in the story, of bringing the Jewish authorities to arrest Jesus. But his role in this crucial scene is, compared to the other Gospels, minimal. There is no kiss of death. He does his thing and disappears from history, as far as the Gospel of John is concerned.

## JUDAS IN THE CANONICAL GOSPELS AND ACTS

From this survey of the canonical Gospels and the book of Acts, we can see how each handles the figure of Judas, how they are the genesis of the horrible image of Judas down through the centuries, and yet how, upon inspection, they do not present that image as being as one-sidedly horrible as we have usually assumed.

To be sure, they do not in any sense of the word vindicate him, much less make him into the hero, as the *Gospel of Judas* at times seems almost to do. Modern efforts point out that he is not (with the one exception of Luke 6:16) actually said to betray Jesus as a "traitor" and that he is only carrying out his role as prophesied in the Hebrew scriptures, predicted by Jesus, even ordered by Jesus. But the canonical texts also pronounce a woe on him for his evil deed and present him in such remorse that he kills himself. This is not what one normally does in fulfilling the Hebrew scriptures or obeying Jesus! But a presentation in which Judas is to be praised, not just blamed, calls for a rather complete reversal of values such as is to be found in the *Gospel of Judas*.

5

# The Historical Judas

*Judas* is the Greek spelling of the Hebrew name *Judah,* meaning "praised." Judah is about as popular a name as one can find in all of Judaism. Indeed, Judaism itself is named after Judah! Judah is, after all, the origin of the word *Jew.* Paul points out that he grew up "in Judaism" (Gal. 1:13–14), though he was of the tribe of Benjamin (Phil. 3:5).

Judah was the fourth son of Jacob and Leah, and Judah was the name of one of the twelve tribes of Israel. When the Israelites entered the Promised Land, the tribe of Judah was awarded the southern part. After the reign of Solomon, the Israelite kingdom that David had created was divided into two kingdoms: Judah was the Southern Kingdom and Israel the Northern Kingdom. The Northern Kingdom was overrun by the Assyrians and disappeared from the pages of history. But after the Babylonian captivity of the Southern Kingdom, Judah was repopulated by those who returned from captivity. The Roman emperor Augustus named it Judea, and so its inhabitants became "Judeans" (John 7:1). In our day, Judea is the name used by the modern state of Israel to designate its southern part, though the United Nations, the United States, and hence the media, usually refer to much of it as part of the "occupied West Bank."

Understandably enough, Judas, as the Greek spelling of the Hebrew word *Judah,* was a very popular Jewish name indeed. The Maccabean revolt against Syrian armies was led by Judas Maccabee (167–160 B.C.E.), so of course the name was especially popular among the Maccabeans. The Jewish historian Josephus reports that the terrorists of his day, the Zealots, whom Josephus calls

Sicarii, often used the name Judas for their leaders. In the New Testament, six people named Judas are mentioned.

Actually, Jesus had a brother named Judas. This has been somewhat hidden from view by the fact that the translators of the King James Bible wanted, at all costs, to keep the two persons named Judas separate. So the King James Bible entitled the Letter ascribed to Jesus's brother as "Jude." The Letter begins: "Jude, a servant of Jesus Christ and brother of James." James is of course another brother of Jesus, as the list in Matthew 13:55 indicates:

> Is not this the carpenter's son? Is not his mother called Mary? And are not his brothers James and Joseph and Simon and Judas?

Furthermore, in Luke's list of the twelve apostles, two are named Judas:

> ... and Judas the son of James, and Judas Iscariot, who became a traitor. (6:16)

Of course, after the crucifixion when Luke lists only eleven apostles, there is only one Judas:

> ... and Judas the son of James. (Acts 1:13)

Because of the number of persons named Judas, and especially because there are two named Judas in Luke's list of the Twelve, not to speak of Jesus's brother Judas, it was obviously necessary to distinguish one Judas from the other. A comparison of various lists of the Twelve shows that most apostles are given only one name. But when there are more than one with the same name, for example, Simon Peter and Simon the Cananaean or James the son of Zebedee and James the son of Alphaeus, these clarifications are appended to their names to distinguish between them. So it is with Judas the son of James and Judas Iscariot.

What, then, does *Iscariot* mean? There are various theories, so many in fact that none can be counted on as definitive. Perhaps it means "man (*ish-*) from Karioth," if Karioth really is the name of a town of southern Judea mentioned in Joshua 15:25. But what is written there could just mean "town," as suggested by the rather free New Revised Standard Version (NRSV) translation, "Kerioth-hezron (that is, Hazor)." The NRSV also lists, in a note to "Judas son of Simon Iscariot" (John 6:71), a second choice: "Judas son of Simon from Karyot (Kerioth)." There is a Tel Qirrioth on the current map in the Negev. And there is an Askaroth or Askar near Shechem. Another suggestion has been that it just meant a person from the "city," that is, Jerusalem, as attested in later Jewish sources. Any of these derivations would make Judas the only one of the twelve apostles from Judea and would help explain how it was that he was known to the Jerusalem authorities.

Or *Iscariot* may mean one of the Sicarii, the name Josephus used for the Zealots of his day. And there are still other explanations for *Iscariot.* In sum, there is so much uncertainty about the derivation of the term that nothing can be made of it, other than that it was used to distinguish this Judas both from the other Judas listed among the Twelve and from Jesus's brother Judas.

The Gospel of John also lists the name of Judas's father, for it was customary then, just as it is now, to use a father's name (or ancestor's name) as the "second" name of a person. My own name has two such "patronymics." Of course "-son" is the most common English way to produce a patronymic. Robinson goes back to the Scottish nickname for Robert, Robin. But even my middle name, McConkey, uses the Gaelic patronymic, Mc or Mac. In Greek, the patronymic is put in the genitive, meaning "*X* (the son) of *Y*." So the Gospel of John refers to "Judas (son of) Simon Iscariot" (6:71; 13:2, 26). But since this Simon is unknown, that bit of information does not help us further. Yet it does weaken the case for Judas being a terrorist of the day: "Iscariot," if related to "Sicarii," would have been used of his father, Simon. It would simply have been taken over by Judas in taking over his father's name and epithet, customary at the time.

## JUDAS IN THE INNER CIRCLE

There is of course discussion as to whether Judas was one of "the Twelve." It has seemed to many that it would be unreasonable for Jesus to admit such a person into that inner circle. Yet the Gospel of John, which is the Gospel most critical of Judas, explicitly scores the point that Jesus did choose him:

> Jesus answered them, "Did I not choose you, the twelve? Yet one of you is a devil." He was speaking of Judas son of Simon Iscariot. (6:70–71)

But John's having to score the point that Jesus really did choose him assumes Judas to have been a notorious scoundrel, which is precisely what one would now like to question.

Celsus, a pagan critic of Christianity in the second century, listed Jesus's betrayal by a disciple as a reason that Jews used to discredit Jesus:

> How could we have accepted as God one who, as was reported, did not carry out any of the works he announced, and when we had evidence against him and denounced him and wanted to punish him he hid himself and tried to escape; who was captured in a disgraceful manner and even was betrayed by one whom he called his disciple? Surely if he was God he would not have needed to flee, or been taken away bound, and least of all to be left in the lurch and deserted by his companions, who shared everything with him personally, considered him their teacher.[1]

Nonetheless, Judas is after all given in each list of the Twelve in the Gospels (Matt. 10:4; Mark 3:19; Luke 6:16). His credentials are solid!

The question of his being in the Twelve has less to do with Judas than with whether Jesus ever really created an inner circle of disciples consisting of precisely twelve persons. The number twelve used of the inner circle seems to have come from the twelve tribes of Israel. One can detect the beginnings of such an idea at the conclusion of the sayings Gospel Q:

> You who have followed me will sit on thrones judging the twelve tribes of Israel. (Q 22:28, 30)

Then Matthew edited this conclusion of Q to suggest that, since a disciple of Jesus was judging each of the twelve tribes, there would surely be twelve judgment seats:

> You who have followed me will also sit on twelve thrones, judging the twelve tribes of Israel. (19:28)

Here the idea of judging the twelve tribes of Israel clearly preceded the idea of there being twelve thrones, which in turn would engender the idea of twelve members of the inner circle. So one may assume that the number twelve was arrived at not by counting those in the inner circle, but by counting tribes. In fact, Paul simply refers to the Twelve on an occasion when in fact no more than eleven could have been involved. In the list of resurrection appearances, Paul says:

> He appeared to Cephas, then to the twelve. (1 Cor. 15:5)

But at the time of the resurrection appearances, Judas was no longer a member of the Twelve. At most, Jesus appeared to eleven. But Paul's point is only that Jesus appeared to the inner circle of disciples, which was named the Twelve. In fact, some of the persons named in the Twelve are names only—they never crop up in specific stories. Names that usually crop up in stories of the inner circle are Peter, James, and John.

A Jewish Christian Gospel that did not gain admission into the New Testament, the *Gospel of the Ebionites,* lists only nine disciples, including Judas, but in the calling of Matthew it refers to there being "twelve apostles as a witness to Israel." Here again the association with the twelve tribes of Israel is implied.

Irrespective of whether the Twelve was an actual number of members in the inner circle during Jesus's public ministry, it seems clear that Judas was a member of that inner circle. His name would hardly have been inserted into the list later, after he had given Jesus over. But what can we know about him?

## DID JUDAS ACTUALLY HAVE THE MONEYBAGS?

The Gospel of John presents Judas as the treasurer of the Jesus movement as a way to discredit him in the story of Mary and Martha:

> But Judas Iscariot, one of his disciples (the one who was about to give him over), said, "Why was this perfume not sold for three hundred denarii and the money given to the poor?" (He said this not because he cared about the poor, but because he was a thief; he kept the common purse and used to steal what was put into it.) (12:4–6)

There is then a flashback to this story at the Last Supper:

> Jesus said to him, "Do quickly what you are going to do." Now no one at the table knew why he said this to him. Some thought that, because Judas had the common purse, Jesus was telling him, "Buy what we need for the festival"; or, that he should give something to the poor. (13:27–29)

But since this report of Judas having the common purse is only in John and is used there just to discredit Judas, we have questioned whether there is any truth to this detail. It is more probably a creation of John than a historical fact.

## DID JUDAS FULFILL SCRIPTURE?

Mark had explained that the Jewish authorities wanted to find a way to arrest Jesus privately, for fear of the supportive crowds at the festival (14:1–2). Jesus then alludes to this in the Garden of Gethsemane:

> Day after day I was with you in the temple teaching, and you did not arrest me. But let the scriptures be fulfilled. (14:49)

Yet the historical Jesus of course did not know about the authorities' comment:

> Not during the festival, or there may be a riot among the people. (14:2)

And which scripture needing to be fulfilled would Jesus have had in mind? Did he really know as much scripture as modern scripture scholars ascribe to him? Certainly not! Nor would he have developed such skill in applying everything to himself.

Mark had presented Jesus predicting at the Last Supper that Judas would give him over:

> When they had taken their places and were eating, Jesus said, "Truly I tell you, one of you will give me over, one who is eating with me.... For the Son of Man goes as it is written of him, but woe to that one by whom the Son of Man is given over! It would have been better for that one not to have been born." (14:18, 21)

The Gospel of John describes the scene in much more detail:

> The disciples looked at one another, uncertain of whom he was speaking.... Jesus answered, "It is the one to whom I give this piece of bread when I have dipped it in the dish." So when he had dipped the piece of bread, he gave it to Judas son of Simon Iscariot. After he received the piece of bread, Satan entered into him. Jesus said to him, "Do quickly what you are going to do." ... So, after receiving the piece of bread, he immediately went out. And it was night. (13:22, 26–27, 30)

Here Jesus is apparently presented as fulfilling a prophecy from the Old Testament:

> Even my bosom friend in whom I trusted, who ate of my bread, has lifted the heel against me. (Ps. 41:9)

This, then, is a really odd situation. The Hebrew scriptures predict what Judas will do, and Jesus knows this scriptural passage to be referring to himself, but does nothing to prevent it, since it obviously is the prophesied will of God. So why does he proceed to pronounce a woe on the one who fulfills the prophecy? Would it really have been better for Judas never to have been born? Perhaps better for Judas, but not better for carrying out Jesus's God-willed destiny to die!

All of this sounds much more like what the learned Evangelists could compose, with the help of the Hebrew scriptures in front of them (in Greek translation), than like an actual dialogue in the upper room at the Last Supper, where literacy and exegetical skill were at a much lower level!

## DID JUDAS ISCARIOT "BETRAY" JESUS?

The Gospel of Mark presents in graphic detail the scene in the Garden of Gethsemane in which Judas plays the central role:

> Immediately, while he was still speaking, Judas, one of the twelve, arrived; and with him there was a crowd with swords and clubs, from the chief priests, the scribes, and the elders. Now the one who gave him over had given them a sign, saying, "The one I will kiss is the man; arrest him and lead him away under guard." So when he came, he went up to him at once and said, "Rabbi!" and kissed him. And they laid hands on him and arrested him. (14:43–46)

What is actually going on here in the case of Judas? Several recent books about Judas have turned a sympathetic ear to him, sensing that what he is reported to have done was not all that wrong, after all. The more fictional presentation of Ray S. Anderson presents a dialogue between Jesus and Judas in which Jesus forgives Judas—and his book already bore the title *The Gospel According to Judas*![2] Hans-Josef Klauck, a German professor who has recently joined the faculty of the University of Chicago's Divinity School, laid out a very balanced assessment of Judas as "a disciple of the Lord" in a work that unfortunately is not available in English.[3] William Klassen's book *Judas: Betrayer or Friend of Jesus?* defends the thesis that Judas was indeed more friend than betrayer.[4] And Kim Paffenroth, who specializes in the area of religion and film, gives a very sympathetic though partly fictional presentation in *Judas: Images of the Lost Disciple*.[5]

The thesis of Klassen's book is that Judas did not *betray* Jesus, but only *gave* him *over* to the appropriate Jewish authorities to evaluate his claims, a quite appropriate and understandable transaction within the Judaism of that day. Hence we are wrong to understand Judas as a *traitor*, as if what the Gospels present him doing is a *betrayal*. Klassen points out:

> Not one ancient classical Greek text ... has the connotation of treachery. Any lexicon that suggests otherwise is guilty of theologizing rather than assisting us to find the meaning of Greek words through usage.[6]

Hence, the Greek word in the Gospels that is translated as "betray" (*paradidomi*) does not actually have that basically negative meaning that we associate with betrayal in English.

In the standard Greek-English dictionary of the New Testament that all scholars use,[7] the first meaning is listed neutrally as "hand over, turn over, give up" a person. But it has also the decidedly positive meaning "give over, commend, commit," for example, to commend a person "to the grace of God" (Acts 14:26; 15:40). It often means "hand down, pass on, transmit, relate, teach" the oral or written tradition. It is in fact most familiar to us in the liturgy of the Lord's Supper, "For I received from the Lord what I also *handed on* to you" (1 Cor. 11:23), and in the way Paul introduced a list of resurrection appearances, "For I *handed on* to you as of first importance what I in turn had received" (1 Cor. 15:3). It is consistent with this double meaning of the verb that the noun means a *handing over* or a *handing down* both in the sense of an *arrest* and in the sense of the *transmission of tradition*. It is clear from the use of this verb that Judas *handed* Jesus *over*. The etymology of the Greek word is neutrally *give over*, which I hence use, so as not to prejudice us unduly against Judas. But what that *giving over* actually meant is the question at issue.

In the whole of the New Testament, the literal term *traitor* is applied to Judas Iscariot only once, in Luke's naming him as the last in the list of the Twelve: "Judas Iscariot, who became a traitor" (6:16). Is this a mistake on Luke's part?

## JUDAS ISCARIOT GAVE JESUS OVER TO THE JEWISH AUTHORITIES

There have been a lot of efforts to define in theological detail what it was that Judas "betrayed" about Jesus, such as the fact that Jesus was the Messiah. But the record is clear in this regard: Judas did not reveal anything about who Jesus was or what he taught or did. Judas simply revealed where Jesus was. Mark makes this quite clear:

> It was now two days before the Passover and the festival of Unleavened Bread. The chief priests and the scribes were looking for a way to arrest Jesus by stealth and kill him; for they said, "Not during the festival, or there may be a riot among the people." (14:1–2)

This in turn is a flashback to an earlier comment at the cleansing of the temple:

> And when the chief priests and the scribes heard it, they kept looking for a way to kill him; for they were afraid of him, be-

> cause the whole crowd was spellbound by his teaching. And when evening came, Jesus and his disciples went out of the city. (11:18–19)

Klassen's main point is that for Judas to turn Jesus in to the proper Jewish authorities is not necessarily a hostile "betrayal," but rather a proper procedure in the Jewish world of that day. He comes to the following conclusion:

> What precisely was Judas's contribution? I submit that in the grand scheme of things, it was quite modest. In discussions with Jesus, he had often heard Jesus criticize the Temple hierarchy. When Judas reminded Jesus that his own advice had always been to rebuke the sinner directly, Jesus may have said that an occasion to confront the high priest directly had not appeared. Perhaps at that point Judas offered to arrange it, hoping that the process of rebuke would work. At the same time, he may have questioned Jesus about his own faithfulness to his mission. All of this could have led to a plan whereby Judas would arrange a meeting with Jesus and the high priests, each agreeing to that meeting on their own terms and with their own hopes for the outcome. This role in the "handing over" was later transformed into a more sinister one, especially after Judas died at his own hand. Whether the reader is able to accept this interpretation of the earliest tradition available to us, I submit that it is at least as plausible as the very negative view of Judas that still pervades the church but rests on a very shaky foundation.[8]

This alternative is of course fleshed out with undocumented speculation about what might have gone on between Jesus and Judas, and therefore is hardly a convincing argument. Yet it does illustrate the other alternative to the standard view, that Judas was radically disloyal and simply *betrayed* Jesus. And it does show how the *Gospel of Judas* could, without too much fantasy, have made Judas more nearly a positive figure.

## THE DEATH OF JUDAS

Whereas the Gospel of Mark reports nothing more specific about Judas's fate than Jesus pronouncing woe on the one who gives him over (14:21), Matthew proceeds to describe in some detail Judas's remorse and suicide:

> When Judas, the one giving him over, saw that Jesus was condemned, he changed his mind and brought back the thirty pieces of silver to the chief priests and the elders. He said, "I have sinned by giving over innocent blood." But they said, "What is that to us? See to it yourself." Throwing down the pieces of silver in the temple, he departed; and he went and hanged himself. But the chief priests, taking the pieces of silver, said, "It is not lawful to put them into the treasury, since they are blood money." After conferring together, they used them to buy the potter's field as a place to bury foreigners. For this reason that field has been called the Field of Blood to this day. Then was fulfilled what had been spoken through the prophet Jeremiah, And they took the thirty pieces of silver, the price of the one on whom a price had been set, on whom some of the people of Israel had set a price, and they gave them for the potter's field, as the Lord commanded me." (27:3–10)

This story may be a strikingly exact fulfillment of a prophecy from the Old Testament, but, as with several other details in the passion narrative, it is more likely to be the other way around: the prophecy engendered the detail in the story. We do not need to waste our time speculating whether this was a large enough bribe to explain Judas's giving Jesus over to the Jewish authorities, since the amount simply comes from the prophecy. The Old Testament was considered a thoroughly reliable source for facts fulfilled by Jesus. The proof-text in question is Zechariah 11:12–13 (though Matthew inaccurately ascribed it to Jeremiah):

> Then I said to them, "If it seems right to you, give me my wages; but if not, keep them." So they weighed out as my wages thirty shekels of silver. Then the Lord said to me, "Throw it into the treasury"—this lordly price at which I was valued by them. So I took the thirty shekels of silver and threw them into the treasury in the house of the Lord.

An additional instance of a detail being derived from the Old Testament is that those who crucified Jesus "divided his clothes among them, casting lots to decide what each should take" (Mark 15:25). It comes from Psalm 22:18:

> They divided my clothes among themselves, and for my clothing they cast lots.

Such details from the crucifixion story probably do not reflect eyewitness reports. But only in modern times have historians changed their methods enough to question the factuality of details derived only from Old Testament quotations.

Luke also writes of Judas's death, in a report that diverges somewhat from that of Matthew:

> In those days Peter stood up among the believers (together the crowd numbered about one hundred twenty persons) and said, "Friends, the scripture had to be fulfilled, which the Holy Spirit through David [Ps. 41:9] foretold concerning Judas, who became a guide for those who arrested Jesus—for he was numbered among us and was allotted his share in this ministry." (Now this man acquired a field with the reward of his wickedness; and falling headlong, he burst open in the middle and all his bowels gushed out. This became known to all the residents of Jerusalem, so that the field was called in their language Hakeldama, that is, Field of Blood.) (Acts 1:15–19)

These two narratives of Judas's death would seem to confirm the fact that he did indeed promptly die, though the specifics of the two stories are mutually exclusive. In Matthew, he hangs himself; in Acts, he falls forward and ruptures himself. Both reports associate the death (in different ways) with the place-name "field of blood," purchased with the thirty pieces of silver, but in one instance it is purchased by the Jewish authorities with the money he threw back at them (Matt. 27:5–7), in the other it is purchased by Judas himself with the money he was given, to become the place where he died (Acts 1:18). Since the details are mutually exclusive, one is hardly copying the other. Rather, we should assume that they share a tradition with the overlapping facts that Judas soon died and that the term "field of blood" is in some way associated with his death.

## THE REHABILITATION OF JUDAS ISCARIOT

No one in our history has such a bad name as Judas Iscariot. You only have to sneer "Judas!" or say "thirty pieces of silver" or "Judas kiss" to score your put-down, without going into detail. People who have never read the Gospels know what you mean! It is like referring to someone who betrays one's country as a "Benedict Arnold," without needing to know any details of his betrayal of the American colonies to the British.

Maybe Judas Iscariot needs to be rehabilitated! After all, the Evangelists presented the Twelve as quite dull about Jesus's mission, yet they have become honorific names used to accredit the Gospels of Matthew and John. Peter is said to have rebuked Jesus when he foretold his passion, but Peter's reputation has shifted from "Satan" to "rock." Jesus's family tried to restrain him early in his ministry, but now it is dogma that Mary has been assumed into heaven, where she can be appealed to: "Hail, Mary, mother of God," as one recites in the Rosary. Thus the dubious characters in the story have all become saints—except for Judas Iscariot! Has his time not come?

I have used with much appreciation the appealing and scholarly book by the Mennonite theologian William Klassen. As indicated above, he has argued convincingly that the translations *betray* and *betrayal* are simply not what the Greek term means. Rather it means *give over, hand over, turn in*.

This neutral translation is then defended by the account itself. Jesus has been telling the Twelve again and again in great detail that he must go to Jerusalem to die and reproached Peter for not accepting the fact: it is prophesied in the Hebrew scriptures and hence is the will of God, which Jesus must fulfill. Judas is playing an indispensable role in the divine plan and surely must know it. He himself had been prophesied already in the Hebrew scriptures according to John 13:18: "The one who ate my bread has lifted his heel against me" (Ps. 41:9). He is just doing what Jesus tells him to do: "Do quickly what you are going to do" (John 13:27). What's so wrong with that?

Of course much of this is John's theology rather than historical fact, which is sometimes overlooked in the effort to exonerate Judas. And even Mark, although fitting Judas into the plan of salvation, does actually pronounce woe on him as well (14:21). Yet, on the other hand, one notices the bad press Mark gives to the stupid Twelve, Peter (i.e., Satan), and Jesus's family, who are embarrassed by the bad impression Jesus is making as a fanatic and want to take him home to keep him out of circulation (though his mother does stick by him on Good Friday to the bitter end, and his brother James surfaces as a leader of the Jerusalem church). But Christianity has rehabilitated all of them, and so it is a bit inconsistent to leave Judas Iscariot on the hook!

The argument has been made by Klassen that Judas may have thought that having the official Jewish authorities investigate Jesus's claims was the appropriate thing to do, for they would surely understand his message and endorse his ministry. Yet the Gospels do not say so. Jesus's triple prediction of the details of Good Friday in Mark refers explicitly to "the chief priests and the scribes" as perpetrators of the evil, so that Judas would have been the most stupid of the Twelve not to know what would happen if he gave Jesus over to them. It is very difficult to interpret the canonical Gospels as being on Judas's side. Matthew and Luke do not really clean up Mark's story to exonerate Judas, and the

Gospel of John is the worst of all. To be sure, Matthew and the book of Acts report Judas's remorse, hurling back the thirty pieces of silver to the Jewish authorities or buying with the money a place to die. Does this not help a bit to exonerate him?

Perhaps the most fruitful way to go at giving Judas a better place in our minds and hearts is to recall what Jesus himself said about forgiveness. Not only is there his comment in Luke 23:34 about those who were doing him in: "Father, forgive them, for they do not know what they are doing" (emulated by the first Christian martyr, Stephen, at his stoning, Acts 7:60). And not only did he tell one of the criminals being crucified with him: "Today you will be with me in Paradise" (Luke 23:43). His own teachings pointed in the same way in saying after saying, many of which we venerate as part of the Sermon on the Mount:

> Love your enemies and pray for those persecuting you, so that you may become sons of your Father, for he raises his sun on bad and good and rains on the just and unjust.
>
> The one who slaps you on the cheek, offer him the other as well; and to the person wanting to take you to court and get your shirt, turn over to him the coat as well. And the one who conscripts you for one mile, go with him a second. To the one who asks of you, give; and from the one who borrows, do not ask back what is yours.
>
> And the way you want people to treat you, that is how you treat them.
>
> If you love those loving you, what reward do you have? Do not even tax collectors do the same? And if you lend to those from whom you hope to receive, what reward do you have? Do not even the Gentiles do the same?
>
> Be full of pity, just as your Father is full of pity.
>
> Do not pass judgment, so you are not judged. For with what judgment you pass judgment, you will be judged. And with the measurement you use to measure out, it will be measured out to you.

> Which person is there among you who has a hundred sheep, on losing one of them, will not leave the ninety-nine in the mountains and go hunt for the lost one? And if it should happen that he finds it, I say to you that he rejoices over it more than over the ninety-nine that did not go astray.
>
> Or what woman who has ten coins, if she were to lose one coin, would not light a lamp and sweep the house and hunt until she finds? And on finding she calls the friends and neighbors, saying: Rejoice with me, for I found the coin which I had lost. Just so, I tell you, there is joy before the angels over one repenting sinner.
>
> If your brother sins against you, rebuke him; and if he repents, forgive him. And if seven times a day he sins against you, also seven times shall you forgive him. (Q 6:27–38; 15:4–5, 7–10; 17:3–4)

So should we forgive Judas? Love our enemy? I do not think the efforts to argue that what he did was the right thing to do under the circumstances have proven their case. But I do think we can stop using him as a whipping boy and seek a fairer, more forgiving relation to him.

# 6

# The Gnostic Judas

The first thing we hear about Judas after the New Testament is—his vindication! In the middle of the second century, a *Gospel of Judas* was written by the Gnostics. Of course that *Gospel of Judas* was promptly suppressed as heretical, but it is apparently this *Gospel of Judas* that is involved in what has been rediscovered in our own time. It is unclear whether the newly discovered text is identical with that original text, which of course is not available for comparison, especially in view of the composite nature of the newly discovered text. That question will be analyzed in our final chapter devoted to the *Gospel of Judas.* In the present chapter we propose to lay out what we already knew about the *Gospel of Judas* from the heresy-hunting church fathers who condemned it and from what we know about how books were written back then.

The *Gospel of Judas* is first mentioned by Irenaeus. He wrote his *Refutation of All Heresies* in Lyon, France, around 180 C.E. The *Gospel of Judas* is then documented by another heresy hunter, Epiphanius, bishop of Salamis on the island of Cyprus, in the fourth century. So we have to begin with them.

The horrified report by Irenaeus tells us a good deal about how the Bible was interpreted by those who wrote the *Gospel of Judas* and hence how they would interpret the biblical accounts of Judas. It is in this connection that Irenaeus actually mentions the *Gospel of Judas:*

> And others say that Cain was from the superior realm of absolute power, and confess that Esau, Korah, the Sodomites,

> and all such persons are of the same people (or nation) as themselves; for this reason they have been hated by their maker, although none of them has suffered harm. For wisdom (Sophia) snatched up out of them whatever in them belonged to her. And furthermore—they say—Judas the betrayer was thoroughly acquainted with these things; and he alone was acquainted with the truth as no others were, and (so) accomplished the mystery of the betrayal. By him all things, both earthly and heavenly, were thrown into dissolution. And they bring forth a fabricated work to this effect, which they entitle the *Gospel of Judas*.[1]

Cain, Esau, Korah, and the Sodomites are of course very bad company for Judas to keep—and we know people by the company they keep! Judas's associates were so terrible that the God of the Hebrew scriptures punished them severely. Let's look at the specifics.

Esau is the older son of Isaac and Rebekah who sold his birthright for a "mess of pottage" to his younger brother, Jacob. As Paul summarizes it:

> As it is written, "I have loved Jacob, but I have hated Esau." (Rom. 9:13)

Or as Hebrews puts it:

> See to it that no one becomes like Esau, an immoral and godless person, who sold his birthright for a single meal. (12:16)

Korah was the son of Esau (Gen. 36:5, 14; 1 Chron. 1:35), if not his grandson (Gen. 36:16). Perhaps it is basically the name of a clan. But in any case Korah is given credit/blame for instigating a revolt against Moses and Aaron, about which we will hear more later.

The Sodomites? This is the name about which you may already be best informed, if you know what is named after them: sodomy.

Abraham's nephew Lot lived in Sodom. He extended oriental hospitality to two angels as house guests. But before bedtime, things suddenly took a turn for the worse:

> But before they lay down, the men of the city, the men of Sodom, both young and old, all the people to the last man, surrounded the house; and they called to Lot, "Where are the men who came to you tonight? Bring them out to us, so that we may 'know' them." (Gen. 19:4–5)

God's destruction of Sodom was notorious already in antiquity, as a warning against committing abominations deserving equal or worse punishment:

> For Sodom it shall be more bearable on that day than for that town. (Q 10:12)

Sodom and its sister city Gomorrah went down in history as the worst cities of antiquity. As a result, their punishment was legendary:

> And as Isaiah predicted, "If the Lord of hosts had not left survivors to us, we would have fared like Sodom and been made like Gomorrah." (Rom. 9:29)

Their condemnation continued even more explicitly in the postapostolic age:

> Likewise, Sodom and Gomorrah and the surrounding cities, which, in the same manner as they, indulged in sexual immorality and went after other flesh, serve as an example by undergoing a punishment of eternal fire. (Jude 7)

Then, in 2 Peter, probably the last New Testament book to be written, in the second century, one gets the fullest formulation of their depravity:

> For if God did not spare the angels when they sinned, but cast them into hell and committed them to chains of deepest darkness to be kept until the judgment;... and if by turning the cities of Sodom and Gomorrah to ashes he condemned them to extinction and made them an example of what is coming to the ungodly;... then the Lord knows how to rescue the godly from trial, and to keep the unrighteous under punishment until the day of judgment—especially those who indulge their flesh in depraved lust, and who despise authority. (2:4, 6, 9–10)

This, then, is the Sodom that Irenaeus puts in association with Cain ... and Judas!

Sodom was a large city at the southern end of the Dead Sea that obviously was already in antiquity a notorious ruin. I participated in the archeological excavation of the most probable site, Bab edh-Dhra, back in 1965, though we found no incriminating evidence, of course.

Two centuries after Irenaeus, Epiphanius also quotes and refutes the Gnostic sect that produced the *Gospel of Judas:*

> And others say, "No, he [Judas] betrayed him despite his goodness because of heavenly knowledge. For the [evil] archons knew," they say, "that the weaker power would be drained if Christ were given over to crucifixion. And when Judas found this out," they say, "he was anxious, and did all he could to betray him, and performed a good work for our salvation. And we must commend him and give him the credit, since the salvation of the cross was effected for us through him, and the revelation of the things which that occasioned."
>
> Hence Judas did not betray the Savior from knowledge, as these people say; nor will the Jews be rewarded for crucifying the Lord, though we certainly have salvation through the cross. Judas did not betray him to make him the saving of us, but from the ignorance, envy and greed of the denial of God.

> "And therefore," they say, "Judas has found out all about them [the higher powers]." For they claim him as kin too and consider him particularly knowledgeable, so that they even attribute a short work to him, which they call the *Gospel of Judas*.[2]

Here, Epiphanius is presupposing a very familiar Gnostic dualism in which this world is evil and the heavenly world is good. The death of Christ's earthly body of flesh could have been seen by Judas as the necessary event to release Christ's heavenly nature. This is in fact the point scored in the newly discovered *Gospel of Judas*. But none of what Epiphanius apparently presents as quotations occurs in the *Gospel of Judas* we now have. Of course Epiphanius rejects any notion of Judas as being motivated by anything other than ignorance and greed, but acknowledges that there are some, to the contrary, who commend Judas as "knowledgeable" (the Gnostics' essential theme), give him some credit for Christ's salvific act, and attribute a Gospel to him.

## WHAT SCHOLARS ALREADY KNEW ABOUT THE *GOSPEL OF JUDAS*

There is a standard scholarly reference work about such Gospels that were not accepted into the canon of the New Testament. It reports, in all too academic a way, but nonetheless succinctly and exhaustively, all that has been known thus far about those who promulgated the *Gospel of Judas*. Let me quote this reference work, with all due apologies for its pedantry:

> **Attestation:** The most important and oldest source here is Irenaeus (*adv. Haer.* I 31.1 = Theodoret of Cyrus, *Haereticorum fabularum compendium* I 15, PG LXXXIII 368 B): certain gnostic sectaries possessed in addition to other works of their own composition, a 'gospel' under the name of the traitor Judas (*Judae euangelium,...*); these sectaries are elsewhere identified with the Cainites, and reckoned among

the 'Gnostics' of Epiphanius, the Nicolaitans, Ophites, Sethians, or Carpocratians. The existence and title of the document ... are also attested by Epiphanius (*Pan.* 38.1.5; II, 63.13f. Holl.).

**Content:** It would be rash to ascribe to the Gospel of Judas a quotation derived by Epiphanius from a Cainite book (*Pan.* 38.2.4; II, 64.17–19 Holl. 'This is the angel who blinded Moses, and these are the angels who hid the people about Korah and Dathan and Abiram, and carried them off'). Still less reason is there for ascribing to this gospel a formula reproduced by Irenaeus (I 31.2 and Epiphanius 38.2.2), which accompanied the sexual rite practiced by the sect for the attainment of the 'perfect gnosis.' As to the subject and content of the apocryphon, we are reduced to simple conjecture, supported at best by some characteristics of Cainite doctrine as it is known from the notices of the heresiologues. It is possible, but far from certain, that this 'gospel' contained a passion story setting forth the 'mystery of the betrayal' (*proditionis mysterium,...*) and explaining how Judas by his treachery made possible the salvation of all mankind: either he forestalled the destruction of the truth proclaimed by Christ, or he thwarted the designs of the evil powers, the archons, who wished to prevent the crucifixion since they knew that it would deprive them of their feeble power and bring salvation to men (ps.-Tertullian, *adv. Omn. Haer.* 2; Epiphanius, *Pan.* 38.3.3–5; Filastrius, *Haer.* 34; Augustine, *de Haer.* 18; ps.-Jerome, *Indiculus de haer.* 8; cf. Bauer, *Leben Jesu,* p. 176). However that may be, the work was probably in substance an exposition of the secret doctrine (licentious and violently antinomian in character) ostensibly revealed by Judas, a summary of the Truth or of the superior and perfect Gnosis which he was supposed to possess by virtue of a revelation (Irenaeus, I 31.1; Epiph., *Pan.* 38.1.5; Filastrius, *Haer.* 34).

**Dating:** The *Gospel of Judas* was of course composed before 180, the date at which it is mentioned for the first

> time by Irenaeus in *adv. Haer.* If it is in fact a Cainite work, and if this sect—assuming that it was an independent Gnostic group—was constituted in part, as has sometimes been asserted, in dependence on the doctrine of Marcion, the apocryphon can scarcely have been composed before the middle of the 2nd century. This would, however, be to build on weak arguments. At most we may be inclined to suspect a date between 130 and 170 or thereabouts.[3]

Obviously, very little was actually known about the *Gospel of Judas.* But more can be known about those who produced the text. Irenaeus classified them as Gnostics, and Epiphanius associated them with "the people about Korah and Dathan and Abiram." This is of course guilt by association. But at least it shows how they were seen by the early church fathers.

What had Dathan and Abiram done that was so terrible, and what happened as a result? The Hebrew scriptures tell the story in all its gory details:

> Dathan and Abiram came out and stood at the entrance of their tents, together with their wives, their children, and their little ones. And Moses said, "This is how you shall know that the Lord has sent me to do all these works; it has not been of my own accord: If these people die a natural death, or if a natural fate comes on them, then the Lord has not sent me. But if the Lord creates something new, and the ground opens its mouth and swallows them up, with all that belongs to them, and they go down alive into Sheol, then you shall know that these men have despised the Lord."
>
> As soon as he finished speaking all these words, the ground under them was split apart. The earth opened its mouth and swallowed them up, along with their households—everyone who belonged to Korah and all their goods. So they with all that belonged to them went down alive into Sheol; the earth closed over them, and they perished from the midst of the assembly. (Num. 16:27–33)

The story is told again in a simple listing of the Israelites who came out of Egypt with Moses:

> The descendants of Eliab: Nemuel, Dathan, and Abiram. These are the same Dathan and Abiram, chosen from the congregation, who rebelled against Moses and Aaron in the company of Korah, when they rebelled against the Lord, and the earth opened its mouth and swallowed them up along with Korah, when that company died, when the fire devoured two hundred fifty men; and they became a warning. Notwithstanding, the sons of Korah did not die. (Num. 26:9–11)

Even when Deuteronomy summarizes what God had done for the chosen people, this has to be repeated:

> Remember today that ... it is you who must acknowledge his greatness, his mighty hand and his outstretched arm, ... what he did to Dathan and Abiram, sons of Eliab son of Reuben, how in the midst of all Israel the earth opened its mouth and swallowed them up, along with their households, their tents, and every living being in their company. (11:2, 6)

A psalm recalls:

> Our ancestors, when they were in Egypt, did not consider your wonderful works; they did not remember the abundance of your steadfast love, but rebelled against the Most High at the Red Sea.... They were jealous of Moses in the camp, and of Aaron, the holy one of the Lord. The earth opened and swallowed up Dathan, and covered the faction of Abiram. Fire also broke out in their company; the flame burned up the wicked. (Ps. 106:7, 16–18)

What these terrible people did was to seek to share with the family of Aaron the priestly function in the tabernacle. Terrible? Is it just our modern sensitivities that take offense when God takes *credit* for 250 Israelites "going down alive" into hell "together with their wives, their children, and their little ones"? Is that also something that could have offended readers at an earlier time, making them even wonder just how good and loving their God really was? But watch out—I may have just about talked you into becoming a Gnostic!

All one has to do, or had to do back then, is to be very painfully aware of just how terrible the world really is, so terrible in many ways that one is unconvinced that poor old Adam and Eve could take the blame for all of it. God must have made it that way—if not before Adam and Eve, then in any case as terrible punishment after Adam and Eve. Rather than singing "praise God from whom all blessings flow," the Gnostics would sing "blame god from whom all curses flow."

## A GNOSTIC CREATION STORY

Is what Adam and Eve wanted to do really so terrible as to warrant the blame for all the evil that is in the world? A thinking person (their term: a Gnostic) could give a literal interpretation of the creation story of Genesis 3 that turns it upside down:

> It is written in the Law about this: God commanded Adam, "From every tree you may eat, [but] from the tree that is in the middle of paradise do not eat, for on the day that you eat from it, you will certainly die." But the snake was wiser than all the other animals in paradise, and he persuaded Eve by saying, "On the day that you eat from the tree that is in the middle of paradise, the eyes of your mind will be opened." Eve obeyed; she stretched out her hand, took from the tree, and ate. She also gave some fruit to her husband who was with her. Immediately they realized that they were naked. They took some fig leaves and put them on as aprons.
>
> But at [evening] time [God] came along, walking in the middle [of] paradise. When Adam saw him, he went into hiding. And God said, "Adam, where are you?" He answered,

"I have come under the fig tree." At that very moment God [realized] that he had eaten from the tree about which he had commanded him, "Don't eat from it."

And God said, "Who is it who instructed you?" Adam answered, "The woman you gave me." And the woman said, "It is the snake who instructed me." He cursed the snake and called him "devil." And God said, "Look, Adam has become like one of us now that he knows evil and good." Then he said, "Let's throw him out of paradise so he doesn't take from the tree of life, eat, and live forever."

What kind of a god is this? First, he begrudged Adam's eating from the tree of knowledge. Second, he said, "Adam, where are you?" God does not have foreknowledge; otherwise, wouldn't he have known from the beginning? He has certainly shown himself to be a malicious grudger. And what kind of a god is this?

Great is the blindness of those who read such things, and they don't know him. He said, "I am the jealous God; I will bring the sins of the fathers upon the children up to three and four generations." He also said, "I will make their heart thick, and I will cause their minds to become blind, that they might not understand or comprehend the things that are said." But these are things he says to those who believe in him and worship him![4]

The Gnostics would ask of us: Are you also the victim of blindness, not knowing that god is a jealous god, making your heart thick, your mind blind, so that you will not understand? Don't you realize that god himself is not all that smart, not even knowing where Adam is? What's wrong with the eyes of your mind being opened? What's wrong with Adam becoming like "one of us," like a divine being, godlike? What's so wrong with eating from the tree of life and living forever? Are you really against the immortality of the soul? What kind of god is this—is he, after all, "a malicious grudger"? A malevolent god like that would surely explain how the world he created is so terrible.

Is that really the last word? Isn't there some hope somewhere? Maybe high above the heavens—the same evil god who made the earth also made the heavens—and so, *beyond* the heavens? Some really decent, good, loving God that the Hebrew scriptures don't know about, a hidden God? Yet a hidden God who did reveal himself, on rare occasions, to persons who resisted the evil god, hence got punished by the evil god, and got terrible reputations in the scriptures composed by the evil god?

## THE MALIGNED CAIN

Who got worse notoriety in the scriptures than Cain? Just listen to the way he is portrayed:

> Now the man knew his wife Eve, and she conceived and bore Cain, saying, "I have produced a man with the help of the Lord." Next she bore his brother Abel. Now Abel was a keeper of sheep, and Cain a tiller of the ground. In the course of time Cain brought to the Lord an offering of the fruit of the ground, and Abel for his part brought of the firstlings of his flock, their fat portions. And the Lord had regard for Abel and his offering, but for Cain and his offering he had no regard. So Cain was very angry, and his countenance fell. The Lord said to Cain, "Why are you angry, and why has your countenance fallen? If you do well, will you not be accepted? And if you do not do well, sin is lurking at the door; its desire is for you, but you must master it."
>
> Cain said to his brother Abel, "Let us go out to the field." And when they were in the field, Cain rose up against his brother Abel, and killed him. Then the Lord said to Cain, "Where is your brother Abel?" He said, "I do not know; am I my brother's keeper?" And the Lord said, "What have you done? Listen; your brother's blood is crying out to me from the ground! And now you are cursed from the ground, which has opened its mouth to receive your brother's blood from your hand. When you till the ground, it will no longer yield

> to you its strength; you will be a fugitive and a wanderer on the earth."
>
> Cain said to the Lord, "My punishment is greater than I can bear! Today you have driven me away from the soil, and I shall be hidden from your face; I shall be a fugitive and a wanderer on the earth, and anyone who meets me may kill me." Then the Lord said to him, "Not so! Whoever kills Cain will suffer a sevenfold vengeance." And the Lord put a mark on Cain, so that no one who came upon him would kill him. (Gen. 4:1–15)

What kind of a God is that who even back at the beginning of the story rejects the farmer's offering, even though it is all the farmer has produced that he could offer? Cain may have overreacted, but did not God also overreact—condemning Cain to be a fugitive and a wanderer on the earth, no longer able to make a livelihood out of farming? And would you like to walk around the rest of your life with the "mark of Cain" on you, whatever that was?

Cain, who gets overly punished by a vengeful God, is a precursor of Korah, Dathan, and Abiram, who suffered such a terrible fate along with their families, simply because they wanted a more important role in worshiping God in the temple. They get the bad press, whereas their opponents, Moses and his brother Aaron, stay in power. But is that then really the last word? They might well have taken hope for, after all, "The sons of Korah did not die!"

The Gnostics might well have said: we who are in the know, who think for ourselves and see through the sham, have been enlightened by a hidden God far above, who is free of all this impossible system under which the world suffers. This hidden God frees us—he does not enslave us!

And if you read not only the Hebrew scriptures with these glasses on, but also read the Christian scriptures this way, whom do you light upon as the defamed hero who is damned for doing the only decent thing, namely, seeing to it that prophecy is fulfilled, God's will done, Jesus obeyed, and thus humanity saved?

Well, Judas, of course! Maybe the Gospels of Matthew, Mark, Luke, and John need to be replaced by—the *Gospel of Judas*?

## HOW TO MAKE A PAPYRUS BOOK

We know that the *Gospel of Judas* is from an early papyrus codex. The Nag Hammadi Codices are in this regard very similar—both discoveries in Middle and Upper Egypt are of third- and fourth-century papyrus codices with Coptic translations of Gnostic tractates originally composed in Greek. Since I worked intensively for years restoring and publishing for UNESCO the Nag Hammadi Codices,[5] I do know a lot about the kind of book that contains the *Gospel of Judas*.[6] So let me tell you about how papyrus books were made in late antiquity, both the original second-century Greek book containing the *Gospel of Judas* and the third- or fourth-century Coptic copy that has now surfaced.

Papyrus is a plant that grew in antiquity in the shallow waters along the edge of the Nile River. It produced a long stalk that was cut and peeled, and then its pith cut into thin strips. These strips were laid vertically side by side on a flat surface, and then a second layer of strips was rowed up on top horizontally. This was then pressed together, indeed pounded, until the juice in the pith formed a kind of glue that held both layers together as a flat surface on which one could write. One such writing surface could be as long as six feet, to judge by those whose length I calculated in the process of conserving the Nag Hammadi Codices. At the end of such a piece of papyrus, another piece could be pasted on, with an overlap of about half an inch. Piece after piece of papyrus could be added, to produce as long a writing surface as one wished.

People back then wrote on the surface with the horizontal fibers, since writing horizontally with the flow of the fibers was easier than having to bump across from fiber to fiber going against the grain. Writing was done in columns about the width of a column in a book today, then a space of an inch or so was left, then the next column followed, and so on, for as long a book as one wished. Then the long papyrus strip was rolled up, with the writing surface on the inside to protect it, and *voila!* There you have a papyrus scroll!

A rolled-up scroll would be hard to identify, especially if there were several lying side by side. So on the outside, at the end that was visible when the scroll was rolled up, an identifying phrase was written; this phrase, at right angles to the text on the inside, was still going in the direction of the fibers, since on the outside these were in the opposite direction to the fibers on the inside. This is the origin of what we would think of as a book "title." It may not have been chosen by the person who wrote the text of the book itself, but probably by the copyist or the person who needed to distinguish this scroll from other scrolls. The original author would tend to suggest in the body of the text itself, at its beginning or ending (or both), the gist of what the book was all about. Sometimes it would be this that the later scribe would summarize as the label on the outside of the scroll.

These papyrus scrolls had been used for thousands of years (literally!) by the time Christianity began. But technology was advancing, and scrolls were, after all, rather cumbersome. Rolling a scroll up every time you want to put it away and then unrolling it again to resume reading the next time were time-consuming chores. And rolling and unrolling were hard on the papyrus, durable though it was.

About the time of the beginning of Christianity, people had developed a kind of notebook for schoolchildren, first attested in Rome. Two small thin planks of wood were each covered on one side with wax, then laid together with the wax surfaces on the inside, to protect them. The schoolchild would write on the wax surfaces, then scrape them clean, add new wax to harden overnight, and reuse them the next day. (I remember as a child having my own small blackboard and chalk for the same purpose!)

Then it occurred to people that they could replace the wax between the planks with a few leaves of papyrus to write on. The leaves were then attached together and to the wooden planks on the side, so they would not fall out and get lost. The boards developed into leather covers, the few papyrus sheets became quires, and there you have something that is like a modern book: pages you can turn! They called it a *codex,* plural *codices,* to distinguish them from scrolls. "Codex" just meant a "fistful," a book you could hold in your left fist and turn pages with your right hand as you read—much easier than laying out a long piece of papyrus on a table and unwinding with both hands.

Bit by bit books that had been composed to fit the length of a not too long scroll were copied into codices. Usually a scroll had to be relatively short, so that one did not have to scroll and scroll endlessly to find one's place. But a codex was easier to use—one could simply open it in the middle and go on reading where one had left off, especially since the pages were usually numbered. So several scrolls could be copied into one codex.

That is how the "books" of the Bible became one book, the Bible—originally they had been written on separate scrolls (which is still today the preferred form of book for Jewish scriptures). Now they could be copied into a single codex! This is why we have the habit of talking about the "books" of the Bible—they were originally composed each as a book in its own right, though in the Bible they are really just the length of what we might call chapters or, as we call them in the case of the Nag Hammadi Codices, "tractates." This is also the case with the newly discovered copy of the *Gospel of Judas,* since it is in a codex that also included three other texts, two of which have parallel copies in the Nag Hammadi Codices. The table of contents is as follows: Pp. 1–9, the *Letter of Peter to Philip;* pp. 10–30, the (*Revelation of*) *James;* pp. 33–58, the *Gospel of Judas;* and pp. 59–66, the *Book of Allogenes,* or the *Book of the Stranger.* And one may recall that Epiphanius referred to the *Gospel of Judas* as "a short work."

The phrase that had been put on the outside of a roll to identify what text was inside could be carried over to the codex. When a number of "books" or tractates are included in a single codex, they need to be distinguished one from the other. An identifying phrase would be copied at the beginning or end (or both) of a text, set off by blank space and >>>> as decoration, as a superscript and/or subscript title.

You can see what I mean by "hatch marks" by looking at the photograph facing the first page of the Preface of the book in your hands, at the end of the last line of the text of the *Gospel of Judas* as well as on the otherwise blank line between the end of the text and the subscript title: >>>>.

## "GOSPELS" AND THEIR "AUTHORS"

Since the author of the individual book was usually not the person who wrote the label on the outside of the scroll or the title that was set off at the beginning and/or end of a tractate in a codex, there is often a slight discrepancy between the text of the tractate itself and its secondarily attached title. This is even the case with the four Gospels in the New Testament. Their titles inform us that they are the Gospels according to Matthew, Mark, Luke, and John. But in the body of the texts of these four tractates, they are all anonymous. In John 21:24 we are told that the beloved disciple wrote the tractate, which is why we are sure John wrote it—until we notice that the beloved disciple is never identified as John. In fact, John is never mentioned in the Gospel of John!

There may be reasons why a Gospel was associated with a certain apostle. The calling of Levi the tax collector in Mark 2:13–17 becomes the calling of Matthew the tax collector in Matthew 9:9–13, and so, in Matthew's list of the Twelve, the apostle "Matthew" (Mark 3:18) becomes "Matthew the tax collector" (Matt. 10:3). This may have been intended as a hint by the person who wrote the Gospel of Matthew to claim apostolicity, irrespective of whether it was the tax collector Levi/Matthew or not. In any case, it would have been taken as sufficient reason to ascribe this Gospel to Matthew. But there is no place in this Gospel, or in any of the others, where the name of the Evangelist is actually said to have been the author. Rather, we now assume that the name of the apostle to whom a Christian community appealed for its own "apostolicity" was ascribed to the Gospel that the community used and cherished as its authority. Usually by this time people no longer knew who had first composed the text. All they knew was that their community was "apostolic."

The same situation prevails with regard to the title "Gospel" that we automatically associate with the four Gospels in the New Testament. The word *gospel* of course means "good news." Paul contrasts his *good news* with the false *good news* of his opponents, which is not to be believed, even if it comes from angels (Gal. 1:6–10). But he is not referring to a book entitled *Gospel* that he (or they) had written. In Paul's time, no Gospels had yet been written!

Mark's Gospel begins with the word *gospel* in the very first verse. But he is not saying that the book that follows is a Gospel, rather that he is writing down the *good news.* Hence in Mark 1:1 *gospel* is somewhat of a mistranslation (down to and including the Revised Standard Version) or at least misleading: "The beginning of the *gospel* of Jesus Christ." The NRSV has more correctly translated: "The beginning of the *good news* of Jesus Christ." Mark's first verse means that his whole book is the beginning of the good news that Christianity has to offer. To be sure, that use of the word *gospel* in the first verse of the oldest Gospel is no doubt the reason that copyists in later centuries used *Gospel* in the titles ascribed to each. But that means that the title *Gospel* is a creation of copyists, not of the Evangelists themselves.

When we look at the opening of the other Gospels, we find them describing what they are doing with other nouns, indicating that they do not yet have in mind *Gospel* as the name for what they are writing. Matthew begins: "*Book* of the genealogy of Jesus Christ" (1:1). Luke bases what he is writing on records from those "compiling a *narrative,*" who were "eyewitnesses and servants of the *word*" (1:1). And at the opening of Acts, Luke refers back to his first volume, which we call the Gospel of Luke, as "the first *book,*" literally "the first *word,*" a way of saying volume one, not as his "Gospel." The Gospel of John begins its Prologue with "In the beginning was the *Word*" (1:1). Thus the Evangelists are thinking about the message when they introduce their "Gospels." They were not aware of creating a literary genre to which their book belongs, namely, the Gospel genre. Actually, the *Gospel of Judas,* like Luke-Acts and John, begins by referring to itself as "the secret *word* of the revelation that Jesus spoke," though this is obscured in the initial translation, which is quite free: "The secret account of the revelation that Jesus spoke," which is improved to read in the final critical edition, "the secret word of declaration by which Jesus spoke."

However, the name Gospel did get attached to the four canonical Gospels, and as they moved toward the authoritative status of being included in the New Testament, the designation Gospel could readily be attached to other writings in an effort to accredit them as being of equal (or superior) authority. But here too an examination of the body of the text of such noncanonical "Gospels" indicates that they were not called Gospels by their original authors.

This can be illustrated by the four "Gospels" found outside the New Testament in the Nag Hammadi Codices. The best known by far is the *Gospel of Thomas.* It exists, almost completely intact, both in a papyrus codex of the mid-fourth century in Coptic translation (Nag Hammadi Codex II,2) and in three very fragmentary Greek vestiges from the third century (Oxyrhynchus Papyri 1, 654, and 655). Ralph Pöhner, in his journalistic essay sensationalizing the *Gospel of Judas,* also plays up the *Gospel of Thomas:*

> This dialogue of Jesus with Thomas counts today as very important for the history of religion: Some researchers name it "the fifth Gospel," and it could be that here even lies the original text on which the official Gospels built.[7]

Though the *Gospel of Thomas* is less a "dialogue" than a collection of 114 sayings ascribed to Jesus, it is indeed a very important discovery, no doubt the most important Gospel outside the New Testament. Though it is not "the original text on which the official Gospels built," some scholars have argued that a first draft may have been known to some of the canonical Evangelists. In any case, it may well have older readings than the same sayings in the canonical Gospels and in this sense be nearer to Jesus himself. In fact, I for one have made just such an argument.

Saying 36 contains at one place an older text than does the New Testament. In the familiar sayings about the ravens and lilies, which demonstrate their trust in God in that they do not work (Q 12:22–31), the first example of the lilies not working is "they grow"—hardly what one would expect! But in the *Gospel of Thomas,* saying 36 reads (in the Greek original, P.Oxy. 655): "They do not card." This is precisely the first work women did back then in making the wool of sheep into clothing. The difference in spelling between the two Greek words is very slight. It seems probable that here the *Gospel of Thomas* has the correct text, and the New Testament has the corrupted text. I have published seven articles arguing this point alone.[8]

Another instance is the parable of the vineyard, which in the New Testament (Mark 12:1–12) has a secondary allegorizing interpretation imbedded in the parable itself. The *Gospel of Thomas,* saying 65, presents a more nearly original form of the parable prior to that allegorization.[9]

But there are also sayings in the *Gospel of Thomas* that seem to presuppose the New Testament Gospels. One is saying 16, in which the number of five in the household of those who disagree among themselves seems based on Luke 12:52–53, though Luke seems here to have made a late addition to the sayings Gospel Q.[10] The current scholarly view is hence that the *Gospel of Thomas* contains some material that is older than the canonical Gospels and some material that is newer.

The idea of calling the *Gospel of Thomas* the "fifth Gospel," to which Pöhner refers with obvious approval, is in fact the title of a book I edited (though the idea was not original with me), containing a new translation of the text and an essay I wrote on the fiftieth anniversary of its discovery.[11] But that is not what the original author/collector of these 114 *sayings* ascribed to Jesus would have called his tractate.

Another noncanonical Gospel that Pöhner lists is the *Gospel of Mary* (Magdalene). This is a very important second-century apocryphal Gospel and plays an important role in the modern feminist movement. The author of this standard kind of Gnostic dialogue refers to the preaching of the "*gospel* of the kingdom," but also to Jesus's *words* and a *vision,* so it is not clear whether the original author chose the title *Gospel of Mary* or this was secondarily added. The first six pages are missing, so it is impossible to determine how the opening line read. But at the end there is the subscript title: "The Gospel of Mary." I was the first to make the *Gospel of Mary* available in English, in *The Nag Hammadi Library in English.*[12] The *Gospel of Mary* is not among the Nag Hammadi Codices, but is found in a similar Gnostic codex, Papyrus Berolinensis 8502. Hence I thought it would be beneficial to include it with the Nag Hammadi Codices, especially since it had been available for a long time in German but not yet in English.

I mention here such details of my involvement not to draw attention to my work, but rather to make it clear that my criticism of Pöhner is not the standard conservative prejudice in favor of limiting oneself to the canonical Gospels by the exclusion of the noncanonical Gospels. My concern is quite the reverse. The attention we are giving to the noncanonical Gospels today should not be discredited by those who, like Pöhner, make use of this scholarly material in a nonscholarly way.

We name it the *Gospel of Thomas* because the subscript title at the end reads "The Gospel According to Thomas." But this tractate does not tell the stories of Jesus, as do the canonical Gospels; it is limited to sayings of Jesus. This has led scholars to make a distinction between narrative Gospels, which tell the story of Jesus (as do Matthew, Mark, Luke, and John), and sayings Gospels (such as the source used by Matthew and Luke called Q and the *Gospel of Thomas*).

The *Gospel of Thomas* consists of 114 sayings ascribed to Jesus, each introduced with the stereotypical phrase, "Jesus says: . . ." The word *gospel* occurs nowhere in the text! Rather, sayings themselves refer to Jesus's *sayings* or *words*. Both *saying* and *word* are translations of the same word in Coptic and Greek. It is just a distinction we sometimes make in translating. For example, where it occurs in the opening of Luke and John, we translated it *word*. But in the *Gospel of Thomas* it probably fits the meaning best to translate it *saying*.

Saying 19 of the *Gospel of Thomas* reads:

> If you become disciples of mine and listen to my *sayings*, these stones will serve you.

Saying 38 reads:

> Many times you have desired to hear these *sayings*, these that I am speaking to you, and you have no one else from whom to hear them.

The opening of the text of the *Gospel of Thomas* reads: "These are the hidden *sayings* that the living Jesus spoke." The term *sayings* actually occurs in the very first saying:

> Whoever finds the interpretation of these *sayings* will not taste death.

This indicates that it is Jesus's *sayings* that are what saves! The author or collector of these sayings thought that the work he or she was producing was a collection of Jesus's *sayings*, not a *Gospel*.

The saying that is no doubt responsible for the *Gospel of Thomas* being ascribed to Thomas is saying 13:

> Jesus said to his disciples: "Compare me and tell me whom I am like."
>
> Simon Peter said to him: "You are like a just messenger."
>
> Matthew said to him: "You are like an especially wise philosopher."
>
> Thomas said to him: "Teacher, my mouth cannot bear at all to say whom you are like."

> Jesus said: "I am not your teacher. For you have drunk, you have become intoxicated at the bubbling spring that I have measured out."
>
> And he took him, and withdrew, and he said three sayings to him.
>
> And when Thomas came back to his companions, they asked him: "What did Jesus say to you?"
>
> Thomas said to them: "If I tell you one of the sayings he said to me, you will pick up stones and throw them at me, and fire will come out of the stones and burn you up."

As a result of this preeminence given to Thomas, the *Gospel of Thomas* begins:

> These are the hidden sayings that the living Jesus spoke, and Didymos Judas Thomas wrote them down.

Though the *Gospel of Thomas* was not designated by its original author or compiler as a Gospel, it was secondarily named a Gospel in the effort to get it accredited by the church as being on a par with or superior to the Gospels gaining canonicity in the emerging New Testament.

The situation with another Nag Hammadi tractate, the *Gospel of Philip,* is similar. It does not narrate the stories of Jesus either, as we might expect of a Gospel, based on what is in the Gospels of the New Testament. Rather, it is engrossed in other issues, though at times it refers to a saying or action of Jesus. The text never even uses the word *gospel.* However, there is one saying ascribed to Philip, which is probably why the whole text came to be ascribed to him:

> Philip the apostle said: "Joseph the carpenter planted a garden for he needed wood for his trade. He is the one who made the cross from the trees he planted, and his own offspring hung on what he planted. His planting was the cross."[13]

Normally a Nag Hammadi tractate has a title separated off from the body of the text, at the top or bottom (or both), surrounded by blank papyrus and with >>>> to decorate it, as we have described earlier and as you can see on the photograph opposite the Preface. But the title "The Gospel According to Philip" is jammed into the end of the last line of the text. This suggests that it was secondarily added, as a kind of afterthought, by the scribe of Nag Hammadi Codex II who copied out this tractate. It was apparently not the title intended by the anonymous author of the tractate.

In the case of the *Gospel of the Egyptians,* whose real title is the *Holy Book of the Great Invisible Spirit,* the situation is similar. The actual text of the tractate begins: "The holy book of the Egyptians about the great invisible Spirit."[14] And it concludes with a subscript title: "The Holy Book of the Great Invisible Spirit. Amen."[15] But then the scribe of Nag Hammadi Codex III has inserted a note just before the subscript title, in which he writes:

> The Egyptian Gospel, a holy secret book, writtem by God. Grace, intelligence, perception, and understanding be with the copyist Eugnostos the beloved in the Spirit—my worldly name is Gongessos—and my fellow luminaries in incorruptibility. Jesus Christ, Son of God, Savior, ICHTHUS. The Holy Book of the Great, Invisible Spirit is written by God. Amen.[16]

Codex III was the first codex to reach the Coptic Museum in Cairo. It was delighted to put p. 69 on display, with the "title" *The Egyptian Gospel* clearly legible. So this quite secondary title has stuck with the tractate ever since! But the author of the tractate did not intend to be writing a Gospel, and his text has nothing to do either with the story of Jesus or with the sayings of Jesus. The text contains the myth of a Gnostic sect that venerated Seth, the third son of Adam and Eve after Cain had killed Abel and had himself been banished (Gen. 4:25–26).

The fourth "Gospel" in the Nag Hammadi Codices is the *Gospel of Truth*. It is quite well known, because the Jung Institute of Zürich "baptized" the codex containing it the "Jung Codex" in honor of their founding hero, the psychologist Carl Jung, who maintained that the *Gospel of Truth* made sense in the light of his psychology. The tractate, which had no title of its own in the Jung Codex (Nag Hammadi Codex I), was given the title the *Gospel of Truth* on the basis of the opening line:

> The gospel of truth is joy for people who have received grace from the Father of truth that they might know him through the power of the Lord.[17]

There is apparently already an allusion to the tractate to be found in Irenaeus. He recognizes that "The Gospel of Truth" is of course not the title of the tractate, but only the author's opening blast announcing the message of the tractate as "the *true* gospel," in distinction from the orthodox Gospels that falsely claim to be true.

One may conclude that the term "gospel" was not part of the original titles of the four canonical Gospels or those of the four Nag Hammadi "Gospels." Both the branch of the church that was moving toward what came to be called orthodoxy and the branch that was moving toward what came to be called heresy designated their texts Gospels to accredit them in the ongoing competition.

## "GOSPEL"? BY "JUDAS"?

It should come as no surprise to learn that the text of the *Gospel of Judas* does not begin with a reference to itself as a *gospel,* but rather refers to itself as the *word,* the same term used in Luke and Acts to refer to what we today call the *Gospel* of Luke. In all probability, the original author of the *Gospel of Judas* did not himself name it a *Gospel*.

The *Gospel of Judas* was composed after the canonical Gospels were written, at about the same time as the Nag Hammadi Gospels. No doubt, like them, the *Gospel of Judas* secondarily made use of the title *Gospel* to accredit itself over against the canonical Gospels, which had secondarily popularized the title in their own quest for accreditation. As a result, one can say that the *Gospel of Judas* was not written by Judas—after all, he had been dead for over a century—and is not what the public assumes a Gospel would be—a collection of the stories and/or sayings of Jesus. The four Gospels among the Nag Hammadi Codices have shown that the honorific title could be ascribed to works that we today would never call Gospels if that title had not been attached to them in the tradition. The *Gospel of Judas* teaches us a lot more about the Gnosticism of the second century than about the public ministry of Jesus, the sayings of Jesus, Holy Week, or the like.

## JUDAS DOWN THROUGH THE CENTURIES

How has Judas been understood down through the centuries, after the New Testament presented him as giving Jesus over to the Jewish authorities and the *Gospel of Judas* tried to vindicate him? Actually, Kim Paffenroth's book *Judas: Images of the Lost Disciple* attempts to answer just that question with a series of chapters entitled "Judas the Obscure: Object of Curiosity," "Judas the Arch-Sinner: Object of Horror," "Judas the Villain: Object of Hatred and Derision," "Judas the Tragic Hero: Object of Admiration and Sympathy," and "Judas the Penitent: Object of Hope and Emulation." Paffenroth ends with an epilogue that does not claim to be history, but only "a story that ends the way I would like it to," with Judas living a rather normal life.[18]

In antiquity, to fall on one's sword when one's leader is slain was considered a noble death. Should not Judas's suicide after Jesus's crucifixion be accorded this distinction of being a noble death? Apparently it was first St. Augustine who decided that Judas's suicide was in fact a sin.[19] Listen to the way Augustine put it:

> He did not deserve mercy; and that is why no light shone in his heart to make him hurry for pardon from the one he had betrayed.[20]

And so, irrespective of what one might think of Judas giving Jesus over to the Jewish authorities as implementing God's plan of salvation or as a traitor betraying his friend, he cannot be forgiven for his suicide!

The most generous that early Christian monasticism could be toward Judas was to suggest that Jesus forgave him, but ordered him to purify himself with "spiritual exercises" in the desert like those the monks themselves practiced. In the seventh century, the Bible commentator Theophylact thought Judas had not expected things to turn bad once he arranged a hearing between Jesus and the Jewish authorities, and in anguish at the outcome he killed himself to "get to Hades before Jesus and thus to implore and gain salvation":

> Some say that Judas, being covetous, supposed that he would make money by betraying Christ, and that Christ would not be killed but would escape from the Jews as many a time he had escaped. But when he saw him condemned, actually already condemned to death, he repented since the affair had turned out so differently from what he had expected. And so he hanged himself to get to Hades before Jesus and thus to implore and gain salvation. Know well, however, that he put his neck into the halter and hanged himself on a certain tree, but the tree bent down and he continued to live, since it was God's will that he either be preserved for repentance or for public disgrace and shame. For they say that due to dropsy he could not pass where a wagon passed with ease; then he fell on his face and burst asunder, that is, was rent apart, as Luke says in the Acts.[21]

A Dominican preacher, Vinzenz Ferrer, in a sermon in 1391, had a similar explanation for the suicide, that Judas's "soul rushed to Christ on Calvary's mount" to ask and receive forgiveness:

> Judas who betrayed and sold the Master after the crucifixion was overwhelmed by a genuine and saving sense of remorse

> and tried with all his might to draw close to Christ in order to apologize for his betrayal and sale. But since Jesus was accompanied by such a large crowd of people on the way to the mount of Calvary, it was impossible for Judas to come to him and so he said to himself: Since I cannot get to the feet of the master, I will approach him in my spirit at least and humbly ask him for forgiveness. He actually did that and as he took the rope and hanged himself his soul rushed to Christ on Calvary's mount, asked for forgiveness and received it fully from Christ, went up to heaven with him, and so his soul enjoys salvation along with all elect.[22]

Yet the all too rampant anti-Semitism of the Middle Ages exploited Judas as the archbetrayer in order to arouse just such anti-Semitic sentiments by painting him as a caricature of a Jew, with exaggerated features, a large hooked nose, red hair, and of course greed for money.

William Klassen has tracked down the sources primarily responsible for the terrible track record of the Dark Ages regarding Judas.[23] First, he lists the *Carmen Paschale,* written by Sedulius shortly before 431:

> It is highly likely that Sedulius, more than any other person, is responsible for the negative portrait of Judas so common among the educated, especially the theologians and clergy. "[The *Carmen Paschale*] was required reading in schools throughout the Middle Ages and a source of inspiration for Latin and the vernacular Biblical epics well into the 17th century.... It was a work which centuries of European readers found of enduring value," writes a modern student of the epic.
>
> Sedulius shows no moderation in connection with Judas. His longest literary "intrusion" deals with Judas. His imprecation against Judas, for which there is no biblical precedent, sets the standard for later writers.

The other baleful influence listed by Klassen is the *Legenda Aurea,* the *Golden Legends:*

> The *Legenda Aurea,* a collection of apocryphal stories first gathered by the Dominican Jacob of Virragio (1230–1298), was widely circulated from the fourteenth and fifteenth centuries and beyond. What the *Carmen Paschale* did for the educated, this collection did for the uneducated. It "enveloped the whole intellectual life of the Middle Ages" and, according to one writer, remains the most popular book of edification of the West.

Dante Alighieri (1265–1321), in his *Divine Comedy,* relegated Judas into his inferno, the lowest (seventh) pit of hell, where his head is being gnawed off for all eternity by a three-headed monster. No doubt he is reunited down there for all eternity with his infamous predecessors, Korah, Dathan, and Abiram, "together with their wives, their children, and their little ones." Those of you who could not help being a bit sympathetic with these poor people will be appalled by the obvious satisfaction Dante and others have taken in all this. But those of you who were even more appalled by the Gnostics turning the Bible on its head in order to make the bad guys into the good guys cannot help but have a bit of sympathy for Dante's presentation. And this side of the argument has largely prevailed down until relatively modern times.

In 1991 Klassen lit upon the sermons of Abraham Santa Clara (actually the Austrian Hans-Ulrich Megerle, 1644–1709), the most eloquent preacher of his day. The title of the work defaming Judas, when first published (1686–95), was *Ertz-Schelm,* roughly translated *Prime Slime.* His complete works were published in twenty-one volumes from 1834 to 1854 as well as in a six-volume abbreviated edition (1904–1907), and his writings have been translated into many languages. Klassen's summary:

> Virtually every Sunday for an entire decade he preached about him, or, perhaps better said, *against* him. By way of

> warning to his faithful, Santa Clara proclaimed that Judas' mother had talked too much; listeners were urged not to let this happen to them lest they bring forth another Judas!
>
> The concluding sermons in his interminable series consist of cursing all parts of Judas's anatomy, beginning with his red hair and ending with his toes.

Part of the blame/credit for this goes to the King James translation of the Bible. King James I of England commissioned a new translation, familiarly known as the "Authorized Version," which appeared in 1611. It has determined the understanding of the Bible for the English-speaking world ever since. Although the language today sounds quaint, it is perhaps for that very reason still preferred by many who read the Bible. The idea of Judas "betraying" Jesus is deeply imbedded in the King James translation and its successors, and so will be very difficult to eliminate from our cultural tradition. To give you a sense for the language problem, I quote Matthew's treatment of Judas in the King James translation, complete with all its quaintness of "thee and thou" language ("ye," "verily," "dippeth," "goeth," "spake," "wherefore," "art")—even its pedantic use of italics for words with no equivalent in the Greek original. I reproduce Matthew, since it has probably been the most widely used by average people over the ages:

> Then one of the twelve, called Judas Iscariot, went unto the chief priests,
>
> And said *unto them*, What will ye give me, and I will deliver him unto you? And they covenanted with him for thirty pieces of silver.
>
> And from that time he sought opportunity to betray him. . . .
>
> And as they did eat, he said, Verily I say unto you, that one of you shall betray me.
>
> And they were exceedingly sorrowful, and began every one of them to say unto him, Lord, is it I?

> And he answered and said, He that dippeth *his* hand with me in the dish, the same shall betray me.
>
> The Son of man goeth as it is written of him: but woe unto that man by whom the Son of man is betrayed! It had been good for that man if he had not been born.
>
> Then Judas, which betrayed him, answered and said, Master, is it I? He said unto him, Thou hast said....
>
> And while he yet spake, lo, Judas, one of the twelve, came, and with him a great multitude with swords and staves, from the chief priests and elders of the people.
>
> Now he that betrayed him gave them a sign, saying, Whomsoever I shall kiss, that same is he: hold him fast.
>
> And forthwith he came to Jesus, and said, Hail, master; and kissed him.
>
> And Jesus said unto him, Friend, wherefore art thou come? Then came they, and laid hands on Jesus, and took him. (26:14–16, 21–25, 47–50)

In this imprecise translation, for centuries held as the "gospel truth" by English speakers around the world, Judas comes off as unquestionably dishonorable.

In more recent times, especially since the Enlightenment, views somewhat sympathetic to Judas have emerged. Roger Thiede reports:

> Nonetheless the history of the Judas material teaches that the "super-knave," the alleged greedy forefather of all informers and spies, always also found revisionist defenders: Poets such as Klopstock and Goethe, authors such as Walter Jens, belonged here. Also modern theologians, such as the American William Klassen or the German Hans-Josef Klauck, laid out in voluminous monographs the Judas material of the New Testament they interpreted.
>
> Hence "Judas did not betray Christ" is the inference even of the newspaper *Bild*. Basis for the acquittal is especially the significance of the ancient Greek verb *paradidomi*. In most

> Bible translations the term is translated, in connection with Jesus and Judas, as "betray." To be sure, if one puts the term on the philological gold scales, it is clear that the word in question would be translated as "hand out" or "give over."

Yet the traditional repudiation of Judas continues unabated, as Thiede goes on to point out:

> Yet such subtleties have thus far changed nothing in this, that the name of the perfidious table-companion of Jesus, on the basis of a barely 2000-year-old tradition, is treated by and large as the sum total of the underhandedly disloyal double-dealer.
>
> If an ungrateful football player who is on the rise changes teams behind the back of the team to which he belongs, disillusioned fans still today bawl the name Judas. Also the member of the Kiel assembly, who last week torpedoed the reelection of the SPD Minister President Simonis by his secret abstention, promptly received the biblical reproach.[24]

Thiede also points to a change in attitude in modern times. He captions a picture of Cain killing Abel:

> **Protest against the Good:** The murder of a brother by Cain against Abel has provoked readers of the Bible again and again to risk flirting with evil. Distant influences of Gnosticism showed up also in modern literature.

He then quotes two modern European authors on the *Gospel of Judas,* the German author Hermann Hesse and the French poet Charles Baudelaire. Following the caption "Murderers of Brothers and Betrayers," there is the highlighted preview: "Whether there really was the 'Cainite' sect of the church father Irenaeus? In any case it developed literary influence." He points out that Hesse's *Demian* "picked up the theme of Cain":

> Using the name "Emil Sinclair" as the author, there appeared in 1919 the novel *Demian*. In reality the author was Hermann Hesse. His book told about a High School student who runs across the theory that one could also conceive of Cain quite differently. "What the story took as its point of departure was the sign. There was a man there who had something in his face that aroused fear in others ( ...). So one explained the sign, not as that which it was, as a distinction, but rather as the opposite. One said that the folk with this sign were weird, and they really were that. People with courage and character are always very weird to the other people. It was very uncomfortable for a race of fearless and weird people to be running around, and so one hung on this race a nickname and a fable, to avenge oneself on it—to hold oneself a bit indemnified for all the fear one endured.

Baudelaire is introduced: "The French lyricist became world famous for his 'Blossoms of Evil'":

*O, race of Abel, your remains*
*Rot, wherever the sun burns!*
*Race of Cain, your works*
*Are thus not yet at an end;*
*Race of Abel, in the fray*
*The lance bored through your flesh!*
*Race of Cain, go up to heaven,*
*And hurl God down to earth!*[25]

Will Baudelaire's wish come true, thanks to the *Gospel of Judas*?

In fact, this modern shift in attitude toward Judas is further evidenced by several fictional versions of the long-lost *Gospel of Judas* that have been published over the past century. The Polish novelist Henryk Panas published the *Gospel of Judas* in 1973.[26] The Irish writer Michael Dickinson wrote the *Lost Testament of Judas Iscariot,* purporting to be Judas's self-defense written to Peter, in 1994.[27] The best was written in 1929 by Ernest Sutherland Bates, the *Gospel of Judas,* portraying Judas as an Essene who continued to reject the God of the Hebrew scriptures, which had originally been Jesus's own view.[28] Hugh S. Pyper published in 2001 a very critical survey of such literature, charging it with being symptomatic of today's alienation from traditional Christianity and its limitation to the canonical text, now that the Dead Sea Scrolls and the Nag Hammadi Codices have opened up the much broader world of Jewish and Christian texts of the times.[29]

Actually, Marvin Meyer presents a list of such modern studies of Judas:

> The literature on Judas is rich and includes well-known works of academic scholarship and modern literature—Jorge Luis Borges's *Three Versions of Judas,* Mikhail Bulgakov's *The Master and Margarita,* Hans-Josef Klauck's *Judas: Ein Jünger des Herrn,* William Klassen's *Judas: Betrayer or Friend of Jesus?,* Hyam Maccoby's *Judas Iscariot and the Myth of Jewish Evil,* and Marcel Pagnol's play *Judas.* In the rock musical *Jesus Christ Superstar,* Judas Iscariot nearly steals the show, and his presence and music provide a more sympathetic view of the depth of his devotion to Jesus. In the song "With God on Our Side," Bob Dylan sings of Judas:
>
> *You'll have to decide*
> *Whether Judas Iscariot*
> *Has God on his side.*[30]

Although it may well strike us as a new and challenging idea, it seems that the attempt to understand Judas's "betrayal," to give him the benefit of the doubt, and perhaps even to redeem him has a long-standing and continuing tradition.

# 7

# The *Gospel of Judas*

The "official" edition of the *Gospel of Judas* has gone out of its way to "prove" that Codex Tchacos is not a modern forgery. Yet no one in the academic world ever thought that it was! But for the broader public it is an easy confusion to assume that proof of authenticity means that its contents are historically true. It seems to have been the Waitt Foundation that required proof that Codex Tchacos was not a modern forgery before it agreed to make a major financial contribution to the National Geographic Society.[1] Of course the more relevant question is the relation between the copy of the *Gospel of Judas* in Codex Tchacos and the original *Gospel of Judas* generally assumed to have been composed in the middle of the second century.

## THE *GOSPEL OF JUDAS* OF IRENAEUS AND OF TCHACOS

Scholars in the field are of course familiar with the fact that Gospels are often revised, enlarged, or adapted to new situations. Indeed, this may be more the rule than the exception. The Gospel of Mark was merged with the sayings Gospel Q, first from the perspective of the Jewish Christian church to become the Gospel of Matthew, and then by the gentile Christian church to become the Gospel of Luke. Indeed, the Gospel of Mark as used by Matthew and Luke may have been revised in a more spiritualistic direction for the inner circle of the church in Alexandria, then expanded still further by the Carpocratian Gnostics to conform to their form of Gnosticism, then pruned back by the more orthodox Alexandrian church to become the Gospel of Mark canonized into the New Testament. This might explain the differences between the original Gospel of Mark used to produce Matthew and Luke and the canonical Gospel of Mark—for Matthew and Luke, when quoting Mark, at times agree with each other over against Mark (the so-called minor agreements).

It may also be the case that an early collection of miracle stories, the so-called Signs Source, was spiritualized and enlarged into the Gospel of John, to which chapter 21 was subsequently added. An early edition of the sayings Gospel Q has been proposed, as has an early edition of the *Gospel of Thomas*. With regard to other apocryphal Gospels, the question is in most cases moot, since these Gospels are no longer extant in either their original or any expanded version.

All of this is enough to indicate that, in the case of the *Gospel of Judas,* such a question is far from irrelevant. Indeed, different versions are at least as probable as the reverse, that there had been only one version. Of course the fact that there is only one extant copy makes it more difficult to investigate this question.

Gregor Wurst refers to those attacked by Irenaeus for producing the *Gospel of Judas* as "Cainites."[2] He examined the third-century Pseudo-Tertullian description of the "Cainite" heresy and pointed out that it presents two alternate explanations of Judas's betrayal. One was to prevent Jesus from "subverting the truth," the other "to enable salvation for humanity." He hence raised the question whether there were two diverging drafts of the *Gospel of Judas* in the early centuries:

> But it is important to note that Pseudo-Tertullian does not mention the Gospel of Judas at all. His discussion is limited to what he believes to be the teaching of the Cainites. So that poses the question of whether we should regard the Gospel of Judas, mentioned by Irenaeus, as a Cainite work containing this kind of reevaluation of salvation or not. If so, the identification of Irenaeus's Gospel of Judas with the text within Codex Tchacos will be difficult, because in the newly discovered text there is no mention of Cain or the other antiheroes

> from the Jewish Scriptures mentioned by Irenaeus. As a result, we would have to assume the existence of more than one Gospel of Judas circulating within Gnostic communities in antiquity.[3]

Since Pseudo-Tertullian does not mention the *Gospel of Judas* and Irenaeus does not mention Cainites, there is not sufficient evidence to postulate a draft of the *Gospel of Judas* containing what Pseudo-Tertullian ascribes to Cainites. As John D. Turner has pointed out, there is no cogent reason to assume there was a distinct Gnostic group that identified itself as "Cainite." Rather "Cainite" seems to have been simply a pejorative term secondarily attached to the view described by Irenaeus, as Turner has indicated in an e-mail of August 14, 2006:

> The major reason, aside from the obvious content of the Judas Gospel and its apparent lack of interest in Cain, is that Irenaeus, and probably even Hippolytus in his lost *Syntagma,* called their opponents "Gnostics"; it was only their later epitomators Theodoret and Epiphanius for Irenaeus, and Pseudo-Tertullian, Filastrius, and Epiphanius for Hippolytus, that glossed Irenaeus's "other gnostics" with names such as Barbeloites, Ophites, Cainites, and Sethites.

Birger Pearson, in an unpublished paper entitled "Judas Iscariot and His New Gospel: Some Conclusions," makes the same point. But whether there ever was a Gnostic sect called "Cainites" does not affect the issue here. We can leave Wurst with that as his problem. Suffice it to say that what is assigned to the "Cainites" does not occur in the *Gospel of Judas* from Codex Tchacos.

The more relevant question is how the *Gospel of Judas* from Codex Tchacos relates to the *Gospel of Judas* mentioned by Irenaeus in *Adversus Haereses:*

> They bring forth a fabricated work to this effect, which they entitle the *Gospel of Judas*. (I 31.1)

The text with this same striking title in Codex Tchacos is presumably the *Gospel of Judas* to which Irenaeus referred. But, given the way that texts, and especially Gospels, were revised and "improved" at will, it is not necessarily the case that Irenaeus's *Gospel of Judas* and the *Gospel of Judas* from Codex Tchacos are identical.[4] Of course we do not know whether Irenaeus's copy, if indeed he had a copy in writing, was itself identical with the original *Gospel of Judas*. But the comparison must begin with what Irenaeus reports, since that is all we have.

Irenaeus begins with a description of the views of a group that produced the *Gospel of Judas:*

> And others say that Cain was from the superior realm of absolute power, and confess that Esau, Korah, the Sodomites, and all such persons are of the same people (or nation) as themselves; for this reason they have been hated by their maker, although none of them has suffered harm. For wisdom (Sophia) snatched up out of them whatever in them belonged to her. And furthermore—they say—Judas the betrayer was thoroughly acquainted with these things.

None of this Old Testament background of the Gnostics in question is reflected in the *Gospel of Judas* from Codex Tchacos, since none of these bad-guys-turned-good-guys are mentioned in the *Gospel of Judas*. Of course Irenaeus does not say that this background is included in the *Gospel of Judas*. But he does go on to maintain that the Gnostics say that Judas was "thoroughly acquainted with these things." But there is no confirmation of this fact in the *Gospel of Judas* from Codex Tchacos.

Irenaeus continues:

> He alone was acquainted with the truth as no others were, and (so) accomplished the mystery of the betrayal. By him all things, both earthly and heavenly, were thrown into dissolution. And they bring forth a fabricated work to this effect, which they entitle the *Gospel of Judas*.

Since Irenaeus says that they produced the *Gospel of Judas* "to this effect," one may ask what in the *Gospel of Judas* could be described in that way. It does in fact present Judas in a way that could be described as his being "thoroughly acquainted with these things," "acquainted with the truth as no others were." Judas is indeed separated off from "the Twelve" for instruction. And it is said of Judas that he "accomplished the mystery of the betrayal." In Codex Tchacos, "mysteries beyond the world" are what Jesus teaches the disciples: "He began to speak with them about the mysteries beyond the world and what would take palce at the end" (p. 33). But this promptly narrows down to Judas, whom Jesus tells on the third day: "Look, I have explained to you the mysteries of the kingdom" (p. 45). "Look, you have been told everything" (p. 57). And of course the *Gospel of Judas* ends with Judas giving Jesus over: "And Judas received money and handed him over to them" (p. 58). Thus the information provided by Irenaeus can be harmonized with the *Gospel of Judas* from Codex Tchacos, meager though it is.

## TITLE, INTRODUCTION, AND CONCLUSION

The four Gospels in the New Testament and the four Gospels in the Nag Hammadi library did not originally bear the title "Gospel" or the name of an author.[5] The label on the outside of the scroll or the title set off at the beginning and/or end of a tractate in a codex was usually first done by a copyist, not by the original author. In the case of "Gospels," author and title were added secondarily to accredit them as of equal (or superior) authority to the others that were coming to be called "Gospels" and to be ascribed to authoritative apostles.

Often the original author of a text had indicated in the opening and/or closing lines of the text itself how he thought the work should be identified. At times it was that opening and/or closing that later came to be summarized by a copyist, to arrive at a title that both distinguished one text from another and provided the right focus and authority that the copyist wished the text to have.

The *Gospel of Judas* has the by now famous subscript title the *Gospel of Judas.* So let us seek to correlate that with the opening and closing lines of the text itself:

> The secret word of declaration by which Jesus spoke in conversation with Judas Iscariot, during eight days, three days before he celebrated Passover. When Jesus appeared on earth, he performed miracles and great wonders for the salvation of humanity. And since some [walked][6] in the way of righteousness while others walked in their transgression, the twelve disciples were called.
>
> [And] their high priests murmured because [...] had gone into the guest room for his prayer. But some of the scribes were there watching carefully in order to arrest him during the prayer. For they were afraid of the people, since he was regarded by all as a prophet. They approached Judas and said to him, "What are you doing here? You are Jesus' disciple." And he answered them as they wished. And Judas received money and handed him over to them.

This sounds quite like a Gospel, with familiar details such as "Jesus," "Judas Iscariot," "Passover," "he performed miracles and great wonders," "the twelve disciples were called," "high priests," "scribes ... were afraid of the people, since he was regarded by all as a prophet," then Judas "received money" and "handed him over to them"—almost everything in the introduction and conclusion is familiar!

Of course this introduction and conclusion suggest that the body of the text would be limited to Holy Week. In any case one could hope to find much more information about that last week of Jesus's life. Then comes the big surprise, and disappointment—the introduction and conclusion are really the only parts of the *Gospel of Judas* that sound like a Gospel! There are no sayings of Jesus like those in the sayings Gospel Q and the *Gospel of*

*Thomas,* no baptism, parables, healings, exorcisms, feedings, or debates like those in the Gospel of Mark—much less infancy narratives or even the crucifixion story and resurrection appearances like those in the Gospels of Matthew and Luke! The body of the text consists only of second-century Gnostic thought with a focus on criticizing the emerging orthodox church.[7]

The subscript title the *Gospel of Judas* does indeed pick up the opening and closing sections of the text and could have been added by a copyist to do just that. But these opening and closing sections seem more related to the canonical Gospels than to what comprises the rest of the text in the *Gospel of Judas*! Indeed, one could even wonder if a secondary focus on turning a competitive Gnostic tractate into a Gospel could be responsible not only for the title, but even for the opening and closing sections themselves. A purely Gnostic dialogue of Jesus and Judas could have been embellished at beginning and end with summaries familiar from the canonical Gospels, leading to the concluding title the *Gospel of Judas,* intended to mislead the orthodox church, much as its sensational re-publication last Easter was intended to mislead modern Christians.

It is striking what Gospel-like materials are *not* included in these opening and closing summaries, which suggests that their content is of no real interest to their author. Jesus "performed miracles and great wonders," but none are recorded. "The twelve disciples were called," but they are not listed, nor are they sent on their mission or taught, as they are in the canonical Gospels—indeed in the *Gospel of Judas* they are there only to become the villains of the story. Similarly, at the conclusion, Jesus "had gone into the guest room for his prayer." But what happened in the Upper Room in the canonical Gospels is all absent—the Last Supper, the parting discourses, Judas leaving to get the Jewish authorities, then Jesus going to Gethsemane, and the prayerful scene there! The last scene of the *Gospel of Judas,* the betrayal itself, apparently takes place still in the guest room. The thirty pieces of silver, the Judas kiss, the actual arrest, trial, crucifixion, and resurrection are all absent.

What is actually present in the body of the text could be there even without that Gospel-like beginning and end and without the title the *Gospel of Judas*. The body of the text begins quite differently: "He began to speak with them about the mysteries beyond the world and what would take place at the end" (p. 33). This does not sound like a Gospel, but instead, it is like the typical introduction of the standard Gnostic genre, a dialogue of the Resurrected with his disciples.

The body of the text then takes up: "But often he does not appear to his disciples as himself, but you find him among them as a child" (p. 33). This sounds like an ascetic saying symbolizing prepubescent purity, alluded to, for example, in *Gospel of Thomas* saying 4: "The person old in his days will not hesitate to ask a child seven days old about the place of life, and he will live." But this lead-in does not lead into the public ministry of Jesus, by which time he was about thirty years old (Luke 3:23). Furthermore, the word translated "child" is unclear in its meaning, and the whole sentence has been conjectured to be "a secondary gloss."[8] It leads nowhere.

The twofold temporal reference at the opening of the text, "during eight days" and "three days before he celebrated Passover," may point to two distinct dimensions of the text itself: the Gospel is apparently confined to "Holy Week," if indeed that is what the reference to "eight days" is intended to indicate. Be that as it may, the preceding Galilean ministry is not mentioned at all. Instead, the text begins with a place reference to Judea (p. 33). The body of the text does list a sequence of Jesus appearing on three days. This is the best one can do by way of making sense of the opening time references.

It is an obvious question as to whether these more Gospel-like paragraphs at beginning and end are dependent on the canonical Gospels, or whether they reflect some noncanonical source material. Of course Gospel material, canonical and noncanonical, written and oral, was well known in Christian communities of the second century. Much of it in the *Gospel of Judas* does not call for us to assume dependence on a written source, such as the Last Supper being a Passover meal (found in the Synoptic Gospels, but not in the Gospel of John), Jesus performing "miracles and great wonders," there being twelve disciples, Jesus being given over by Judas Iscariot, and the like. But when one looks more closely at the references, a dependence on the two-volume work of Luke, namely his Gospel and his Acts of the Apostles, does seem probable.

Only Luke has a reference to "scribes" in connection with not arresting Jesus because they were "afraid of the people" (20:19). Only Luke adds to the scene of the Jewish authorities engaging Judas to turn Jesus over the condition that it be "in the absence of the crowd" (22:6). Luke 9:8 (and Mark 6:15) report the rumor that Jesus is a "prophet." When this is repeated, only Luke retains the singular, "some prophet of the ancients" (9:19), whereas Matthew (16:14) and Mark (8:28) use the plural, "one of the prophets." The reference to the upper room as the "guest room" occurs in Luke 22:11 (and Mark 14:14). Also Luke 22:5 (and Mark 14:11) refers to giving Judas "money" (literally, "silver"), rather than "thirty pieces of silver" (Matt. 26:15), much as the *Gospel of Judas* ends with "he received money," with no mention of thirty pieces. Thus again and again the *Gospel of Judas* seems to echo Luke[9] (and less frequently a Markan parallel). No other Gospel presents any significant unique parallels that would suggest that the author had access to that Gospel.[10]

Furthermore, reference in the book of Acts to a replacement for Judas seems to have been used: "For someone else will replace you, in order that the twelve [disciples] may again come to completion with their god" (p. 36). Acts 1:23–26 reports the choice of Matthias to replace Judas. Since this is the only early Christian reference to this idea, the *Gospel of Judas* must have gotten it from Acts.

Of course Luke-Acts was originally written and copied together as a two-volume work. This probably continued into the second century. Hence, the *Gospel of Judas* may have had access to a codex containing only Luke-Acts. By the third century this seemed to have changed. In the papyrus codex $\mathfrak{P}^{75}$ John instead of Acts followed Luke. In the papyrus codex 𝔓[45] all four Gospels are followed by Acts. In the papyrus codex 𝔓[53] there are fragments of both Matthew and Luke. But the familiar sequence that became standard, Matthew, Mark, Luke, John, Acts, should not be presupposed in the second century, for which there is no relevant manuscript evidence. Perhaps the *Gospel of Judas* itself is the best evidence we have that Luke-Acts continued to be copied and used together, without the other Gospels, down to the middle of the second century.

Nor do other New Testament texts, such as letters of Paul, seem to be presupposed.[11] We are all familiar with the great parchment uncials from the fourth century that present a complete New Testament, but this cannot be unconsciously read back into the earlier period.

One should also not overlook the divergences from all the canonical Gospels that occur in these opening and closing paragraphs. The conclusion opens with a comment not otherwise attested: "Their high priests murmured because he had gone into the guest room for his prayer." In the canonical Gospels, the high priests are not portrayed as aware of the Last Supper. The next comment, "But some scribes were there watching carefully in order to arrest him during the prayer," is also unattested elsewhere. The *Gospel of Judas* has no Last Supper in the guest room, but only "prayer," in spite of the reference in the opening paragraph, "before he celebrated Passover." The scribes' statement to Judas is not in the canonical Gospels: "What are you doing here? You are Jesus' disciple."[12] The arrest is apparently carried out by the scribes, since there is no mention of an armed crowd (in the Synoptics; in John 18:3, "a band of soldiers and some officers"). But the most obvious divergence between the *Gospel of Judas* and the canonical Gospels is that Jesus and the Twelve never leave the guest room to go to the Garden of Gethsemane for Jesus's tearful prayers and the arrest there. The giving over of Jesus apparently takes place in the guest room, not in the Garden of Gethsemane.

One may suspect that some of the canonical story is omitted from the conclusion because of the Gnostic proclivities of the author. There is no Last Supper, since the saying over the bread, "This is my body, which is given for you" (Luke 22:19), would be inappropriate in the Gnostic context: the body is not the divine part, but only that from which the divine part is trying to escape. For the same reason there are no bodily resurrection appearances. But this may also explain the absence of the scene in the Garden of Gethsemane. Jesus there is clearly anything but eager to die, to put it mildly: "Remove this cup from me." But the Gnostic Jesus longs to be free from the body so as to be able to ascend back home. Hence one may suspect that these most glaring omissions from the conclusion of the book are tendentious, due to the Gnostic orientation of the *Gospel of Judas*. The arrest in the guest room is not an ancient tradition omitted in the canonical Gospels but preserved for posterity in the *Gospel of Judas*, but rather just a secondary solution called for by what Gnosticism had of necessity to exclude from the canonical tradition.

## THE BODY OF THE TEXT: THREE ODD DAYS

We preface the substantive analysis of the *Gospel of Judas* in later sections of this chapter with a mere analysis of the flow of thought, or lack of same, in the body of the text. First, with regard to the three days in the body of the text, the narrative begins: "And one day he was with his disciples in Judea" (p. 33). Then: "Now, the next morning, after this happened, he [appeared] to his disciples (again)" (p. 36). Then: "Another day Jesus came to [them]" (p. 37). These time references are what the reference to "three days" at the opening could have in mind.

This division into three days before Passover turns out to be very wooden, as if it were superimposed where there is no real narrative continuity, just to divide the units one from the other. On the first day, after the disciples repudiate Jesus, he takes Judas aside and says, "I shall tell you the mysteries of the kingdom" (p. 35). Judas asks when he will tell him these things, whereupon "Jesus left him." Not only does Jesus fail to tell Judas the mysteries of the kingdom; he is not even polite enough to tell him when he will! Then: "Now, the next morning, after this [. . . ?] happened, he [appeared] to his disciples (again)." If Jesus withdrew from the disciples to instruct Judas alone, why is this instruction bypassed? And why does Jesus promptly disappear and then appear not to Judas alone, but to all the disciples again? There simply does not seem to be any train of thought!

When the disciples ask where Jesus had gone, he replies: "I went to another great and holy generation" (p. 36). When they ask what that great generation is, Jesus laughs, because "[the] generation of people among [you] is from the generation of humanity" (p. 37). This seems to indicate that he not only fails to answer the question about the holy generation, but that he goes out of his way to put them down as from another, purely human, generation. It is understandable enough that this leaves the disciples "troubled in [their] spirit. They did not find a word to say." That ends the second day.

But immediately, without a break: "Another day Jesus came up to [them]" (p. 37). They ask him to explain their vision of twelve men, priests, at the altar (p. 38). Jesus interprets the vision as referring to the disciples themselves: "It is you who are presenting the offerings on the altar you have seen" (p. 39), which p. 40 spells out in somewhat more detail. (The next leaf, pp. 41–42, is largely missing.) Then there are two very brief exchanges between Jesus and Judas (p. 43–44), which are cut off abruptly: "After Jesus said this, he departed" (p. 44). (The editors of the critical edition of Codex Tchacos propose in a footnote an emendation of the text to help it make sense: not "he" departed but "they" departed.) Thereupon Judas addresses the absent "Master," wanting to tell his vision—to whom? Jesus—not absent, after all—responds that Judas is to "speak up" (p. 44). Judas then reports his vision of the twelve disciples stoning him (pp. 44–45). Jesus responds: "I have explained to you the mysteries of the kingdom" (p. 46). Have we missed something in the intervening dozen pages? There are some holes in the papyrus, but not large enough to have contained an intelligible train of thought. The flow of the text, or absence of a flow to the text, simply does not make sense.

All this is more like resurrection appearances in the canonical Gospels, where Jesus appears from nowhere, then disappears again, without anyone inquiring where he had been (presumably on high). But the *Gospel of Judas* does not have resurrection appearances, though its Jesus has the same ghostlike manner as does the resurrected Christ, who suddenly appears in a room behind locked doors (John 20:19). Jesus escaping from his physical body at the end of the text comes as a bit of an anticlimax, since he seems to have come and gone at will all along.

What takes place on these three days leading up to Passover in the *Gospel of Judas* has nothing to do with what takes place during Holy Week in the canonical Gospels, and indeed has nothing to do with the life of Jesus. Though it is cast in the form of a dialogue between Jesus and Judas, this can be no more than a secondary convention to lend Christian authority to the text's teaching. One may recall a secondarily Christianized dialogue between Jesus and his disciples, the *Wisdom of Jesus Christ* (Nag Hammadi Codex III,*4*; P.Berol. 8502,*3*), which is a Christian reworking of the non-Christian treatise *Eugnostos the Blessed* (Nag Hammadi Codices III,*3*; V,*1*).

This third day does seem to end on an upbeat note for Judas. He asks: "Master, could it be that my seed is under the control of the rulers?" (p. 46). Jesus's encouraging reply is: "You will become the thirteenth, and you will be cursed by the other generations, and you will come to rule over them. In the last days they < will . . . > to you, and that you will not ascend on high to the holy [generation]" (pp. 46–47). This not only has at least a very brief reference to the opening prediction, "what would take place at the end" (p. 33). It also puts Judas as "the thirteenth" over against "the Twelve," which seems to be the connection with the rest of the body of the text that follows.

Thereupon Jesus launches into a long discourse based on the Sethian theogony and cosmogony (pp. 47–53). This then is followed by a dialogue between Jesus and Judas that functions as a commentary (pp. 53–57). This all concludes with a claim that is anything but obvious: "Look, you have been told everything" (p. 57).

The *Gospel of Judas* concludes with what is assumed to be the ascension of Judas: "So Judas lifted up his eyes and saw the luminous cloud, and he entered it" (p. 57). This is then followed by the tractate's conclusion, quoted above. But this transition to that conclusion creates problems. After Judas has entered the luminous cloud above, he has to be in the guest room, down on earth again, to turn Jesus over to the scribes.[13]

Thus the body of the text, with its three empty days and then the long Sethian concluding section (still on the third day?), seems to fit poorly into the more Gospel-like introduction and conclusion. In fact, the overall organization of the *Gospel of Judas*, or, more exactly, what seems to be its lack of organization, makes one wonder if it is what the original author wrote. If it is, he was a very poor author when compared, for example, with the authors of the Gnostic tractates from Nag Hammadi! But the emptiness of the text does suggest that there may have been deletions along the way. But where, why, by whom, when? And, if not, why does the text read the way it does? What did its awkward form achieve?

## SETHIAN NAG HAMMADI TRACTATES

It is of course recognized that the *Gospel of Judas* is a Gnostic text similar to the Nag Hammadi Gnostic texts. It is therefore relevant to investigate just which Nag Hammadi tractates show the closest affinity. According to the "official" presentation, the *Gospel of Judas* is a Sethian text. A generation ago, Hans-Martin Schenke identified the largest cluster of texts in the Nag Hammadi library as Sethian,[14] that is, belonging to a group that claimed Seth, the third son of Adam and Eve, as its ancestor. The most authoritative list of Sethian Nag Hammadi tractates to date has been provided by John P. Turner:

> *The Apocryphon of John* [= *The Secret Book of John*] (*Ap. John:* four copies in two versions: short [BG 8502,2; NHC III,*1*]; long [NHC II,*1*; NHC IV,*1*]);

*The Hypostasis of the Archons* [= *The Nature of the Rulers*] (*Hyp. Arch.*: NHC II,*4*);
*The Holy Book of the Invisible Spirit*, customarily named the *Gospel of the Egyptians* (*Gos. Egypt.*: NHC III,*2*; NHC IV,*2*);
*The Apocalypse* [*Revelation*] *of Adam* (*Apoc. Adam:* NHC V,*5*);
*The Three Steles of Seth* (*Steles Seth:* NHC VII,*5*);
*Zostrianos* (*Zost.*: NHC VIII,*1*);
*Marsanes* (NHC X,*1*);
*Melchizedek* (*Melch.*: NHC IX,*1*);
*The Thought of Norea* (*Norea:* NHC IX,*2*);
*Allogenes* (NHC XI,*3*); and
*The Trimorphic Protennoia* [= *Three Forms of First Thought*] (*Trim. Prot.*: NHC XIII,*1*).

A proposal to add another Nag Hammadi treatise to the Sethian corpus has been made recently by B. Layton, namely, *The Thunder, Perfect Mind* (NHC VI,2), which he hypothesizes to be an offshoot (along with certain materials in the *Hypothesis of the Archons* [= *The Nature of the Rulers*] and the untitled text dubbed *On the Origin of the World*, NHC II,*5*) of a certain *Gospel of Eve* cited by Epiphanius (*Panarion* 26.2.6). Although the untitled treatise from NHC II, *On the Origin of the World*, contains no distinctive Sethian mythologumena, and therefore should be excluded from membership in this group, it is nonetheless closely related to the *Hypostasis of the Archons* [= *The Nature of the Rulers*]; indeed they both may stem from a common Sethian parent.[15]

There is one reference to Seth in the *Gospel of Judas*, "the incorruptible [generation] of Seth" (p. 49). However, in the critical edition of Codex Tchacos there is another reference to Seth (p. 52), part of which is a restoration in a lacuna. It is probably not an accurate restoration, since in a parallel list of mythological names in Sethian tractates from Nag Hammadi it is not Seth, but Yaoth,

Haoth, or Athoth. Gregor Wurst maintains that the final vowel is ē, and so it should perhaps it left undecided, as [...]ēth, or, as John Turner suggests, transcribed [Ath]ēth.

## THE SETHIAN SECTION OF THE *GOSPEL OF JUDAS*

The question of whether the *Gospel of Judas* is to be considered a Sethian Gnostic text does not depend on the frequency of the name of Seth, but rather on whether the *Gospel of Judas* does in fact contain Sethian mythology. This does seem to be the case, though it is largely confined to one central section that seems to be a major digression from the main thrust of the *Gospel of Judas*. It begins on p. 47, includes the sections in the translation published at Easter 2006 entitled "Jesus Teaches Judas About Cosmology: The Spirit and the Self-Generated," "Adamas and the Luminaries," "The Cosmic Chaos, and the Underworld," "The Rulers and Angels," and "The Creation of Humanity," and ends on p. 53. It is then followed by Judas asking questions about what has gone before, which Jesus answers, in what amounts to a catechism, which extends onto p. 57. To quote Attridge's unpublished footnote: "The structure of the text, in which a catechism dealing with questions about salvation follows an account of origins, is similar to the organization of the *Apocryphon* [*Secret Book*] *of John*." Indeed, this is the section that turns out to have the closest affinities to Sethianism. But it may not justify the sweeping assertion of the "official" edition that the *Gospel of Judas* is a Sethian tractate, which in turn has led to the reading of Sethianism into the text as a given.

One can get at the unusually strong Sethianism of this section of the *Gospel of Judas* by looking at the mythological names in the text. Whereas the *Gospel of Judas* does not name any disciples other than Judas, the text has a flood of names of mythological personages: Barbelo (p. 35), Sophia (p. 44), Self-Generated (Autogenes) (p. 47 three times, 50), Adamas (p. 48), Seth (p. 49), El (p. 51), Nebro (p. 51 twice), Yaldabaoth (p. 51), Saklas (p. 51 twice, 52, 54, 56); Sakla (p. 52), [S]eth, (probably [Ath]ēth, p. 52), Harmathoth

(p. 52), Galila (p. 52), Yobel (p. 52), Adonaios (p. 52), Adam (pp. 52, 53, 54), Eve (p. 52), Michael (p. 53), and Gabriel (p. 53). From the placement of these mythological names, it is apparent that pp. 47–53 are a kind of Gnostic mythological intrusion into the dialogue of Jesus and Judas. Since these names are familiar from the Nag Hammadi tractates, their distribution there will help to reveal this section of the *Gospel of Judas* to be a Sethian section in the *Gospel of Judas,* surrounded by non-Sethian sections. With all due apologies for a battery of detailed data, here is the list of Coptic page references in the Nag Hammadi tractates in the sequence in which they occur in the *Gospel of Judas.* Feel free to skip over these lists, indented just for this purpose, and move to the conclusions that can be derived from this data:[16]

**Barbelo** (p. 35): II,*1* (*Secret Book of John*): 4, 5 (five times), 6 (four times), 7 (three times); VII,*5* (*Revelation of Adam*): 121; VIII,*1* (*Zostrianos*): 14, 36 (twice), 37, 53, 62, 63, 83, 87, 91, 118, 119, 122, 124, 129; IX,*1* (*Melchizedek*): 5, 16; X,*1* (*Marsanes*): 4, 8, 43; XI,*3* (*Allogenes the Stranger*): 51, 53, 56, 58, 59 (twice); XIII,*1* (*Three Forms of First Thought*): 38; **Barbalo:** XI,*3* (*Allogenes the Stranger*): 46; **Barbelon:** III,*2* (*Holy Book of the Great Invisible Spirit*): 42, 62, 69.

**Sophia** (p. 44): II,*1* (*Secret Book of John*): 8, 9, 23, 28; II,*3* (*Gospel of Philip*): 59 (twice); II,*4* (*Nature of the Rulers*): 94, 95 (four times); II,*5* (*On the Origin of the World*): 98, 102 (twice), 103, 112, 113, 115, 122; III,*2* (*Holy Book of the Great Invisible Spirit*): 57, 69; III,*3* (*Eugnostos the Blessed*): 77, 81, 82 (five times), 88, 89; III,*4* (*Wisdom of Jesus Christ*): 90, 101, 102, 104 (twice), 106 (twice), 107 (three times), 112, 113, 114, 119; V,*1* (*Eugnostos the Blessed*): 9, 35, 36 (twice); VI,*4* (*The Concept of Our Great Power*): 44 (twice); VII,*1* (*Paraphrase of Shem*): 31; VII,*2* (*Second Discourse of Great Seth*): 50, 51, 52, 68, 70; VIII,*1* (*Zostrianos*): 9, 10 (twice), 27; XI,*2* (*Valentinian Exposition*): 31, 33, 35 (three times), 39 (seven times); XIII,*1* (*Three Forms of First Thought*): 40, 47; BG,*3* (*Wisdom of Jesus Christ*): 109, 120;

**Pistis Sophia:** II,*4* (*Nature of the Rulers*): 87, 95; II,*5* (*On the Origin of the World*): 100 (three times), 104 (twice), 106, 108; III,*3* (*Eugnostos the Blessed*): 82, 83; **Sophia Pistis:** II,*5* (*On the Origin of the World*): 106; **Sophia, who is called Pistis:** II,*4* (*Nature of the Rulers*): 94; **Sophia Zoe:** II,*5* (*On the Origin of the World*): 113, 115, 121; **Wisdom:** II,*3* (*Gospel of Philip*): 60 (four times), 63; VII,*4* (*Teachings of Silvanus*): 88, 89, 91, 106, 107 (twice), 112, 113; XI,*1* (*Interpretation of Knowledge*): 12; XII,*1* (*Sentences of Sextus*): 16.

**Self-Generated = Autogenes** (pp. 47 [three times], 50): II,*1* (*Secret Book of John*): 7 (five times), 8 (five times), 9 (twice); III,2 (*Holy Book of the Great Invisible Spirit*): 41, 49, 50 (twice), 52 (twice), 53, 55, 57, 62, 65, 68; III,*3* (*Eugnostos the Blessed*): 82, 106; VII,*5* (*Three Steles of Seth*): 119; VIII,*1* (*Zostrianos*): 6 (twice), 7, 12, 15, 17, 18, 19, 20, 30 (four times), 34, 35 (twice), 41 (twice), 44, 53, 56, 58, 127; IX,2 (*Thought of Norea*): 28; X,*1* (*Marsanes*): 5; XI,*3* (*Allogenes the Stranger*): 46, 51, 58.

**Adamas** (p. 48): II,*5* (*On the Origin of the World*): 108; III,2 (*Holy Book of the Great Invisible Spirit*): 49, 50, 51 (twice), 55, 65; IV,2 (*Holy Book of the Great Invisible Spirit*): 61; VIII,*1* (*Zostrianos*): 6, 30 (twice), 33, 51; IX,2 (*Thought of Norea*): 27, 28.

**Seth** (p. 49): II,*1* (*Secret Book of John*): 9 (twice), 25; II,*4* (*On the Origin of the World*): [91]; III,2 (*Holy Book of the Great Invisible Spirit*): 51, 54, 55, 56, 59, 60 (five times), 61 (twice), 62 (three times), 63, 64 (three times), 65 (twice), 68 (twice); V,*5* (*Revelation of Adam*): 64 (twice), 67, 77, 85 (twice); IV,2 (*Holy Book of the Great Invisible Spirit*): 59; VII,2 (*Second Discourse of Great Seth*): 70; VII,*5* (*Three Steles of Seth*): 118 (three times), 121 (twice), 124, 127; VIII,*1* (*Zostrianos*): 6, 7, 30, 51, 130; IX,*1* (*Melchizedek*): 5.

**El** (p. 51): **Eloaios:** II,*5* (*On the Origin of the World*): 101; **Eloai:** II,*5* (*On the Origin of the World*): 101; **Eloaio:** II,*1* (*Secret Book of John*): 12; **Eloaiou:** II,*1* (*Secret Book of John*): 11; **Elohim:** VII,*3*

(*Revelation of Peter*): 82; **Eloim:** II,*1* (*Secret Book of John*): 24 (twice); IV,*1* (*Secret Book of John*): 38.

**Nebro** (p. 51 [twice]): **Nebrith:** II,*1* (*Secret Book of John*): 16; **Nebruel:** III,2 (*Holy Book of the Great Invisible Spirit*): 57 (twice).

**Yaldabaoth** (p. 51): II,*1* (*Secret Book of John*): 24; II,*4* (*Nature of the Rulers*): 95, 96; II,*5* (*On the Origin of the World*): 100 (three times), 102, 103 (twice); VII,2 (*Second Discourse of Great Seth*): 53, 68; BG,*3* (*Eugnostos the Blessed*): 119; **Aldabaoth:** II,*1* (*Secret Book of John*): 23; **Yaltabaoth:** II,*1* (*Secret Book of John*): 10, 11 (twice), 14, 19 (twice); II,*4* (*Nature of the Rulers*): 95; XIII,*1* (*Three Forms of First Thought*): 39.

**Saklas** (pp. 51 [bis], 52, 54, 56; **Sakla** 52): II,*1* (*Secret Book of John*): 11; XIII,*1* (*Three Forms of First Thought*): 39; **Sakla:** II,*4* (*Nature of the Rulers*): 95; III,2 (*Holy Book of the Great Invisible Spirit*): 57 (three times), 58; V,*5* (*Revelation of Adam*): 74 (twice).

**Harmathoth** (p. 52): **Harmas:** II,*1* (*Secret Book of John*): 10; III,2 (*Holy Book of the Great Invisible Spirit*): 58; **Armas:** II,*1* (*Secret Book of John*): 17.

**Galila** (p. 52): III,2 (*Holy Book of the Great Invisible Spirit*): 58; **Kalila:** II,*1* (*Secret Book of John*): 17; **Kalila-Gumbri:** II,*1* (*Secret Book of John*): 10.

**Yobel** (p. 52): II,*1* (*Secret Book of John*): 10; III,2 (*Holy Book of the Great Invisible Spirit*): 58. **Yubel:** III,2 (*Holy Book of the Great Invisible Spirit*): 58.

**Adonaios** (p. 52): II,*5* (*On the Origin of the World*): 101; III,2 (*Holy Book of the Great Invisible Spirit*): 58; V,*3* (*First Revelation of James*): 39; VII,2 (*Second Discourse of Great Seth*): 52, 55 (twice); **Adonaiou:** II,*1* (*Secret Book of John*): 10.

**Adam** (pp. 52, 53, 54): II,*1* (*Secret Book of John*): 15, 20 (twice), 22 (twice), 24 (three times); II,2 (*Gospel of Thomas*): 41, 47; II,*3* (*Gospel of Philip*): 55, 58, 68, 70 (twice), 71 (four times), 74; II,*4*

(*Nature of the Rulers*): 88 (five times), 89 (five times), 90 (three times), 91 (three times); II, *5* (*On the Origin of the World*): 108, 111, 112 (twice), 115 (five times), 116 (six times), 117 (three times), 118 (three times), 119 (three times), 120 (five times), 121 (twice), 122; III,2 (*Holy Book of the Great Invisible Spirit*): 60; III,*3* (*Eugnostos the Blessed*): 81; III,*4* (*Wisdom of Jesus Christ*): 105; V,*5* (*Revelation of Adam*): 64 (twice), 66 (twice), 85 (three times); VII,2 (*Second Discourse of Great Seth*): 53 (twice), 54, 62, 63; IX,*1* (*Melchizedek*): 9, 10, 12; IX,2 (*Thought of Norea*): 29; IX,*3* (*Testimony of Truth*): 45, 46 (twice), 47 (four times), 50, 67; XI,*1* (*Interpretation of Knowledge*): 14; XI,2 (*Valentinian Exposition*): 38; BG,*3* (*Wisdom of Jesus Christ*): 108.

**Eve** (p. 52): II,*1* (*Secret Book of John*): 24; II,*3* (*Gospel of Philip*): 68, 70; II,*4* (*Nature of the Rulers*): 91 (twice), 92 (twice); II,*5* (*On the Origin of the World*): 113, 114, 115, 116 (three times), 117 (twice), 118 (twice), 119 (three times); V,*5* (*Revelation of Adam*): 64 (twice), 65 (twice), 66 (three times), 69; IX,*1* (*Melchizedek*): 10, 46.

**Michael** (p. 53): II,*1* (*Secret Book of John*): 17.

**Gabriel** (p. 53): III,2 (*Holy Book of the Great Invisible Spirit*): 52, 53, 57, 64; VIII,*1* (*Zostrianos*): 57, 58.

When one thumbs through this list of mythological personages, almost all of them fall within this Sethian section on pp. 47–53. Only Barbelo and Sophia are mentioned before it. But the reference to "the immortal aeon of Barbelo" is isolated, without Barbelo playing the standard active role familiar in Sethianism. And the reference to "corruptible Sophia" may not involve a personification at all, but only refer to "corruptible wisdom." Only Michael and Gabriel occur after the Sethian section, although these two are included in the "catechism" on pp. 53–57. Almost all of these mythological names are specifically Sethian in that they occur almost exclusively in Sethian tractates. In this sense it would perhaps be preferable to speak of a large section of the *Gospel of*

*Judas* as Sethian, rather than saying simply that the *Gospel of Judas* is a Sethian tractate. Yet this large section with these many parallels of mythological characters does not constitute the major thrust with which the *Gospel of Judas* begins and ends. Furthermore, there are a few parallels between the *Gospel of Judas* and Nag Hammadi tractates that are not Sethian. An instance is *Eugnostos the Blessed,* of which two copies occur in the Nag Hammadi library. One parallel is so close as to indicate some kind of dependence.[17]

One prominent dimension of this "Sethian" section of the *Gospel of Judas* is the astrological "numbers magic" that begins with Seth and the number twelve. First on the positive side:

> He made the incorruptible [generation] of Seth appear [ … ] the twelve [ … ] 24 [ … ]. He made 72 luminaries appear in the incorruptible generation, in accordance with the will of the Spirit. And the 72 luminaries themselves made 360 luminaries appear in the incorruptible generation, in accordance with the will of the Spirit, that their number should be five for each. And the twelve aeons of the twelve luminaries constitute their father, with six heavens for each aeon, so that there are 72 heavens for the 72 luminaries, and for each [of them five] firmaments, [for a total of] 360 [firmaments]. (p. 49)

Attridge in a footnote explains this numbers magic:

> There is therefore a mathematical progression in the unfolding of the luminous spiritual world. The initial 12 x 2 = 24 x 3 = 72 x 5 = 360 Illuminators. The multipliers are the first three primes, excluding 1, which occupies a special position in the numerical hierarchy. Factors, i.e., 6 and 12, of 72, the intermediate number in this sequence, also have symbolic significance. Neo-Pythagorean numerical theory probably lurks behind this sequence. The same number of heavenly realities in the same configuration is found in the Nag Hammadi tractate *Eugnostos* [*the Blessed*], NHC 3,*3*: 83.10–20;

> 5,*1*: 11.20–12.1. The *Apocryphon* [*Secret Book*] *of John* (NHC 2,*1*: 11.25) mentions 365 angelic powers.

One should note that the closest parallel to this numbers magic is not in the Sethian text the *Secret Book of John,* but rather in the non-Sethian text *Eugnostos the Blessed*!

Corresponding to the positive mathematics, there is an evil imitation:

> "Let twelve angels come into being [to] rule over chaos and the [underworld]." And look, from the cloud there appeared an [angel] whose face flashed with fire and whose appearance was defiled with blood. His name was Nebro, which means in translation "rebel"; others call him Yaldabaoth. And another angel, Saklas, also came from the cloud. So Nebro created six angels—as well as Saklas—to be assistants, and these produced twelve angels in the heavens, with each one receiving a portion in the heavens. (p. 51)

Here there are twelve evil angels in the astrology, with names distinctive of Sethianism in the Nag Hammadi tractates. It would seem to be "the twelve [positive] aeons of the twelve luminaries" and even more the "twelve [negative] angels in the heavens" that provide the point of contact between the Sethian section of the *Gospel of Judas* and "the Twelve" in the more down-to-earth beginning and end of the text.

## "THE TWELVE"

"The Twelve" is of course an honorific title in the New Testament. Already the sayings Gospel Q closes with Jesus's followers sitting "on thrones judging the twelve tribes of Israel" (22:30). Here the number twelve obviously derives from the number of Israelite tribes, not from the counting up of the individual disciples. But then Matthew glossed the conclusion of Q to read "*twelve* thrones" (19:28), which brings to expression the logical inference that if one is judging the twelve tribes of Israel, there must be a judge for each tribe, a total of twelve judges.

Thus the New Testament concept of "the Twelve" is no doubt secondary. In fact, the lists of "the Twelve" in the various Gospels and Acts do not agree. Furthermore, several of those named among "the Twelve" play no role in the Gospels other than being included in the listing of "the Twelve." Or consider Paul's report of "the Twelve" having a resurrection experience even after Judas was no longer in the picture, when there would have been only eleven disciples (1 Cor. 15:5). Clearly, "the Twelve," like "apostles," had simply become an honorific title.

As a result, the title "the Twelve," like the title "apostle," became a term for legitimizing the authority of the orthodox church. It is orthodox in going back to the authority of "the Twelve," whereas contrary groups that are heretical do not go back to "the Twelve." Such heretical groups for their part would either have to validate their "apostolicity" by claiming to go back to "the Twelve" or they would have to discredit the title "the Twelve." Hence, a polemic against "the Twelve" in the *Gospel of Judas* can be recognized as a Gnostic effort to put down the orthodox church, which claimed to go back to "the Twelve."

We can see this taking place in the numerous references to "the Twelve" in the *Gospel of Judas.* The text begins with a rather normal reference to "the Twelve": "And since some [walked] in the way of righteousness while others walked in their transgression, the twelve disciples were called" (p. 33). One would of course assume that "the Twelve" are the ones who walk "in the way of righteousness"—until one learns more: Jesus laughs at their prayer of thanksgiving "because it is through this that your god [will receive] thanksgiving" (p. 34). Then the disciples turn vehemently against Jesus: "And when his disciples heard this, [they] started getting angry and infuriated, and began blaspheming against him in their hearts. And when Jesus observed their lack of understanding ..." (p. 34). A lack of understanding on the part of the disciples has its precedent in the Gospel of Mark.[18] But in the *Gospel of Judas* their ignorance is quite different—they stupidly worship the orthodox church's biblical god! This becomes explicit when referring to the choice of Matthias to replace Judas: "For someone else will replace you, in order that the twelve [disciples] may again come to completion with their god" (p. 36). The appended comment "with their god" makes clear that "the Twelve" do not worship the unknown good God of the Gnostics, but rather the evil creator god of the orthodox church.

One of the major sections of the *Gospel of Judas* that forms a unity for itself is a vision the disciples have of "a great house [with a] large altar [in it, and] twelve men—they are the priests, we would say" (p. 38). This is taken to refer to the temple in Jerusalem, since "a crowd of people is waiting at that altar, [until] the priests [finished presenting] the offerings" (p. 38). Yet the priests carrying on the functions are apparently disciples of Jesus: "[And] the men who stand [before] the altar invoke your [name]" (p. 38). This interpretation of the "twelve men" in the vision as referring to the twelve disciples is then made explicit: "That one is the god you serve, and you are the twelve men you have seen" (p. 39). Finally, the identification of "the Twelve" as those opposed to Judas becomes explicit: "Judas said to him, 'In the vision I saw the twelve disciples stoning me and persecuting [me severely]'" (p. 44).

It is familiar in the writings of the heresy hunters that the orthodox church caricatured the "heretics" as grossly immoral in their conduct. But now the orthodox in turn are smeared:

> [others] sacrifice their own children, others their wives, in praise [and] in humility with each other; some sleep with men; some are involved in slaugh[ter]; still others commit a multitude of sins and deeds of lawlessness. (p. 38)

Then Jesus presses home the polemical point: "It is you who are presenting the offerings at the altar you have seen" (p. 39). They in turn symbolize the orthodox church: they "invoke my name" (p. 39). "[And] they have planted trees without fruit, in my name, in a shameful manner" (p. 39). Jesus then explicitly repudiates this orthodox church:

> For to the human generations it has been said, "Look, God has received your sacrifice from the hands of priests, that is, a minister of error. But the Lord who commands, it is he who is the Lord of the universe, On the last day they will be put to shame. (p. 40)

Thus the whole concept of "the Twelve," representing orthodox Christianity, becomes a negative category from which Judas is clearly distinguished.

## JUDAS, THE THIRTEENTH

In the *Gospel of Judas,* the twelve evil angels derived from Sethian Gnosticism have been combined with the twelve apostles familiar from the New Testament, so as to condemn orthodox Christianity both on the cosmogonic and on the earthly level. As a result, the whole concept of "the Twelve" is so associated with the ignorant orthodox church that Judas cannot be included in that number. It is this that makes sense of the references in the *Gospel of Judas* to Judas as "you thirteenth spirit" (etymologically, "demon"), over against "the twelve disciples" who, he says, were "stoning me" (p. 44). This category outside of "the Twelve" is then used to designate Judas's positive stature: "You will become the thirteenth, and you will be cursed by the other generations—and you will come to rule over them" (p. 46). (Yet, in Sethianism, the thirteenth is actually a negative category.)

Then in the "Sethian" section the number twelve is projected beyond the human sphere into the cosmogony above. This may in fact be how the opening and closing material that fits the title the *Gospel of Judas* came to be connected to the large "Sethian" section, which in other regards seems so unrelated. The hidden, good God above creates "the incorruptible [generation] of Seth," with "twelve aeons of the twelve luminaries" (p. 49). But then the lower evil realm above has its twelve: "Let twelve angels come into being [to] rule over chaos and the [underworld]" (p. 51).

The derivation of the designation of Judas as the thirteenth over against "the Twelve" needed to be projected beyond the earthly into the cosmic sphere, so as to put him over the "twelve [negative] angels in the heavens" (p. 51). Yet a thirteenth does not fit as naturally into the Sethian cosmogony as it does into the on-earth presentation. Much has been made of the comment near the concluding climax of the *Gospel of Judas,* "your star over the [thir]teenth aeon" (p. 55), but just where that is in the grander scheme of things is unclear. A thirteenth aeon may be pretty far down, in the sphere of Saklas, even if in the realm above (where there are after all 12 divided into 72 divided into 360 layers), and thus above the twelve angels ruling over chaos and the underworld, where "the Twelve" of the orthodox church are stuck.

Judas has his "star." Still, today people can understand this metaphor better than some of the other mythological figures. The horoscope is still followed by many, even though modern astronomy has long since eliminated antiquity's personification of stars, and especially planets (literally, "moving" stars), as if they were live superhuman beings. Modern idiom still speaks of being born under a lucky (or unlucky) star, which means one may have good or bad "fortune." For more details, see your fortune-teller. The *Gospel of Judas* is in large part astrological, free of the debunking of modern astronomy. Hence it is no surprise that stars are prominent:

> "No host of angels of the stars will rule over that generation." (p. 37)
>
> "My name has been written on [ . . . ] of the generations of the stars by the human generations." (p. 39)
>
> ". . . since they are over your stars and your angels and have already come to their conclusion there." (p. 41)
>
> "Each of you has his own star." (p. 42)
>
> "Your star has led you astray, Judas." (p. 45)
>
> "I have taught you about the error of the stars." (p. 46)

> "The stars bring matters to completion. And when Saklas completes the span of time assigned for him, their first star will appear with the generations." (p. 54)
>
> "Your star [will rule] over the [thir]teenth aeon." (p. 55)
>
> "I am not laughing [at] you but at the error of the stars, because these six stars wander about with these five combatants, and they all will be destroyed along with their creatures." (p. 55)
>
> "Your star has passed by." (p. 56)
>
> "Lift up your eyes and look at the cloud and the light within it and the stars surrounding it. The star that leads the way is your star." (p. 57)

It is of course this reference to "the star that leads the way is your star" that is played up in the "official" publications,[19] rather than, for example, "Your star has led you astray, Judas." The astrology is not consistent, to put it mildly.

## THE LAUGHING JESUS

One of the striking traits in the *Gospel of Judas* is that Jesus laughs (as he never does in the canonical Gospels).[20] There are four such references. First, Jesus laughs in mockery at the disciples' ignorance in giving praise to their evil god in prayer:

> When he [approached] his disciples, gathered together and seated and offering a prayer of thanksgiving over the bread, [he] laughed.
>
> [And] the disciples said to him, "Master, why are you laughing at [our] prayer of thanksgiving? Or what did we do? [This] is what is right (to do)."
>
> He answered and said to them, "I am not laughing at you. You are not doing this because of your own will but because it is through this that your god [will receive] thanksgiving." (pp. 33–34)

Jesus then laughs in mockery at the disciples' ignorance of the holy generation:

> Jesus said to them, "I went to another great and holy generation."
>
> His disciples said to him, "Lord, what is the great generation that is superior to us and holy, that is not now in these aeons?"
>
> And when Jesus heard this, he laughed. He said to them, "Why are you thinking in your hearts about the strong and holy generation? Truly [I] say to you, no one born [of] this aeon will see that [generation]. (pp. 36–37)

Again, Jesus laughs at Judas for trying too hard:

> And when Jesus heard this, he laughed and said to him, "You thirteenth spirit, why do you try so hard? But speak up, and I shall bear with you."

Finally, Jesus laughs in mockery at the error of the stars doomed to destruction:

> And after that Jesus [laughed].
>
> [Judas said], "Master, [why are you laughing at us]?"
>
> [Jesus] answered [and said], "I am not laughing [at] you but at the error of the stars, because these six stars wander about with these five combatants, and they all will be destroyed along with their creatures." (p. 55)

This laughing Jesus is noted frequently in the "official" presentation, since it, like other snippets often quoted, is easily sensationalized, but it is not investigated further. Yet such an investigation leads more nearly to the ultimate point of the *Gospel of Judas*—with Judas's help Jesus, or, more exactly, the divine part trapped in Jesus's human body, is escaping back to heaven.

The heresy-hunting Irenaeus knows of such a Gnostic escape from the prison house of the body, laughing all the way, but he does not associate it with Judas or ascribe it to the Sethians; rather, he attributes it to Basilides:

> He did not suffer, but a certain Simon of Cyrene was compelled to carry his cross for him; and this (Simon) was transformed by him (Jesus) so that he was thought to be Jesus himself, and was crucified through ignorance and error. Jesus, however, took on the form of Simon, and stood by laughing at them.
>
> For since he was an incorporeal power and the Mind of the unborn Father, he was transformed in whatever way he pleased, and in this way he ascended to him who had sent him, laughing at them, since he could not be held, and was invisible to all. Therefore, those who knew these things have been set free from the rulers who made this world.[21]

Jesus was laughing because his opponents thought they were killing him, whereas in reality he was not the one they killed. They were only killing the human body that imprisoned him, thereby setting free the divine person within. They were doing something good in spite of themselves! The story of Simon of Cyrene bearing the cross for Jesus is exploited to conceptualize how this could be possible: Simon and Jesus exchange appearances, and Simon is killed in Jesus's body while Jesus stands by hiding in Simon's body—and laughing, mocking their ignorance. Then Jesus, or, more exactly, God's Mind, ascends back to the highest heaven, laughing at their inability to hold him imprisoned in a human body.

This concept of Jesus, or, more exactly, of his divine self, escaping from the prison house of the body to return on high is the same Gnostic concept that is presupposed in connection with Judas in the *Gospel of Judas*. In both cases, this is done by playing on details in the canonical passion narrative. In the one text Simon of Cyrene is used to facilitate this transaction; in the other it is Judas Iscariot. In both cases Jesus is laughing in mockery at the self-defeating ignorance of the earth-bound humanity. It is this transaction that is ultimately the point of the *Gospel of Judas*. Although the *Gospel of Judas* clearly has Sethian parallels, the "gospel" of the *Gospel of Judas* is not found in Sethian texts, but has its nearest parallel in Basilides!

Since Basilides was active during the second century C.E., this would conform to the usual dating of the *Gospel of Judas* around the middle of the second century. This does not make of the *Gospel of Judas* a Basilidean tractate; it is only that Basilides, like two Nag Hammadi tractates, the *Second Discourse of Great Seth* and the *Revelation of Peter,* documents the same motif in the second century. It is they that should be brought together as the nearest parallels to the main thrust of the *Gospel of Judas*.

The two Nag Hammadi tractates in which one finds the laughing Jesus are in Codex VII,[22] both of which share the same image of the divine escaping from the human prison. (This may in fact be the reason these two tractates were put side by side in Codex VII.) Thus they are of primary relevance for understanding the *Gospel of Judas*.

One of these tractates is the *Second Discourse of Great Seth:*

> They hatched a plot against me, to counter the destruction of their error and foolishness, but I did not give in to them as they had planned. I was not hurt at all. Though they punished me, I did not die in actuality but only in appearance, that I might not be put to shame by them, as if they are part of me. I freed myself of shame, and I did not become fainthearted because of what they did to me. I would have become bound by fear, but I suffered only in their eyes and their thought, that nothing may ever be claimed about them. The death they think I suffered they suffered in their error and blindness. They nailed their man to their death. Their thoughts did not perceive me, since they were deaf and blind. By doing these things they pronounce judgment against themselves. As for me, they saw me and punished me, but

> someone else, their father, drank the gall and the vinegar; it was not I. They were striking me with a scourge, but someone else, Simon, bore the cross on his shoulder. Someone else wore the crown of thorns. And I was on high, poking fun at all the excesses of the rulers and the fruit of their error and conceit. I was laughing at their ignorance. (VII,2: 55–56)

Here various details from the passion narrative are used to distinguish the divine spark from what was being put to death, when "they nailed their man to their death." On the one hand it can be said to be Jesus: "they punished me.... They were striking me with a scourge." But it wasn't really his true self: "I was on high, poking fun at all the excesses of the rulers.... And I was laughing at their ignorance." So the emphasis can be on another, their human father who "drank the gall and the vinegar," Simon of Cyrene, the one "who wore the crown of thorns." One can sense the Gnostic author going through the passion narrative and twisting each detail one way or the other to score the point that the crucifixion is what liberates Jesus's divine self to escape from his human body. It is just a continuation of this same procedure when the *Gospel of Judas* identifies still another person familiar from the passion narrative, to be involved in Jesus's divine self escaping the body. But in this case it is Judas Iscariot!

The other tractate is the *Revelation of Peter*:

> I saw him apparently being arrested by them. I said, "What do I see, Lord? Is it really you they are seizing, and are you holding on to me? And who is the one smiling and laughing above the cross? Is it someone else whose feet and hands they are hammering?"
>
> The Savior said to me, "The one you see smiling and laughing above the cross is the living Jesus. The one into whose hands and feet they are driving nails is his fleshly part, the substitute for him. They are putting to shame the one who came into being in the likeness of the living Jesus...

> Then I saw someone about to approach us who looked like the one laughing above the cross, but this one was intertwined with holy spirit, and he was the Savior....
>
> But the one who is standing near him is the living Savior, who was in him at first and was arrested but was set free. He is standing and observing with pleasure that those who did evil to him are divided among themselves. And he is laughing at their lack of perception, knowing that they were born blind. (VII,*3*: 81–83)

Here "the living Jesus" stands over against "his fleshly part." The center of the ridicule is that the orthodox church thought that the Romans were crucifying Jesus the Son of God, but in actuality they were only liberating him from the physical prison in which his divine spirit was kept captive. This is made explicit in the *Revelation of Peter*:

> But what was set free was my bodiless body. I am the spirit of thought filled with radiant light. (VII,*3*: 83)

Thus both the *Second Discourse of Great Seth* and the *Revelation of Peter* agree with the *Gospel of Judas* on the point decisive for all three: orthodox Christianity worships the crucified Jesus, but Gnostics worship the spark of the divine liberated by the crucifixion from imprisonment in the body of flesh. The orthodox present "the doctrine of a dead man" (*Second Discourse of Great Seth,* VII,*2*: 60), since "they will hold on to the name of a dead man" (*Revelation of Peter,* VII,3: 74), "a mere imitation of the remnant in the name of a dead man" (VII,*3*: 78). But the Gnostics have "the living Savior" (VII,*3*: 82). The Nag Hammadi tractates reach this theological objective in varying ways, but never by reference to Judas. This is the new contribution first documented in the *Gospel of Judas*.

In addition, there is a striking overarching parallel between the *Gospel of Judas* and the *Revelation of Peter*. Of course the two titles are similar, one claiming the canonical title Gospel, the other claiming the canonical title Revelation. In the *Revelation of Peter* it is Peter who plays the role of the enlightened Gnostic that Judas plays in the new text. Thus the *Revelation of Peter* claims the first and foremost apostle of the orthodox church for the Gnostics, whereas the *Gospel of Judas* rescues the defamed Judas Iscariot for the Gnostics.

In both Nag Hammadi tractates the ridicule of the laughing Jesus is directed pointedly at the emerging orthodox church and its literally understood Bible. The *Second Discourse of Great Seth* says:

> We were hated and persecuted both by those who are ignorant [i.e., non-Christians] and by those who claim to be enriched with the name of Christ [i.e., orthodox Christians], though they are vain and ignorant. Like irrational animals they do not know who they are. They hate and persecute those whom I have liberated [i.e., the Gnostics]....
>
> It was a joke, I tell you, it was a joke. The rulers do not know that all this is an ineffable unity of undefiled truth like what is among the children of light. They have imitated it, and they proclaim the doctrine of a dead man....
>
> Adam was a joke.... Abraham was a joke.... David was a joke ... Solomon was a joke.... The twelve prophets were a joke.... Moses was a joke.... None of those before him, from Adam to Moses and John the Baptizer, knew me or my siblings....The ruler was a joke, for he said, "I am God, and no one is greater than I.... He was a joke, with his judgment and false prophecy. (VII,2: 59–60, 62–65)

Thus in the ridiculing of the heroes of the Bible, Adam, Abraham, David, Solomon, the twelve prophets, Moses, and John the Baptist, we have the counterpart to what Irenaeus reports about those responsible for the *Gospel of Judas:* they venerate Cain, Esau, Korah, the Sodomites—and Judas Iscariot.

Similarly in the *Revelation of Peter:*

> And they also praise people who preach this falsehood, people who will come after you [Peter]. They will hold on to the name of a dead man, thinking that in this way they will become pure, but instead they will become more and more defiled. They will fall into a name of error and into the hand of an evil deceiver with complicated doctrines, and they will be dominated by heresy....
>
> Many others, who oppose truth and are messengers of error, will ordain their error and their law against my pure thoughts....
>
> And there are others among those outside our number who call themselves bishops and deacons, as if they have received authority from God, but they bow before the judgment of the leaders. These people are dry canals. (VII,*3*: 74, 77, 79)

This is the same kind of ridicule of the orthodox church, for its blatant ignorance of what really happened at the crucifixion, that is found in the *Gospel of Judas*. Thus Basilides, the *Second Discourse of Great Seth*, and the *Revelation of Peter* are in fact the closest parallels to the main point being scored by the *Gospel of Judas*. Read together, these four texts give the impression of a Bible-study class of the early church in which the elite intelligentsia (the Gnostics) constantly interrupt the presiding bishop to give the higher, spiritual meaning of each detail of the Bible, especially of the passion narrative. It is not hard to see why they were expelled!

This close correlation between the central point of the *Gospel of Judas* and Basilides, the *Second Discourse of Great Seth*, and the *Revelation of Peter* has been overlooked in the all too simple classification of the *Gospel of Judas* as "Sethian." The main point of the *Gospel of Judas* is not Sethian, but rather Basilidean, namely the use of various details of the passion narrative to help explain how the divine spark imprisoned in Jesus escaped back to heaven. They all enjoy a hearty laugh of distain at the ignorant orthodox church in the process.

# Notes

INTRODUCTION: THE EXTRAVAGANZA OF EASTER 2006

1. Hershel Shanks, "Sensationalizing Gnostic Christianity," *Biblical Archaeology Review* 12.4 (July/August 2006): 4, 66.
2. Adam Gopnik, "Jesus Laughed," *New Yorker* (April 17, 2006): 80–81.
3. Herbert Krosney, *The Lost Gospel: The Quest for the Gospel of Judas Iscariot* (Washington, DC: National Geographic, 2006), 177.
4. Peter Watson and Cecilia Todeschini, *The Medici Conspiracy: The Illicit Journal of Looted Antiquities—From Italy's Tomb Raiders to the World's Greatest Museums* (Cambridge, MA: PublicAffairs, Perseus Books Group, 2006), 236.
5. Stephen Emmel, "Antiquity in Fragments: A Hundred Years of Collecting Papyri at Yale," *Yale University Library Gazette* 64 (1989): 38–58.
6. Stephen Emmel, "A Fragment of Nag Hammadi Codex III in the Beinecke Library: Yale Inv. 1784," *The Bulletin of the American Society of Papyrologists* 17 (1980): 53–60.
7. Krosney, *The Lost Gospel,* 5, 177–78.
8. Krosney, *The Lost Gospel,* 219.
9. Krosney, *The Lost Gospel,* 178.
10. The tomb robber Pietro Casasanta, quoted in Watson and Todeschini, *The Medici Conspiracy,* 155.
11. Malcolm Macalister Hall, "The Gospel Truth," *Independent on Sunday,* June 5, 2005, 26.
12. Krosney, *The Lost Gospel,* 213.
13. Krosney, *The Lost Gospel,* 207.
14. Krosney, *The Lost Gospel,* 232.
15. Krosney, *The Lost Gospel,* 231.
16. Rodolphe Kasser, Marvin Meyer, and Gregor Wurst, eds., *The Gospel of Judas: From Codex Tchacos,* with additional commentary by Bart D. Ehrman (Washington, DC: National Geographic, 2006), "Publisher's Note,"183.
17. Krosney, *The Lost Gospel,* 263.
18. Rodolphe Kasser, "The Story of Codex Tchacos and the Gospel of Judas," in Kasser, Meyer, and Wurst, eds., *The Gospel of Judas,* 72.
19. Patrick Jean-Baptiste, "L'évangile de Judas," "Les tribulations d'un manuscrit apocryphe," *Sciences et Avenir* 707 (January 2006): 38–40, 41–45 (41).

20. Mario Jean Roberty, in an interview with Stacy Meichtry, Vatican correspondent of Religion News Service, February 13–14, 2006.
21. Roger Thiede, "Das JUDAS-Evengelium," *FOCUS* 13 (2005): 108–116 (111).
22. Kasser, Meyer, and Wurst, eds., *The Gospel of Judas,* "Publisher's Note," 183.
23. *The Facsimile Edition of the Nag Hammadi Codices,* ed. James M. Robinson et al., 12 vols. (Leiden: Brill, 1972–84), 183–85 (183).
24. Krosney, *The Lost Gospel,* again and again, for example: 136: "Both Robinson and Kasser would figure in the struggle to achieve scholarly dominance over the *Gospel of Judas.*" 155: "His sense that he owned the field would later exasperate some of his rivals, not least Rodolphe Kasser who shrugged his shoulders and said, 'Robinson believes it all belongs to him. *Qu'est-ce qu'on peut faire*? What can one do?'" 234: "In the context of their long-running personal feud, Kasser translating the *Gospel of Judas* would represent a tremendous victory." 242: "longtime rivals."
25. John D. Turner, *Sethian Gnosticism and the Platonic Tradition* (Bibliothèque copte de Nag Hammadi, Section "Études" 6 (Québec: Presses de l'Université Laval; Leuven: Peeters, 2001). Most recently see Turner, "Sethian Gnosticism: A Revised Literary History," in *Actes du Huitième congrès international d'études coptes* (Paris, 2004), vol. 2, *Communications,* ed. Nathalie Bosson and Anne Boud'hors, *Aegyptiaca Monspeliensia* 1 (Montpellier: Université Montpellier III, forthcoming).
26. John D. Turner, in an email to me dated June 1, 2006.
27. Krosney, *The Lost Gospel,* 175.
28. Krosney, *The Lost Gospel,* 165.
29. Krosney, *The Lost Gospel,* 224–25.
30. Krosney, *The Lost Gospel,* 64–65, 70–71.
31. Michel van Rijn, on his Web site (December 2004); http://www.michelvanrijn.nl/artnews/ (February 16, 2006), available also at http://www.tertullian.org/rpearse/manuscripts/gospel_of_judas/ (February 16, 2006).
32. Peter Watson and Cecilia Todeschini, *The Medici Conspiracy: The Illicit Journal of Looted Antiquities—From Italy's Tomb Raiders to the World's Greatest Museums* (Cambridge, MA: PublicAffairs, Perseus Books Group, 2006).
33. *Archaeology* (July–August 2006): 36–43.
34. Watson and Todeschini, *The Medici Conspiracy,* 188–95.

CHAPTER 1: THE *GOSPEL OF JUDAS* SURFACES IN GENEVA

1. Roger Thiede, "Das JUDAS-Evangelium," 114.
2. Ralph Pöhner, "Judas, der Held," *FACTS: Das Schweitzer Nachrichtenmagazin* (January 6, 2005): 76–79.
3. Roger Thiede, "Das JUDAS- Evangelium," *FOCUS* 13 (2005): 108–16.
4. Malcolm Macalister Hall, "The Gospel Truth," *Independent on Sunday, Sunday Review* (June 5, 2005): 24–26, 28, 31.
5. Henri-Charles Puech, revised after his death by Beate Blatz, in *New Testament Apocrypha,* rev. ed., ed. Wilhelm Schneemelcher, English translation ed. R. McL. Wilson, vol. 1, *Gospels and Related Writings* (Cambridge: Clarke; Louisville, KY: Westminster John Knox, 1991), 387.

6. Herbert Krosney, in *The Lost Gospel,* 105, reports that Koenen was known to both: "Perdios contacted him in late 1982 and, following up, sent a set of photographs." "He had met Hanna in Cairo and considered him a credible dealer." Krosney's chap. 6, "Under the Magnifying Glass," 105–20, reports fully on this Geneva event.
7. Henk Schutten, "The Hunt for the Gospel of Judas," in the Dutch newspaper *Het Parool,* translated by Michel van Rijn on his Web site (February 16, 2006); available also at http://www.tertullian.org/rpearse/manuscripts/gospel_of_judas/ (February 16, 2006), misrepresented the involvement of SMU: "Emmel, a leading American coptologist and the German papyrologist Ludwig Koenen was [*sic*] sent from Dallas to Geneva by the Southern Methodist University to have a look at manuscripts that were offered for sale by shadowy merchants." Similarly Pöhner, "Judas, der Held," 78: "The Southern Methodist University in Dallas showed interest, in May 1983 it sent Koenen with the coptologist Stephen Emmel to Geneva."
8. Hans Jonas, *The Gnostic Religion* (Boston: Beacon, 1958, 1963, 1991, 2001).
9. Stephen Emmel, "The Nag Hammadi Codices Editing Project: A Final Report," American Research Center in Egypt, *Newsletter* 104 (1978): 10–32.
10. Roger Thiede, "Ein anderes Frühchristentum?" interview with Stephen Emmel, *FOCUS* 13 (2005): 118–19 (118).
11. Kasser, Meyer, and Wurst, eds., *The Gospel of Judas*, facing the title page.
12. Hall, "The Gospel Truth," 26.
13. Schutten, "The Hunt for the Gospel of Judas."
14. Thiede, "Ein anderes Frühchristentum?" 118.
15. Stephen Emmel, ed., *Nag Hammadi Codex III,5: The Dialogue of the Savior,* The Coptic Gnostic Library, Nag Hammadi Studies 26 (Leiden: Brill, 1984), reprinted in *The Coptic Gnostic Library: A Complete Edition of the Nag Hammadi Codices,* vol. 3 (Leiden: Brill, 2000).
16. This whole episode is also reported by Krosney, *The Lost Gospel,* 117. Since it was an oral communication from Perdios to me, it is clear that in writing his book Krosney used my presentation at the Society of Biblical Literature on November 19, 2005, presumably its preprint, "From the Nag Hammadi Codices to the Gospels of Mary and Judas," in the Coptic newspaper *Watani International* (July 10, 2005), ed. Saad Michael Saad.
17. Quoted in Pöhner, "Judas, der Held," 78.
18. The existence of this work in the codex had already been discovered by Ludwig Koenen on the basis of a few sample photographs that the sellers had sent him when they first offered to show him this material and that Koenen had shared with Gerald M. Brown of the University of Illinois at Champaign-Urbana in order to have the barely legible bits of text transcribed and translated. See Krosney, *The Lost Gospel,* chap. 6, "Under a Magnifying Glass," 105–20.
19. For more details, see my paper "From the Nag Hammadi Codices to the Gospels of Mary and Judas," *Watani International,* July 10, 2005, p. 2. This was updated and presented in the panel on the theme "How Nag Hammadi Changed the World of Early Christianity," in the Nag Hammadi and Gnosticism Section of

the Annual Meeting of the Society of Biblical Literature in Philadelphia on November 20, 2005. A minor updating of that paper was published in February 2006, "From the Nag Hammadi Codices to *The Gospel of Mary* and *The Gospel of Judas*," Occasional Papers 48 (Claremont, CA: Institute for Antiquity and Christianity, 2006).

20. Listed in my Foreword to the reprint of W. E. Crum, *A Coptic Dictionary* (Eugene, OR: Wipf and Stock, 2005). It is on seven unnumbered pages prior to Crum's own Preface. A revised version is published as "Coptic Since Crum" in *Coptica,* journal of the St. Mark Foundation and St. Shenouda the Archimandrite Coptic Society (Los Angeles, 2006): 36–46.
21. Stephen C. Carlson, *Hypotyposeis: Sketches in Biblical Studies,* http://www.hypotyposeis.org/weblog/2005/03/gospel-of-judas-in-news_29.html, "Gospel of Judas in the News, Last Updated: April 7, 2005."
22. James M. Robinson, "The Discovery of the Nag Hammadi Codices," *Biblical Archaeologist* 42.4 (fall 1979): 206–24 (214).
23. Henk Schutten, "Your Life Is at Stake with This Manuscript," in the Dutch newspaper *Het Parool,* translated by Michel van Rijn on his Web site (February 16, 2006); available also at http://www.tertullian.org/rpearse/manuscripts/gospel_of_judas/ (February 16, 2006).
24. The Dutch article "Judasevangelie niet van Judas," listed "From Michel van Rijn, April 1, 2005, from http://www.katholieknieuwsblad.nl/," available also at http://www.tertullian.org/rpearse/manuscripts/gospel_of_judas. The translation is no doubt by van Rijn.
25. *The Facsimile Edition of the Nag Hammadi Codices*: *Introduction,* ed. James M. Robinson et al. (Leiden: Brill, 1984), 21.
26. Michel van Rijn on his Web site (December 9, 2001); also available at http://www.tertullian.org/rpearse/manuscripts/gospel_of_judas/ (February 16, 2006).
27. Hans-Gebhard Bethge, "The Letter of Peter to Philip," in *New Testament Apocrypha,* rev. ed., vol. 1, 342; 347, n. 2.
28. Marvin W. Meyer, "NHC VIII,2: The Letter of Peter to Philip: Introduction," in *Nag Hammadi Codex VIII,* ed. John H. Sieber, Coptic Gnostic Library, Nag Hammadi Studies 31 (Leiden: Brill, 1991), 227–32 (232). This statement is also to be found at the conclusion of his Introduction to the *Letter of Peter to Philip* in James M. Robinson and Marvin W. Meyer, eds., trans. Coptic Gnostic Library Project of the Institute for Antiquity and Christianity, *The Nag Hammadi Library in English* (Leiden: Brill, 1977, paperback 1984; San Francisco: Harper & Row, 1977, paperback 1981).
29. Rodolphe Kasser, "The Story of Codex Tchacos and the Gospel of Judas," in Kasser, Meyer, and Wurst, eds., *The Gospel of Judas,* 54, reports that my "few notes, in several academic publications, signaled the existence of a new Gnostic witness."
30. Krosney, *The Lost Gospel,* 105.
31. Krosney, *The Lost Gospel,* xxv.
32. Krosney, *The Lost Gospel,* 36–37.

33. See my handwritten notes on pp. 1438, 1442–58, 1595–1600 of the black notebooks I always carried with me in Egypt, which are kept in the Nag Hammadi Archives.
34. See my published essays on the topic: "The Discovering and Marketing of Coptic Manuscripts: The Nag Hammadi Codices and the Bodmer Papyri," in *Sundries in Honour of Torgny Säve-Söderbergh,* Acta Universitatis Uppsaliensis, Boreas: Uppsala Studies in Ancient Mediterranean and Near Eastern Civilizations 13 (1984), 97–114, reprinted in *The Roots of Egyptian Christianity,* ed. Birger A. Pearson and James E. Goehring, Studies in Antiquity and Christianity (Philadelphia: Fortress, 1986), 1–25, 182; "The First Christian Monastic Library," in *Coptic Studies: Acts of the Third International Congress of Coptic Studies, Warsaw, 20–25 August 1984* (Warsaw: PWN–Panstwowe Wydawnictwo Naukowe, 1990), 371–78; *The Pachomian Monastic Library at the Chester Beatty Library and the Bibliothèque Bodmer,* Occasional Papers 19 (Claremont, CA: Institute for Antiquity and Christianity, 1990), enlarged reprint in *The Role of the Book in the Civilisations of the Near East,* Manuscripts of the Middle East 5 (1990–91 [1993]): 26–40; "The Manuscript's History and Codicology," in *The Crosby-Schøyen Codex Ms 193 in the Schøyen Collection,* ed. James E. Goehring, Corpus Scriptorum Christianorum Orientalium 521, Subsidia, Tomus 85 (Leuven: Peeters, 1990), xvii–lvii.
35. Michel van Rijn, on his Web site (September 2001); also available at http://www.tertullian.org/rpearse/manuscripts/gospel_of_judas/ (February 16, 2006).
36. Krosney, *The Lost Gospel,* chap. 5, "The Robbery," 83–104.
37. Krosney, *The Lost Gospel,* chap. 8, "Purgatory," 143–52.
38. Thiede, "Das JUDAS-Evangelium," 108–9.
39. Krosney, *The Lost Gospel,* 10; see also 14, 23–27, 31–33, 40, 112, 124.
40. Thiede, "Das JUDAS-Evangelium," 109–10.
41. Krosney, *The Lost Gospel,* 85.
42. Krosney, *The Lost Gospel,* 97–99.
43. Michel van Rijn on his Web site (February 16, 2006); available also at http://www.tertullian.org/rpearse/manuscripts/gospel_of_judas/ (February 16, 2006).
44. Krosney, *The Lost Gospel,* "The Robbery," 85–104.
45. Thiede, "Das JUDAS-Evangelium, 110.
46. Krosney, *The Lost Gospel,* 5, and in more detail 177–78.

CHAPTER 2: THE PEDDLING OF THE *GOSPEL OF JUDAS*

1. Krosney, *The Lost Gospel,* 104.
2. Roger Thiede, "Das JUDAS-Evangelium," 110.
3. Ralph Pöhner, "Judas, der Held," *FACTS: Das Schweitzer Nachrichtenmagazin* (January 6, 2005): 78.
4. Krosney, *The Lost Gospel,* 168–69.
5. Malcolm Macalister Hall, "The Gospel Truth," *Independent on Sunday, Sunday Review* (June 5, 2005): 26. See also Krosney, *The Lost Gospel,* 37, 65–67.

6. Pöhner, "Judas, der Held," 78.
7. Michel van Rijn, December 2004, on his Web site (February 16, 2006); available also at http://www.tertullian.org/rpearse/manuscripts/gospel_of_judas/ (February 16, 2006).
8. Thiede, "Das JUDAS-Evangelium," 111.
9. Krosney, *The Lost Gospel,* chap. 10, "Judas in America," 165–79.
10. Roberty, interview with Stacy Meichtry.
11. Pöhner, "Judas, der Held," 78. See for more details Krosney, *The Lost Gospel,* 146, 168, 176–78.
12. For further details see Krosney, *The Lost Gospel,* chap. 12, "The Ferrini Confrontation," 205–29.
13. Michel van Rijn, on his Web site (February 16, 2006); available also at http://www.tertullian.org/rpearse/manuscripts/gospel_of_judas/ (February 16, 2006).
14. Van Rijn, on his Web site (February 16, 2006).
15. Apparently this letter, available on van Rijn's Web site, is the source of Pöhner's report in "Judas, der Held," 78: "A few years later another American got involved in the matter: James Robinson.... With the Egyptian he agreed on a total price in the area of $900,000 and agreed on a meeting in New York." I did not agree on a price with the Egyptian or Perdios.
16. In e-mails from Charles W. Hedrick to me dated January 24 and February 3, 2006.
17. Pöhner, "Judas, der Held," 77.
18. Charles W. Hedrick, "The ~~Four~~ 34 Gospels: Diversity and Division Among the Earliest Christians," *Bible Review* 18.3 (June 2002): 20–31, 46–47; "The Secret Gospel of Mark: Stalemate in the Academy," *Journal of Early Christian Studies* 11.2 (summer 2003): 133–45.
19. Hedrick, "The ~~Four~~ 34 Gospels," 26; "The Secret Gospel of Mark," 139.
20. Pöhner, "Judas, der Held," 78–79.
21. Charles W. Hedrick and Paul Mirecki, *The Gospel of the Savior: A New Ancient Gospel* (Santa Rosa, CA: Polebridge, 1999).
22. Thiede, "Das JUDAS-Evangelium," 110.
23. Available on the Web site of Michel van Rijn (April 27, 2005), (February 16, 2006), available also at http://www.tertullian.org/rpearse/manuscripts/gospel_of_judas/ (February 16, 2006). See also Krosney, *The Lost Gospel,* 217–23.
24. Michel van Rijn, on his Web site.
25. Krosney, *The Lost Gospel,* chap. 12, "The Ferrini Confrontation," 205–29, especially 222.
26. Michel van Rijn, on his Web site, (April 8, 2005), (February 16, 2006), available also at http://www.tertullian.org/rpearse/manuscripts/gospel_of_judas/ (February 16, 2006).
27. See the Web site of Michel van Rijn (December 9, 2001), (February 16, 2006), available also at http://www.tertullian.org/rpearse/manuscripts/gospel_of_judas/ (February 16, 2006).
28. Hall, "The Gospel Truth," 26.

29. Henk Schutten, "The Hunt for the Gospel of Judas," *Het Parool,* trans. Michel van Rijn on his Web site (February 16, 2006); available also at http://www.tertullian.org/rpearse/manuscripts/gospel_of_judas/ (February 16, 2006).
30. Thiede, "Das JUDAS-Evangelium," 111, 113.
31. Michel van Rijn, on his Web site (December 2004), (February 16, 2006); available also at http://www.tertullian.org/rpearse/manuscripts/gospel_of_judas/ (February 16, 2006).
32. Krosney, *The Lost Gospel,* 64–65, 70–71.
33. Thiede, "Das JUDAS-Evangelium," 113.
34. Thiede, "Das JUDAS-Evangelium," 113.
35. Thiede, "Das JUDAS-Evangelium," 114.
36. Thiede, "Das JUDAS-Evangelium," 114.
37. Kasser, Meyer, and Wurst, eds., *The Gospel of Judas,* 28–29.
38. Schutten, "The Hunt for the Gospel of Judas."
39. Schutten, "The Hunt for the Gospel of Judas."
40. Hedrick, in an e-mail to me dated January 28, 2006.
41. Hedrick, in an e-mail to me dated February 6, 2006.
42. Hedrick, in the e-mail to me dated February 6, 2006.
43. Hedrick, in an e-mail to me dated February 1, 2006.
44. Hedrick, in e-mails to me dated February 6 and 18, 2006.
45. Hedrick, in an e-mail to me dated February 7, 2006.
46. Krosney, *The Lost Gospel,* 253–54.
47. Hedrick, in the e-mail to me dated February 18, 2006.
48. Pöhner, "Judas, der Held," 77.
49. Thiede, "Das JUDAS-Evangelium," 112.
50. Thiede, "Das JUDAS Evangelium," 113.
51. Schutten, "Is there a copy in the Vatican?" Michel van Rijn, on his Web site (February 16, 2006); available also at http://www.tertullian.org/rpearse/manuscripts/gospel_of_judas/ (February 16, 2006).
52. Henk Schutten, "The Shady Side of the Art Trade," Michel van Rijn, on his Web site (February 16, 2006); available also at http://www.tertullian.org/rpearse/manuscripts/gospel_of_judas/ (February 16, 2006).
53. Schutten, "The Shady Side of the Art Trade." Michel van Rijn, on his Web site (February 16, 2006); available also at: http://www.tertullian.org/rpearse/manuscripts/gospel_of_judas/ (February 16, 2006).
54. Roberty, interview with Stacy Meichtry.
55. Thiede, "Das JUDAS-Evangelium," 109: "16 x 29 cm."
56. Marvin Meyer, ed., *The Nag Hammadi Scriptures* (San Francisco: HarperSanFrancisco, 2007).

CHAPTER 3: THE PUBLICATION AND SIGNIFICANCE OF THE *GOSPEL OF JUDAS*

1. Available on the Web site of Michel van Rijn (April 27, 2005), (February 16, 2006); available also at http://www.tertullian.org/rpearse/manuscripts/gospel_of_judas/ (February 16, 2006).

2. See my publications, listed above, on p. 239, chapter 1, note 34.
3. Michel van Rijn, on his Web site (February 16, 2006); available also at http://www.tertullian.org/rpearse/manuscripts/gospel_of_judas/ (February 16, 2006).
4. James M. Robinson, "The Jung Codex: The Rise and Fall of a Monopoly," *Religious Studies Review* 3 (1977), 17–30.
5. Krosney, *The Lost Gospel*, 135.
6. Krosney, *The Lost Gospel*, 242.
7. Van Rijn, on his Web site (February 16, 2006).
8. From the Web site of Michel Van Rijn, April 27, 2005.
9. A minor updating of that paper appeared as "From the Nag Hammadi Codices to *The Gospel of Mary* and *The Gospel of Judas*," Occasional Papers 48 (Claremont, CA: Institute for Antiquity and Christianity, 2006).
10. Patrick Jean-Baptiste, "L'évangile de Judas," "Les tribulations d'un manuscrit apocryphe," *Sciences et Avenir* 707 (January 2006): 38–40, 41–45.
11. The actual publications diverge somewhat from this prediction. *The Gospel of Judas: From Codex Tchacos*, ed. Rodolphe Kasser, Marvin Meyer, and Gregor Wurst, and *The Lost Gospel: The Quest for the Gospel of Judas Iscariot*, by Herbert Krosney, were published around Easter (Washington, DC: National Geographic, 2006). Bart Ehrman, *The Lost Gospel of Judas Iscariot: A New Look at Betrayer and Betrayed* (New York: Oxford University Press, 2006), was published six months later. The "first one: a big book with pictures of the gospel and 3 language translations" still has not appeared, much to the distress of Coptic scholars around the world.
12. Jean-Baptiste, "Les tribulations d'un manuscrit apocryphe," 41.
13. Jean-Baptiste, "L'évangile de Judas," 38.
14. James M. Robinson, "Nag Hammadi: The First Fifty Years," in Stephen J. Patterson, James M. Robinson, and Hans-Gebhard Bethge, *The Fifth Gospel: The Gospel of Thomas Comes of Age* (Harrisburg, PA: Trinity Press International, 1998), 77–110, Section 5, "The New Ethos for Handling Manuscript Discoveries," 95–99.
15. See my review article, "The Jung Codex: The Rise and Fall of a Monopoly," *Religious Studies Review* 3 (January 1977): 17–30.
16. Robert H. Eisenman and James M. Robinson, eds., *A Facsimile Edition of the Dead Sea Scrolls*, 2 vols. (Washington, DC: Biblical Archaeology Society, 1991; rev. ed. 1992).
17. On November 22, 1991, the research and publications committee had (to quote its minutes) "directed that the statement on access be sent to funding agencies, publishers, primary repositories, be published in *Religious Studies News*, and be circulated through the American Council of Learned Societies to other learned societies interested in literary and artifactual remains (encouraging their participation in policy development). The committee approved further distribution as widely as possible." I had it republished in the *Zeitschrift für Papyrologie und Epigraphik* 92 (1992): 296.
18. By pure coincidence I presented an address proposing such policies the same weekend that the Huntington Library made its announcement. It has hence been widely republished: James M. Robinson, *Manuscript Discoveries of the*

*Future,* with an appendix containing the title page, table of contents, introduction, and sample plates from *A Facsimile Edition of the Dead Sea Scrolls,* ed. J. L. Reed, Occasional Papers 23 (Claremont, CA: Institute for Antiquity and Christianity, 1991); abridged by James M. Robinson, "Avoiding Another Scrolls Access Furor," *Los Angeles Times,* September 28, 1991, sec. F, 13–14; abridged as "Handling Future Manuscript Discoveries," *Biblical Archaeologist* (December 1991): 235–40; abridged by Hershel Shanks, "What We Should Do Next Time Great Manuscripts Are Discovered," *Biblical Archaeology Review* 18, no. 1 (January–February 1992): 66–70; reprinted in unabridged form in *Zeitschrift für Papyrologie und Epigraphik* 92 (1992): 281–96.

19. Kasser, Meyer, and Wurst, eds., *The Gospel of Judas*.
20. Krosney has simply projected onto me the monopolistic sensitivities of those with whom he was working when he wrote: "Both Robinson and Kasser would figure in the struggle to achieve scholarly dominance over the Gospel of Judas" (*The Lost Gospel,* 136).
21. *The Facsimile Edition of the Nag Hammadi Codices: Introduction* (Leiden: Brill, 1984), "Addenda et Corrigenda," 103–33 plus 28 plates.
22. Kasser, Meyer, and Wurst, eds., *The Gospel of Judas,* 44, n. 171.
23. Andrew Cockburn, "The Judas Gospel," *National Geographic* (May 2006): 93.
24. Thiede, "Ein anderes Frühchristentum?" an interview with Stephen Emmel, 119.
25. Pöhner, "Judas, der Held," 79.
26. Pöhner, "Judas, der Held," 79.
27. Thiede, "Das JUDAS-Evangelium," 114–15.
28. Stephen C. Carlson, "Gospel of Judas in the News, Last Updated: April 7, 2005," on his Web site, http://www.hypotyposeis.org/weblog/2005/03/gospel-of-judas-in-news_29.html.
29. Pöhner, "Judas, der Held," 79.
30. Summarized in James M. Robinson, *The Gospel of Jesus* (San Francisco: HarperSanFrancisco, 2005), 75–77.
31. Eisenman and Robinson, eds., *A Facsimile Edition of the Dead Sea Scrolls*.
32. For more details see James M. Robinson, "The French Role in Early Nag Hammadi Studies," *Journal of Coptic Studies* 7 (2005): 1–12.
33. *La Bourse Égyptienne,* June 10, 1949.

CHAPTER 4: THE JUDAS OF THE NEW TESTAMENT

1. *The Critical Edition of Q: Synopsis Including the Gospels of Matthew and Luke, Mark and Thomas with English, German, and French Translations of Q and Thomas,* ed. James M. Robinson, Paul Hoffmann, and John S. Kloppenborg (Minneapolis: Fortress; Leuven: Peeters, 2000).
2. Claire Clivaz, "Douze noms pour une main: nouveaux regards sur Judas à partir de Lc 22.21–22," *New Testament Studies* 48 (2002): 400–416.

CHAPTER 5: THE HISTORICAL JUDAS

1. Origen *Against Celsus* 2.9, cited in William Klassen, *Judas: Betrayer or Friend of Jesus?* (Minneapolis: Fortress, 1996, paperback 2002, reprint 2006), 138.

2. Ray S. Anderson, *The Gospel According to Judas* (Colorado Springs, CO: Helmers & Howard, 1991).
3. Hans-Josef Klauck, *Jesus: Ein Jünger des Herrn,* Quaestiones Disputatae 111 (Freiburg: Herder, 1987). A French translation, *Judas un disciple de Jésus: Exégèse et répercussions historiques;* Lectio divina (Paris: Les Éditions du Cerf, 2006), includes a new chapter on *The Gospel of Judas,* 149–59.
4. Klassen, *Judas.*
5. Kim Paffenroth, *Judas: Images of the Lost Disciple* (Louisville, KY: Westminster John Knox, 2001).
6. Klassen, *Judas,* 48.
7. *A Greek-English Lexicon of the New Testament and Other Early Christian Literature,* a translation and adaptation of the fourth revised and augmented edition of Walter Bauer's *Griechisch-Deutsches Wörterbuch zu den Schriften des Neuen Testaments und der übrigen urchristlichen Literatur,* by William F. Arndt and F. Wilbur Gingrich, second edition revised and augmented by F. Wilbur Gingrich and Frederick W. Danker, from Bauer's fifth edition (Chicago and London: University of Chicago Press, 1958).
8. Klassen, *Judas,* 74.

CHAPTER 6: THE GNOSTIC JUDAS

1. Irenaeus, *Refutation of All Heresies* 1.31.1. The translation is from Bentley Layton, *The Gnostic Scriptures: A New Translation with Annotations and Introductions* (Garden City, NY: Doubleday, 1987), 181.
2. Epiphanius, *Panarion* 37.3.4–5; 6.1–2; 38.1.5.
3. Henri-Charles Puech, revised after his death by Beate Blatz, in *New Testament Apocrypha,* rev. ed., vol. 1, 386–87.
4. *The Testimony of Truth,* Nag Hammadi Codex IX,*3*, 45,23–48,15.
5. James M. Robinson, Permanent Secretary of the International Committee for the Nag Hammadi Codices nominated by UNESCO and appointed by the Arab Republic of Egypt, *The Facsimile Edition of the Nag Hammadi Codices,* 12 vols. (Leiden: Brill, 1972–84).
6. See my detailed analysis in *The Facsimile Edition of the Nag Hammadi Codices: Introduction* (1984): chap. 3, "The Quires," 32–44; chap. 4, "The Rolls," 45–60; chap. 5, "The Kollemata," 61–70; chap. 6, "The Covers," 71–86.
7. Pöhner, "Judas, der Held," 76–79.
8. They are reprinted in James M. Robinson, *The Sayings Gospel Q: Collected Essays,* ed. Christoph Heil and Joseph Verheyden, BETL 189 (Leuven: University Press and Uitgeverij Peeters, 2005), 711–883.
9. John S. Kloppenborg, *The Tenants in the Vineyard: Ideology, Economics, and Agrarian Conflict in Jewish Palestine* (Wissenschaftliche Untersuchungen zum Neuen Testament 195; Tübingen: Mohr, 2006).
10. See my "Evaluations," *Q 12:49–59: Children Against Parents—Judging the Time—Settling out of Court;* Documenta Q: Reconstructions of Q Through Two Centuries of Gospel Research Excerpted, Sorted, and Evaluated (Leuven: Peeters, 1997).

11. Stephen J. Patterson, James M. Robinson, and Hans-Gebhard Bethge, *The Fifth Gospel: The Gospel of Thomas Comes of Age* (Harrisburg, PA: Trinity Press International, 1998).
12. *The Nag Hammadi Library in English,* 523–27 (pagination of the most recent, third, edition).
13. *Gospel of Philip,* Nag Hammadi Codex II,*3,* 73,8–19.
14. *The Holy Book of the Great Invisible Spirit,* Nag Hammadi Codex III,*2,* 40,12–13. A second, more fragmentary copy is in Codex IV,2.
15. *The Holy Book of the Great Invisible Spirit,* Nag Hammadi Codex III,*2,* 69,18–20.
16. *The Holy Book of the Great Invisible Spirit,* Nag Hammadi Codex III,*2,* 69,6–17.
17. *Gospel of Truth,* Nag Hammadi Codex I,*3,* 16,31–34.
18. Kim Paffenroth, *Judas,* 2001.
19. A. J. Droge and J. D. Tabor, *A Noble Death: Suicide and Martyrdom Among Christians and Jews in Antiquity* (San Francisco: HarperSanFrancisco, 1992), cited in Klassen, *Judas,* 168, 175.
20. Klassen, *Judas,* 47, quoting Augustine *City of God* 1.17 and *Sermon* 352.3.8 (*Patrologia Latina* 39:1559–63).
21. The translation, by Morton S. Enslin, in "How the Story Grew: Judas in Fact and Fiction," in *Festschrift in Honor of F. W. Gingrich,* ed. E. H. Barth and R. Cocroft (Leiden: Brill, 1972), is quoted in Klassen, *Judas,* 173.
22. Quoted in Klassen, *Judas,* 7.
23. Klassen, *Judas,* 18–20.
24. Thiede, "Das JUDAS-Evangelium," 116.
25. Thiede, "Das JUDAS-Evangelium," 116.
26. English translation by M. E. Heine (London: Hutchinson, 1977).
27. Michael Dickinson, *The Lost Testament of Judas Iscariot* (Dingle: Brandon, 1994).
28. Ernest Sutherland Bates, *The Gospel of Judas* (London: Heinemann, 1929). It had been published already in 1928 in the United States under the title *The Friend of Jesus* (New York: Simon & Schuster, 1928), but *The Gospel of Judas* was Bates's original title.
29. Hugh S. Pyper, "Modern Gospels of Judas: Canon and Betrayal," *Literature & Theology* 15 (2001): 111–22.
30. Marvin Meyer, "Introduction," in Kasser, Meyer, and Wurst, eds., *The Gospel of Judas,* 3.

CHAPTER 7: THE *GOSPEL OF JUDAS*

1. Kasser, Meyer, and Wurst, eds., *The Gospel of Judas,* "Publisher's Note," 183–85.
2. Gregor Wurst, "Irenaeus of Lyon and the Gospel of Judas," in Kasser, Meyer, and Wurst, eds., *The Gospel of Judas,* 121–35 (127–28).
3. Wurst, "Irenaeus of Lyon and the Gospel of Judas," 126–27.
4. Gesine Schenke Robinson posed this question as a member of the panel on the *Gospel of Judas* held at the Institute for Antiquity and Christianity on

September 14, 2006. Remi Gounelle, in his introduction to the French translation of this book, *Les secrets de Judas: Histoire de l'apôtre incompris et de son Évangile* (Paris: Michel Lafon, May 2006), 13–14, also raised this question.

5. See in Chapter 6, "'Gospels' and Their 'Authors'" and "'Gospel'? By 'Judas'?"
6. The "official" translation in the forthcoming critical edition of Codex Tchacos uses the usual scholarly signs in the translation, which are hence followed in quotations in this chapter. Square brackets [ ] indicate that the text has there a hole (we call it by its Latin name, lacuna). Pointed brackets <> indicate that the editors have made a correction of a scribal error. Three dots ... indicate that the letters are too fragmentary or are in a lacuna, and hence the text cannot be restored.
7. The terms "orthodox" and "heretical" are to be understood as if they are in quotation marks, since they are anachronistic and should not be taken literally. Each side in the early church considered itself orthodox and considered the other side heretical. In subsequent centuries it was the winning side that was able to keep the term "orthodox" for itself and brand other views as heretical. Therefore that terminology is not objective and impartial. Similarly it is anachronistic to speak already of the "New Testament," since at the time when the *Gospel of Judas* was composed in the middle of the second century the books comprising the New Testament had not yet been brought together to become the "New Testament" over against the Jewish scriptures as the Christian "Old Testament."
8. Uwe-Karsten Plisch and Hans Gebhard Bethge, in a footnote of the critical edition of Codex Tchacos at 33,21.
9. There may be a parallel to Luke in the obscure opening time reference of the *Gospel of Judas* to "during eight days, three days before he celebrated Passover." There is a similar reference in Luke 9:28 to "about eight days" between the first prediction of the passion and the transfiguration, where Mark 9:2 reads simply "after six days."
10. "The twelve disciples were called" echoes the synoptic Gospels, Matt. 10:1 // Mark 6:7 // Luke 9:1, though only Matthew here refers to the twelve as "disciples": "And he called to him his twelve disciples." Luke never uses the expression "the twelve disciples." But, since Luke refers both to "disciples" and "the twelve," this conjuction in the *Gospel of Judas* need not suggest that it was familiar with Mark.
11. There is a parallel (p. 47) to Saying 17 of the *Gospel of Thomas* found also in Paul, 1 Cor. 2:9. But this saying occurs frequently, such as in the *Prayer of the Apostle Paul,* Nag Hammadi Codex I, p. A.
12. The nearest parallel is Matt. 26:50, where in the Garden of Gethsemane Jesus says to Judas: "Friend, why are you here?" But the parallel is not close enough to suggest a dependence.
13. Gesine Schenke Robinson has suggested an alternative solution that tends to eliminate the problem, ascribing the personal pronoun to Jesus, not to Judas: "I am convinced that we have here to do with two sentences: 'Judas lifted his eyes and saw the luminous cloud. And he (namely Jesus) entered it.' Not Judas but Jesus ascends. He withdraws after having rendered his last revelation—as

he disappeared and reappeared before." She and Sasago Arai are listed for this interpretation in the critical edition of Codex Tchacos at 57,23.

14. Hans-Martin Schenke, "The Phenomenon and Significance of Gnostic Sethianism," in *The Rediscovery of Gnosticism: Proceedings of the International Conference on Gnosticism at Yale New Haven, Connecticut, March 28–31, 1978,* vol. 2, *Sethian Gnosticism* Studies in the History of Religions Supplements to *Numen* 41 (Leiden: Brill, 1981), 588–616.
15. Turner, *Sethian Gnosticism and the Platonic Tradition,* chap. 2, "The Literature of Gnostic Sethianism," 57–92 (61).
16. The titles of the tractates are those that are introduced, some for the first time, in *The Nag Hammadi Scriptures,* ed. Marvin Meyer (San Francisco: HarperSanFrancisco, 2007), since they are more modern, and in some cases more accurate, than those traditionally used in the academic community.
17. This is already noted by Meyer, in "Judas and the Gnostic Connection," in Kasser, Meyer, and Wurst, eds., *The Gospel of Judas,* 148–49.
18. See Chapter 4, "The Gentile Gospel of Mark."
19. This is on the back of the dust jacket of Kasser, Meyer, and Wurst, eds., *The Gospel of Judas.*
20. See John Dart, *The Laughing Savior: The Discovery and Significance of the Nag Hammadi Gnostic Library* (New York: Harper & Row, 1976), esp. chap. 16, "The Laughing Jesus," 107–13. Dart is now news editor for *The Christian Century.* See his report, "Long-lost Gospel of Judas to Be Published," *Christian Century* (December 27, 2005): 12–13. Adam Gopnik's very critical book review of Krosney's *The Lost Gospel* is entitled "Jesus Laughed," *New Yorker* (April 17, 2006): 80–81. Guy Stroumsa, "Le christianisme a transformé l'idée même de religion," *Le Monde de la Bible* (November-December 2006, an issue devoted primarily to *The Gospel of Judas*), 46–49 (46) summarizes his opening essay on the Christ laughing that gave the title to his newest book *Le rire du Christ* (2006): the motif of Christ laughing may be derived from the name of Isaac, which means in Hebrew "he will laugh." Isaac escaped death when his father Abraham was about to sacrifice him, and thus Isaac would be for Gnostics a precursor to a Christ who they maintain escaped crucifixion. In the same issue of *Le Monde de la Bible* Claude Gianotto, "Les interpretations gnostiques de la Passion," 35–36, examines the motif of Christ laughing over the wrong person being crucified as it is found throughout early Christian noncanonical literature.
21. Dart, *The Laughing Savior,* 108–9.
22. Meyer, in "Judas and the Gnostic Connection," 21, n. 10, mentions them, but does not investigate further.

# Index

*Numerals in boldface indicate Bible chapter and verse.*